Gang Prevention in Schools

Katherine De Vito

Gang Prevention in Schools

Creating a Secure Base and Safe Haven

 Springer

Katherine De Vito
Westfield, NJ, USA

ISBN 978-3-030-82913-1   ISBN 978-3-030-82914-8 (eBook)
https://doi.org/10.1007/978-3-030-82914-8

© The Editor(s) (if applicable) and The Author(s), under exclusive license to Springer Nature Switzerland AG 2021

This work is subject to copyright. All rights are reserved by the Publisher, whether the whole or part of the material is concerned, specifically the rights of translation, reprinting, reuse of illustrations, recitation, broadcasting, reproduction on microfilms or in any other physical way, and transmission or information storage and retrieval, electronic adaptation, computer software, or by similar or dissimilar methodology now known or hereafter developed.

The use of general descriptive names, registered names, trademarks, service marks, etc. in this publication does not imply, even in the absence of a specific statement, that such names are exempt from the relevant protective laws and regulations and therefore free for general use.

The publisher, the authors, and the editors are safe to assume that the advice and information in this book are believed to be true and accurate at the date of publication. Neither the publisher nor the authors or the editors give a warranty, expressed or implied, with respect to the material contained herein or for any errors or omissions that may have been made. The publisher remains neutral with regard to jurisdictional claims in published maps and institutional affiliations.

This Springer imprint is published by the registered company Springer Nature Switzerland AG
The registered company address is: Gewerbestrasse 11, 6330 Cham, Switzerland

This book is dedicated to my children, Dylan and Emma. Also, it is dedicated to all of the students whom I have worked with over the years, in the hope that I provided meaningful support and a safe haven while in school.

Preface

Gang involvement is a problem around the world. As a school social worker, my days are very busy filled with working with students on various issues, one of which can include gang involvement. Seeing the repercussions of joining a gang and the issues leading up to that decision to join created a passion in me for gang prevention. This passion sparked my research during my time at Rutgers School of Social Work Doctorate in Social Work (DSW) Program. My research was focused on why former gang members chose to join a gang and why they chose to leave. Through that research, my qualitative study was born, "Seeking a secure base: Gangs as attachment figures," published in *Qualitative Social Work* in 2020. Through that study, I was able to speak to former gang members (whose names have been changed to pseudonyms to protect privacy/confidentiality) about all of their experiences. This book expands on those interviews with former gang members and delves into more research, hearing from experts in the field as well, to inform how we, as school staff members, can intervene in an effort to prevent gang involvement in schools.

Westfield, NJ, USA   Katherine De Vito

Acknowledgments

I would like to thank my family for their unwavering support. I would also like to acknowledge and thank Dr. Edward Alessi, Dr. Michael La Sala, Dr. Erica Goldblatt-Hyatt, and Dr. Miri Jaffe for their mentoring during my research on my topic of gangs and gang prevention in schools during my time at the Doctor of Social Work Program (DSW) at Rutgers University School of Social Work. I would also like to thank Special Agent Edwin Torres, President of the East Coast Gang Investigators Association, for his help with this and many other projects along the way. I would also like to thank both Jay Franklin and Father Greg Boyle for their contribution to this work as well as to my research and for their tireless work with gang-involved youth. I would also like to thank Dr. Gerald Mallon, Dr. Kirk James, Dr. Alexis Dragun, and Dr. Arthur Becker-Weidman for their contributions to this book. I extend a special thank you with gratitude to the participants in my research study for allowing me to create a platform for your voices to be heard.

Contents

1 **Introduction**... 1
   1.1 A School Social Worker's Role... 1
   1.2 Gang Prevalence... 2
   1.3 Violence and Gangs... 3
   1.4 Age of Membership, Gender, Ethnicity, and Age Breakdown... 3
       1.4.1 Age... 3
       1.4.2 Race/Ethnicity... 4
       1.4.3 Gender... 4
   1.5 Gangs and Education... 5
   1.6 My Purpose for This Book... 6
   References... 7

2 **Theories of Gang Involvement**... 9
   2.1 Seeking Theories of Gang Involvement... 9
   2.2 Interactional Theory... 9
   2.3 Developmental Model of Gang Involvement... 10
   2.4 Social Disorganization Theory... 11
   2.5 Multiple Marginalization Theory... 11
   2.6 Strain Theory... 11
   2.7 Social Learning Theory... 12
   2.8 Systems Theory... 12
   2.9 Social Control Theory... 12
   2.10 Self-Control Theory... 13
   2.11 Could There Be Another Possible Theory to Explain Gang Membership?... 13
   2.12 Seeking a Secure Base: Gangs as Attachment Figures... 14
   References... 17

3 **Lack of Family Consistency: Relating Attachment Theory with Gang Involvement**... 19
   3.1 Classical Attachment Theory... 19
   3.2 Types of Attachments... 20

	3.3	Modern Attachment Theory: Affect Regulation	22
	3.4	How Insecure Attachment Has a Lifelong Impact	23
	3.5	Gangs and Attachment Theory	23
	3.6	Clinicians Can Step In	25
	3.7	Lack of Family Consistency	27
		3.7.1 Being Raised in a Single Mother Home, Absent Father	29
		3.7.2 Parents Absent Due to Drug Addiction or Death	31
		3.7.3 Victims of Abuse	33
		3.7.4 Lack of Supervision at Home	34
		3.7.5 Influenced by Family Members in Gangs	35
	References		37
4	"Brotherhood, Sisterhood, Unity:" Gang as Replacement Family		39
	4.1	Gangs and Family Systems	39
	4.2	"Brotherhood, Sisterhood, Unity:" Gang as Replacement Family	41
		4.2.1 Brotherhood, Sisterhood, Unity	41
		4.2.2 Gang as Replacement Family	43
		4.2.3 Growing Up with Gang Members	46
		4.2.4 Conditional Love	48
	References		49
5	"No Other Option:" The Role of Social Environment		51
	5.1	"No Other Option"	51
	5.2	It Is Just the Environment We Grew Up In	53
	5.3	Idolizing Gang Members and Lifestyle	57
	5.4	It's Just a Way of Life	58
	5.5	Playing the Cards They've Been Dealt	59
	5.6	Joining Because They Lost a Friend to Gang Violence	61
	References		61
6	"Death, Jail, or a Turnaround:" Making the Decision to Disengage		63
	6.1	Push and Pull Factors: Reasons Why They Leave	63
	6.2	Consequences for Leaving?	65
	6.3	Making the Decision to Disengage	66
		6.3.1 Wanting a Better Life Outcome for Themselves and Their Families	66
		6.3.2 Witnessing or Experiencing Violence	69
		6.3.3 Experiencing Incarceration	71
		6.3.4 Experiencing Gang Disillusionment	72
		6.3.5 How They Got Out	75
		6.3.6 Moving On	77
	References		78
7	**Case Illustrations**		79
	7.1	Kyle Case Illustration	79
		7.1.1 Kyle	80
		7.1.2 My Work with Kyle	82

		7.1.3	A Tragic and Unexpected Loss	84
		7.1.4	The Aftermath	85
	7.2	Emily Case Illustration		86
		7.2.1	Emily	86
		7.2.2	My Work with Emily	87
		7.2.3	Moving Forward from Grief	89
		7.2.4	A New Beginning	89
		7.2.5	More Losses	90
		7.2.6	Transitioning	91
		7.2.7	The Return of a Familiar Secure Base	92
	7.3	Tying it All Together: Attachment Theory		92
		7.3.1	Anger, Behavioral Difficulties, and Attachment	93
		7.3.2	Counselor Steps in as Secure Base	94
	References			95
8	**Risk Factors and Protective Factors**			**97**
	8.1	Risk Factors		97
		8.1.1	Individual Risk Factors	98
		8.1.2	Family Risk Factors	102
		8.1.3	School Risk Factors	105
		8.1.4	Peer Group Risk Factors	105
		8.1.5	Community/Social Environment Risk Factors	107
		8.1.6	Tying Risk Factors Together	108
	8.2	Protective Factors		109
		8.2.1	Family Protective Factors	111
		8.2.2	School Protective Factors	111
		8.2.3	Peer and Community/Social Environment Protective Factors	111
	8.3	Tying Risk and Protective Factors Together		113
	References			113
9	**Warning Signs of Gang Involvement**			**115**
	9.1	Identifying Warning Signs		115
	9.2	Visible/Physical Signs		115
		9.2.1	Colors	116
		9.2.2	Clothing and Accessories	121
		9.2.3	Hand Signs	121
		9.2.4	Tattoos	122
		9.2.5	Symbols	123
		9.2.6	Graffiti	124
	9.3	Additional Warning Signs		125
		9.3.1	Social Media	125
		9.3.2	Music and Movies	127
		9.3.3	Money/Theft	127
		9.3.4	Safety Worry	127
		9.3.5	New Friends	127

		9.3.6 Use of Street Names...................................	127
		9.3.7 Behavioral Changes....................................	129
		9.3.8 Drug Abuse	129
		9.3.9 Weapons..	129
		9.3.10 Fighting	130
	References..		130

10 Prevention: Building a Safe Haven 133
- 10.1 Building an Oasis... 133
- 10.2 Counselors as Secure Base.............................. 134
- 10.3 Need for Acknowledgment of Gang Problems 135
- 10.4 Components of Gang Prevention in School.................. 136
  - 10.4.1 Target At-Risk Youth 136
  - 10.4.2 Involve Students................................... 137
  - 10.4.3 Incorporate Mentors/Positive Role Models 139
  - 10.4.4 Assess Needs and Create Awareness 141
  - 10.4.5 Engage with Parents and Caregivers 142
  - 10.4.6 Connect with Support Staff 143
  - 10.4.7 Build a Safe Environment 145
  - 10.4.8 Implementing Dress Code 146
  - 10.4.9 Link with Law Enforcement 147
  - 10.4.10 Strengthen Community Ties 148
  - 10.4.11 Teach Students Social Skills 148
  - 10.4.12 Provide Other Options 149
- 10.5 A Word on School Resource Officers 149
- 10.6 Former Gang Members Speak About Prevention 150
  - 10.6.1 Lack of Attachment/Investment to School............. 150
  - 10.6.2 Activities/Mentors 154
  - 10.6.3 Counseling... 155
  - 10.6.4 Community Involvement 156
  - 10.6.5 Former Gang Members Giving Back to the Community: Offering Lessons to Youth 157
  - 10.6.6 Looking Back and Making Different Choices.......... 159
  - 10.6.7 Learning Lessons from the Gang Experience 159
- References.. 160

11 A Piece About Trauma-Informed Practice 163
- 11.1 Adverse Childhood Experiences (ACEs).................... 163
  - 11.1.1 Impacts of ACEs in Childhood 164
  - 11.1.2 Future Impacts of ACEs in Adulthood................ 164
  - 11.1.3 ACEs Are Preventable 169
- 11.2 Effects of Violence on Youth 171
- 11.3 Trauma-Informed Practice................................. 171
- 11.4 How Can Schools Become Trauma-Informed?.................. 173
  - 11.4.1 Administrators 173
  - 11.4.2 Teachers... 174
  - 11.4.3 Support Staff 174

		11.5	The Importance of Trauma-Informed Care	175
			References...	175
12	**School Prevention Programs**			177
	12.1	Let's Talk About Prevention Programs		177
	12.2	Addressing Risk Factors		178
	12.3	Focused Deterrence		178
	12.4	Addressing the Need for Prevention		179
	12.5	When Should Prevention Start?...........................		181
	12.6	Gang Prevention Programs		182
		12.6.1	Promoting Alternative Thinking Strategies (PATHS) (Source: https://pathsprogram.com/)	182
		12.6.2	G.R.E.A.T. Program (Source: https://www.great-online.org/)	183
		12.6.3	Gang-Free Schools and Communities Initiative (Part of the OJJDP Comprehensive Gang Model) (Source: National Gang Center: www.nationalgangcenter.gov) ...	184
		12.6.4	Gang Reduction and Youth Development (GRYD) (Source: https://www.lagryd.org)....................	185
		12.6.5	The City of Chicago's Youth Violence Intervention Plan (Source: https://youth.gov/youth-topics/preventing-youth--violence/forum-communities/chicago/brief)	186
	12.7	Prevention: A Path Forward..............................		187
		References...		188
13	**Being the Change: Making a Difference**........................			189
	13.1	Surrounded by People Who Can Get You to That Next Level....		190
	13.2	Lack of Consistency.....................................		190
	13.3	No Other Option: Gangs Enter the Picture		190
	13.4	Creating a Safe Haven		191
	13.5	Looking Ahead...		191
	13.6	Making a Difference		192
Index...				193

About the Author

Katherine De Vito, DSW, LCSW, is a Licensed Clinical Social Worker (LCSW) working as a school social worker providing mental health counseling to students, crisis intervention, conflict mediation, and case management to special education students, as well as collaborating with families, teachers, administration, law enforcement, and community organizations. She also works in private practice. Prior to becoming a school social worker, she also worked in the nonprofit sector providing individual and group in school counseling and private counseling with adults, children, and their families. She received her Doctorate in Social Work (DSW) from Rutgers University School of Social Work in New Jersey. In her time there, she published two articles: De Vito, K. (2017). Schools fall short: Lack of continuum of care in public schools. *Reflections: Narratives of Professional Helping, 23*(4), 4–19; and De Vito, K. (2020). Seeking a secure base: Gangs as attachment figures. *Qualitative Social Work, 19*(4), 754–769. She also earned a Master of Science in Social Work (MSSW) degree from Columbia University School of Social Work in New York City as well as a Bachelor of Arts degree from Rutgers College and the School of Communication, Information, and Library Studies, with a dual major in Psychology and Journalism/Mass Media. She has interned at various magazines and newspapers and has published articles in both magazines and newspapers as well as worked in children's book publishing for several years. She loves being able to touch the lives of youth in a positive way every day. Gang prevention is a passion for her. Helping to make a difference in the lives of her clients and students is both an honor and a privilege. In her free time, she enjoys spending time with her friends and family, especially her two children, Dylan and Emma.

Chapter 1
Introduction

No hopeful kid has ever joined a gang. It's about a lethal absence of hope. (Boyle, 2020, Unpublished)

– *Father Greg Boyle, Founder of Homeboy Industries*

1.1 A School Social Worker's Role

My office is located in a busy hallway of an urban high school building. I am a school social worker whose primary job is to provide supportive mental health counseling to high school students. Students frequently drop by to sit and talk about their daily worries and issues going on in their lives. My job is to listen and to provide support and intervention. In addition to providing counseling, I also do some case management as part of the Child Study Team and also collaborate with various professionals including private therapists, law enforcement, child protective services, guidance counselors, teachers, and administrators. It is not an easy job. But it is a job that I truly love.

School counseling is such a vital component of public schools. School counselors work with parents; perform individual and group counseling with students, crisis intervention, and skills training; and collaborate with teachers, administration, and parents (Allen-Meares et al., 2013). Counselors work tirelessly every day to be a support system to their students. Students can see counselors as allies and advocates who are great resources and supports. Counseling within the school environment can help in making a difference in children's lives by helping to initiate changes and help in troubled times (Allen-Meares et al., 2013; Rupani et al., 2012; Cooper et al., 2015). It is an honor and a privilege that young people let me into their lives and share their stories and their pain with me. If I can make even one child's life better by being a caring and supportive presence, then that makes every day at this job worthwhile to me.

One of the problems that I have encountered frequently during my career as a school social worker is youth gang involvement. Working in the area of gang prevention has become a passion of mine. I have seen students become involved in gangs and become physically injured or incarcerated. Some lose friends and family, and some even die. I remember getting the call one day that a high school student had been killed at a party due to gang violence. A fight broke out between two rival gang members. Our student was unarmed. The other guy brought a knife. Our student didn't make it. The funeral was packed with many current and former students. I was surprised to see some former high school students there. I was even more surprised and saddened to see them sporting gang beads and colors. That one death impacted so many lives in our current and former student population. My job was there to be a support to grieving students.

The National Gang Center reports that school staff members are on the front line of gang defense within the school. This means that school staff members are in a unique and optimal position to engage in gang prevention efforts. Our job is to intervene as early as we can when we see warning signs or someone shows risk factors. In addition, school social workers can be a consistent figure in a student's life. Many who join gangs are lacking consistency in their lives, which the gangs provide. Sometimes, it can be that one person who can step in and be there for that student, providing support and consistency, and a sense of attachment, which can change that person's life. I believe that prevention and early intervention, even in subtle ways, can be the change in that young person's world.

1.2 Gang Prevalence

Gangs remain a persistent widespread problem throughout many areas of the world. In this book, the focus will be on street gangs. Street gangs can be defined as a group of youth with a shared identity, who are street-oriented, and continually meet to engage in illegal criminal activities (Ruble & Turner, 2000; Alleyne & Wood, 2014; O'Brien et al., 2013). Statistics illustrate how the prevalence of gangs impacts communities. One in twelve youth report gang membership while being a teenager (Howell, 2013). In 2010, one-third (34%) of cities, towns, and counties in rural areas in the United States reported gang problems (Howell, 2013). The National Gang Center reported that in the National Survey of American Attitudes on Substance Abuse XV: Teens and Parents, released in August 2010 by the National Center on Addiction and Substance Abuse, 45% of high school students reported gangs or students who say they were a part of a gang in their schools. In addition, 35% of middle school students reported gangs or students who say they were a part of a gang in their schools. The 2008 National Youth Gang Survey reported a 15% increase in gang activity since 2002, with the United States having 774,000 gang members and 27,900 active gangs and 32.4% of all communities having gang issues

(Egley et al., 2010). These statistics show how invasive the problem has become and support that more needs to be done in terms of prevention with youth today.

1.3 Violence and Gangs

Gang membership has a profound influence on the youth that are involved in gangs, especially since violence is intricately woven into gang culture. The relationship between violence and gangs is strong. Youth involved in gangs commit a large amount of crime, which is a significantly higher amount of crime than their neighborhood peers who are around the same age (Ezell, 2018). Violent offenses, drug usage, and property crime are more likely to be committed by gang members (Hill et al., 1999). Gang members are also more than twice as likely to take part in serious delinquency and to carry a gun and more than three times as likely to sell drugs as non-gang members (Hill et al., 1999). Clark et al. (2018) reported a 100 times greater homicide victimization rate for gang members than in the general population, meaning that a youth's chance of dying earlier in life is much greater if involved in a gang. With the amount of violence that is present that is due to gangs, it makes sense to intervene early and try to prevent youth from joining gangs initially.

1.4 Age of Membership, Gender, Ethnicity, and Age Breakdown

The National Gang Center surveyed law enforcement about the age, race/ethnicity, and gender breakdown of gang members in their jurisdictions between the years of 1996–2011.

1.4.1 Age

Most gang members will initiate membership between the ages of 12 and 15 years (Sharkey et al., 2010). Youth have joined gangs as early as age seven or eight, but involvement ramps up at age 12 or 13 (Estrada et al., 2018). These statistics support getting prevention methods started with youth as early as possible. The National Gang Center also surveyed law enforcement agencies and found them reporting a higher percentage of gang members who are considered adults, over the age of 18, compared to juvenile gang members. Three out of every five gang members were adults. See Fig. 1.1 for a breakdown of ages of gang members from 1996 to 2011 from the National Gang Center.

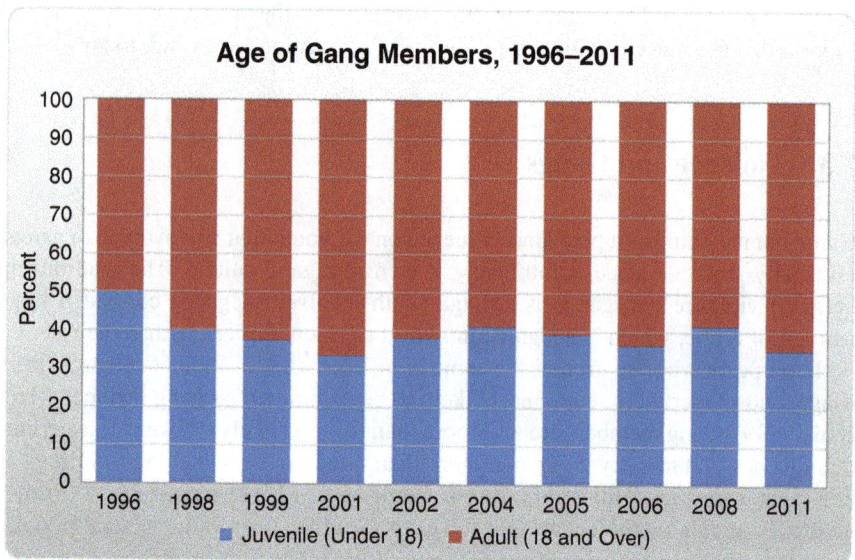

Fig. 1.1 Age of Gang Members, 1996–2011. (National Gang Center. *National Youth Gang Survey Analysis*. Retrieved [8/17/20] from http://www.nationalgangcenter.gov/Survey-Analysis)

1.4.2 Race/Ethnicity

In terms of race and ethnicity, the National Gang Center surveyed law enforcement agencies and found there was a larger percentage of Hispanic/Latino and African American/Black gang members compared to other ethnicities/races. Forty-six percent were Hispanic/Latino, and 35 percent were African American/Black. More than 11 percent were White, and 7 percent another race/ethnicity. Sharkey et al. (2010) reported an ethnic breakdown being 7% of Whites and 12% of Blacks and Latinos involved in gangs by 17 years of age. Please see Fig. 1.2 for a breakdown of race/ethnicity of gang members from 1996 to 2011 from the National Gang Center.

1.4.3 Gender

The majority of gang members are male, but up to 15% are female (Vigil, 2008). Females find their positions within the gang, while males tend to work in areas of gang formation, actions, and hierarchies, being more involved in the more serious street crimes (Miller & Brunson, 2000). Females are found in the more supportive roles of the gang and also criminal activity (Vigil, 2008). The National Gang Center surveyed law enforcement agencies and found that there is an overwhelmingly higher number of males as compared with female gang members. Even though there are fewer gang members that are female, they still do participate in gangs and also

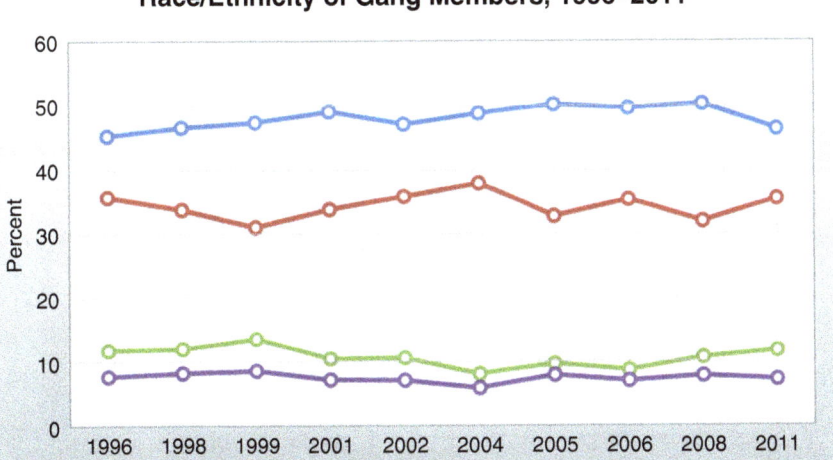

Fig. 1.2 Race/Ethnicity of Gang Members 1996–2011. (National Gang Center. *National Youth Gang Survey Analysis*. Retrieved [8/17/20] from http://www.nationalgangcenter.gov/Survey-Analysis)

need to be included in prevention programs. Please see Fig. 1.3 for a breakdown of gender of gang members from 1998 to 2010 from the National Gang Center.

1.5 Gangs and Education

Youth who become involved in gangs typically have difficulties in school. Gang-involved youth often exhibit lack of motivation for school and an inability to relate to coursework (Clark et al., 2018). Gang members are 30 percent less likely to graduate from high school and 58% less likely to graduate from college (Clark et al., 2018). Since gang-involved youth are typically not as interested in education and school, there will be fewer career options available to them, which then increases the chance of illegal moneymaking (O'Brien et al., 2013). Some may have no other expectations for themselves other than the street life, so school is of little interest. Instead, gang-involved youth may spend their time in school socializing, recruiting, or fighting with gang members (Clark et al., 2018). When youth do not have an interest or motivation for school, there is less of a chance that they will participate or do well.

When youth are not interested in school, it can become problematic. Gang-involved students may be hard to deal with in a school setting because they can defy authority and have behavioral issues, making it more likely that they are placed in

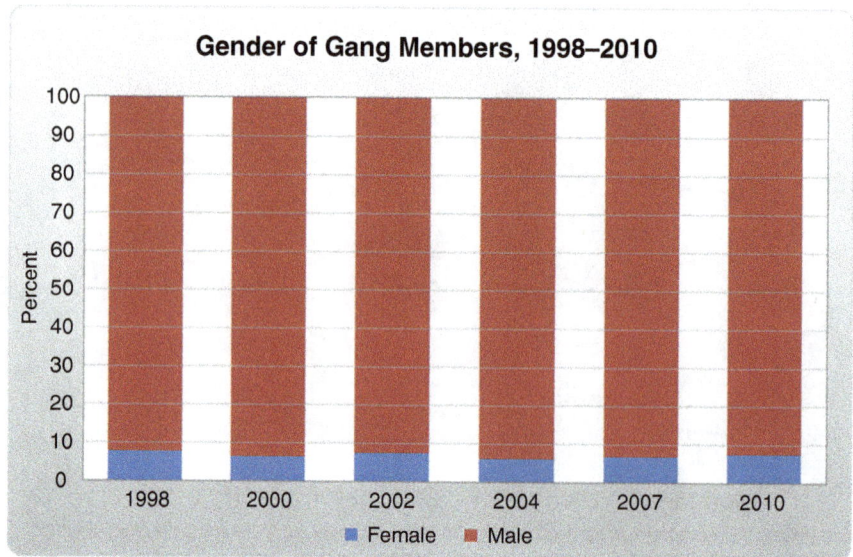

Fig. 1.3 Gender of Gang Members, 1998–2010. (National Gang Center. *National Youth Gang Survey Analysis*. Retrieved [8/17/20] from http://www.nationalgangcenter.gov/Survey-Analysis)

an alternative setting for school, apart from prosocial students (Clark et al., 2018). Being separated from prosocial students means having a lack of positive peer influences. Having a gang presence in schools is linked to a higher level of drug use and violence, less academic achievement and other academic problems, and a feeling of not being safe in school (Fisher et al., 2018). All of these issues are difficult for staff and other students to contend with on a daily basis, making prevention efforts even more important.

1.6 My Purpose for This Book

Gangs are problematic for society. This fact has been well established. What can be done? I believe that the answer lies at the beginning. Prevent the problem before it even becomes a problem. That would mean starting prevention efforts early on in a youth's life. My purpose for this book is to give an inside look into the world of gangs and, within that world, find clues to aid in gang prevention efforts in the world I know best, schools. The key in combating the gang world is prevention. We need to catch these students when they are young. Schools have the best opportunity for prevention because as school staff members, we have access to children daily. There are many things we can do, such as mentoring and getting them invested and interested in school. We can show them that there are opportunities and other options available other than gangs.

Gang members are often portrayed in the media in a certain light. But how did that individual become a gang member? There is not just one sole factor that determines gang membership for an individual youth. Rather, it is often a combination of numerous factors. What are those factors that led that person to choose a path toward gang membership? While I was at Rutgers University School of Social Work earning my Doctorate in Social Work (DSW), I focused my research on youth gang involvement and prevention. I conducted a qualitative research study, "Seeking a Secure Base: Gangs as Attachment Figures," which was published in *Qualitative Social Work* in 2020. This study illustrated some of the voices of former gang members who shared their experiences of life in a gang, what childhood experiences impacted their decision to join a gang, and reasons they chose to leave the gang life. This book will delve deeper into those qualitative interviews as well as interviews with experts in the field and share pieces of the keys to prevention.

I don't believe that anyone grows up truly wanting to be a gang member. There are reasons behind every gang member's story. Those former gang members that have walked those streets have poignant words of wisdom for youth today and offer some hope. They want to help make that change as well. And throughout the book, they, along with me, will tell this story.

References

Allen-Meares, P., Montgomery, K., & Kim, J. (2013). School-based social work intervention: A cross-national systemic review. *Social Work, 58*(3), 253–262.

Alleyne, E., & Wood, J. (2014). Gang involvement: Social and environmental factors. *Crime & Delinquency, 60*(4), 547–568.

Clark, K., Pyrooz, D., & Randa, R. (2018). In H. Shapiro (Ed.), *The Wiley handbook on violence in education: Forms, factors, and preventions.* Wiley.

Cooper, M., Fugard, A., McArthur, K., & Pearce, P. (2015). Estimating effectiveness of school-based counseling: Using data from controlled trials to predict improvement over non-intervention change. *Counseling and Psychotherapy Research, 15*(4), 262–273.

Egley, A., Howell, J. C., & Moore, J. P. (2010). *Highlights of the 2008 National Youth Gang Survey*. U.S. Department of Justice. https://www.ncjrs.gov/pdffiles1/ojjdp/229249.pdf.

Estrada, J. N., Huerta, A. H., Hernandez, E., Hernandez, R. A., & Kim, S. W. (2018). In H. Shapiro (Ed.), *The Wiley handbook on violence in education: Forms, factors, and preventions.* Wiley.

Ezell, M. E. (2018). In H. Shapiro (Ed.), *The Wiley handbook on violence in education: Forms, factors, and preventions.* Wiley.

Fisher, B. W., Curran, F. C., Pearman, A., & Gardella, J. H. (2018). In H. Shapiro (Ed.), *The Wiley handbook on violence in education: Forms, factors, and preventions.* Wiley.

Hill, K. G., Howell, J. C., Hawkins, J. D., & Battin-Pearson, S. R. (1999). Childhood risk factors for adolescent gang membership: Results from the Seattle Social Development Project. *Journal of Research in Crime and Delinquency, 36*, 300–322.

Howell, J. C. (2013). In T. R. Simon, N. M. Ritter, & R. R. Mahendra (Eds.), *Changing course: Preventing gang membership.* US Department of Justice, US Department of Health and Human Services & Centers for Disease Control and Prevention.

Miller, J., & Brunson, R. (2000). Gender dynamics in youth gangs: A comparison of males' and females' accounts. *Justice Quarterly, 17*(3), 419–448.

National Gang Center. (n.d.). https://www.nationalgangcenter.gov/

National Gang Center and Office of Juvenile Justice and Delinquency Prevention. (n.d.). *Gangs in schools*. https://www.nationalgangcenter.gov/Content/Documents/Gangs-in-Schools.pdf

National Gang Center. *National Youth Gang Survey Analysis*. Retrieved [8/17/20] from http://www.nationalgangcenter.gov/Survey-Analysis.

O'Brien, K., Daffern, M., Chu, C., & Thomas, S. (2013). Youth gang affiliation, violence, and criminal activities: A review of motivational, risk, and protective factors. *Aggression and Violent Behavior, 18*(4), 417–425.

Ruble, N., & Turner, W. (2000). A systematic analysis of the dynamics and organization of urban street gangs. *The American Journal of Family Therapy, 28*, 117–132.

Rupani, P., Haughey, N., & Cooper, M. (2012). The impact of school-based counseling on young people's capacity to study and learn. *British Journal of Guidance & Counseling, 40*(5), 514.

Sharkey, J. D., Shekhtmeyster, Z., Chavez-Lopez, Norris, E., & Sass, L. (2010). The protective influence of gangs: Can schools compensate? *Aggression and Violent Behavior, 16*, 45–54.

Vigil, J. (2008). Female gang members from East Los Angeles. *International Journal of Social Inquiry, 1*(1), 47–74.

Chapter 2
Theories of Gang Involvement

> *Some people join gangs for protection...But then some people join gangs for the style, for the publicity, for the popularity...it's like the politics...Some kids don't know how to fight so they got no choice but to join a gang so somebody had their back and it's a family. Some people trust a gang more than they trust their own blood and family. And it's a lifestyle you lead when you were in that type of environment...You from the projects all you know is project stuff. You gonna be considered a project baby to the fullest...Until you start owning projects. (Luis, 2019, Unpublished)*
>
> – Former Gang Member Luis

2.1 Seeking Theories of Gang Involvement

While I was conducting research during my doctoral program, my focus turned to gang prevention. I was curious to learn why would a youth choose to join gang. What are the driving forces? What would make youth choose to leave the gang? I felt that the answers to those questions might aid in research for what could work in gang prevention. In addition to hearing from former gang members, such as Luis, I went to the literature to look at what research has said about what drives gang involvement. There are various theories that have attempted to explain the reason behind delinquent behavior and gang membership.

2.2 Interactional Theory

Thornberry (1987) developed interactional theory as an explanation for delinquent behavior. Different stages in life will yield different priorities. In early adolescence, it is family; in middle adolescence, it is school and peer group; and in adulthood, family and conventional activities become more important (Thornberry, 1987). Interactional theory posits that behavior is part of development, with youth interacting with people and places in their lives, with their behavior being informed by those interactions (Thornberry, 1987). It does not see delinquency as a result of social actions. Rather, it sees human behavior as a result of social interaction. Furthermore, weakened bonds to society, such as weak parental attachment, weak school attachment, and weak traditional values, can increase delinquent behavior (Thornberry, 1987). A youth's position in the social structure of society also plays a role, such as class and neighborhood social disorganization (Thornberry, 1987). Interactional theory can be applied to gang membership, where gang membership is a result of being involved in negative peer relationships, having weak relationships, poor structural environments, and having a lot of crime in the environment (Alleyne & Wood, 2014). Interaction within one's environment and with individuals in the environment can impact life decisions, including delinquency and joining a gang.

Thornberry et al. (2003) also took this theory a step further and developed a life course perspective, which states that behavior that develops in childhood is not cemented there. But instead, it continues to evolve and change over the course of a lifetime because of interactions between the person and the environment. Those interactions can affect the person and thus behavior. Social influences and social-psychological processes are also taken into account in this theory (Howell & Egley, 2005). Therefore, neighborhood and family factors will affect the risk of gang membership through lack of positive social bonds (Howell & Egley, 2005). If there is a lack of positive bonds, there is a greater chance of antisocial influences and values to come into play (Howell & Egley, 2005). Without having those protective factors, youth become more likely to become involved in a gang.

2.3 Developmental Model of Gang Involvement

Howell and Egley (2005) extended the work of Thornberry and colleagues to encompass younger ages and took it a step further to create a Developmental Model of Gang Involvement. Their developmental model has four developmental stages: preschool, school entry, childhood, and adolescence. They discussed how a pathway to gang involvement begins at an early age with a "stepping-stone pattern." One step leads to the next step and so on. Conduct problems begin around age three to four, with school failure during ages six through 12, and joining a gang by age 13 to 15, followed by delinquency onward from there. Conduct problems in preschool can lead to childhood delinquency, which, when combined with other risk factors, increases the chance of adolescent delinquency and gang involvement. It appears as if there is no intervention, then each step will lead to a further step along the path toward gang involvement.

2.4 Social Disorganization Theory

Social disorganization theory focuses on the relationship that exists between a neighborhood and crime, social control, and structure, mainly how the conditions in a neighborhood make it more favorable for crime and delinquency to occur (Kubrin & Weitzer, 2003). This theory states that a community structure does not see the value in residents and therefore does not keep social control in the community (Sampson & Groves, 1989). There will not be a sense of connectedness in a community or social control when there is a high crime rate and juvenile delinquency, which occurs in areas that are more disadvantaged (Sampson & Groves, 1989; Santiago et al., 2011). Social disorganization involves economical destabilization, which leads to breakdown in families and school (Dickson-Gomez et al., 2017). Crime becomes more likely when there are certain conditions that make it more difficult to control public behavior, such as poverty, weak social networks, residential mobility, and ethnic heterogeneity (Kubrin & Weitzer, 2003). Crime is more likely to flourish in a neighborhood that is disadvantaged and disorganized, which also makes gang involvement and activity more prevalent. Social disadvantage and economic inequality may lead to gang involvement (Hill et al., 1999).

2.5 Multiple Marginalization Theory

Multiple marginality is described as the destabilization of urban and minority populations due to societal forces (Vigil, 2004). Those societal forces have an impact on minority populations, causing destabilization. Multiple marginalization is a lack of employment opportunities, poor living conditions, poverty, and family and community stress (Dickson-Gomez et al., 2017). Different events, thoughts, people, and places are associated with push and pull factors for youth gang membership (Vigil, 2004). Therefore, there are many factors causing stress, making it appear as if there is no good way out. A gang might seem like a way to get out of a bleak home situation. Youth turn to gang membership because schools and family do not meet the needs of youth and are unable to form those necessary positive attachments (Dickson-Gomez et al., 2017).

2.6 Strain Theory

Strain theory posits that living in poverty causes strain because one cannot reach the picture of American success in economics (Sharkey et al., 2010). Strain can occur when these goals cannot be attained, such as by living in a poverty community and not having as many opportunities or by a lack of achievement in school (Sharkey et al., 2010). In this situation, people turn to criminal activities, knowing they cannot be successful with typical employment options (Sharkey et al., 2010). If gangs are in the area, they provide a means to achieve these goals. Strain theory community risk factors that go along with this theory include frequent moving, lack of ability and availability of social and economic opportunities, social disorganization, poverty, and organized lower-class communities (Sharkey et al., 2010). Gang involvement and overall delinquency are a result of adapting to structural pressures, such as lack of opportunities leading to frustration, which then leads to illegal antisocial behaviors as a means to attain gains in life (Hill et al., 1999).

2.7 Social Learning Theory

Social learning theory suggests that people exhibit their own behavior by learning and watching role models, especially family (Sharkey et al., 2010). Learning theory suggests that delinquency is not natural but rather learned from watching others (Thornberry, 1987). If youth become involved with peers who are engaged in criminal or delinquent behavior, instead of being around youth who are involved in positive activities, this theory suggests they would be more likely to look to join a gang based on who they hang around and model after (Sharkey et al., 2010). Some risk factors that support this include lack of involvement with positive peers, being socialized to the streets, having gang members in your school classes, and having peers as friends who are involved in drugs (Sharkey et al., 2010).

2.8 Systems Theory

Systems theory can show how gangs resemble a family system (Sharkey et al., 2010). Gangs can take the place of family for at-risk youth and become their only family. Gangs have a certain hierarchy such as age and experience (Sharkey et al., 2010). The hierarchy can resemble a corporation or hierarchy like a family system. For example, there are Big Homies and Little Homies, which are like having a big brother or sister or little brother or sister. The elder members who are more invested and running things can be in more of a parental role doling out orders for the rest of the members.

2.9 Social Control Theory

Social control theory posits that delinquent behavior appears in a community where there are less social and cultural limitations over human behavior (Thornberry, 1987). Social control theorists believe that crime will happen when there is a weak bond between person and society and the weaker the bond, deviant behavior is more likely to occur (Brownfield, 2010). People conform to society based on whether four things are present: attachment, involvement, belief, and commitment (Brownfield, 2010). Youth are less likely to be involved in a gang if the community is on a course of development that is shown to the people and enforced (Sharkey et al., 2010). Youth enter into relationships with deviant peer groups because of a lack of youth social control (Hill et al., 1999). Strong attachment to school, family, and community all help to drive a successful community (Sharkey et al., 2010). If one does not have a stable home environment, with stable sufficient resources, it can cause family stress. One might not attend school, opting to support the family to alleviate stress by working instead. The gang lifestyle may become attractive because it offers a way of making money. However, research that has studied social control has not found that it relates highly to gang membership when compared to others (Sharkey et al., 2010).

2.10 Self-Control Theory

Self-control theory came out of an extension of social control theory (Brownfield, 2010). Self-control theory states that youth who do not have self-control, such as lacking delay of gratification and caution, are more likely to be involved in peer delinquency and criminal activity (Sharkey et al., 2010). Risk factors related to individuals exhibiting a lack of self-control include aggressiveness, deviance, being street-smart, history of delinquency, defiance, social disabilities, alcohol and drug use, owning guns, early sexual activity, exhibiting problem behavior, drinking, victimization, hyperactivity, and wanting rewards that come from being involved in a group such as protection, companionship, and identity (Sharkey et al., 2010). Individuals who lack a high sense of self-control also lack in areas of attachment and commitment, cognitive skills, academic skills, and investment in areas like jobs, family, friends, and relationships (Brownfield, 2010).

2.11 Could There Be Another Possible Theory to Explain Gang Membership?

Youth join gangs for a multitude of reasons. The decision to join is an individual one. All of the theories described above offer some explanation for delinquent and gang behaviors. However, could there be another theory that could be used to explain gang membership? I wanted to conduct my own study to speak to former gang members to see what drove their decision to join and leave gangs. Perhaps there could be more vital information that could be discovered to aid in the areas of prevention.

2.12 Seeking a Secure Base: Gangs as Attachment Figures

As a result of all of my research, a journal article was published. "Seeking a Secure Base: Gangs as Attachment Figures" is a qualitative research study which was published in the journal, *Qualitative Social Work,* in 2020. The goal of the study was to explore several research questions: How the childhood experiences of former gang members shaped their decision to join a gang, and what factors contributed to former gang members' decision to disengage from gang membership? The voices of fourteen former gang members are heard through qualitative interviews. Thematic analysis was used to identify the following themes: "Lack of Family Consistency, Brotherhood, Sisterhood, Unity: Gang as Replacement Family," "No Other Option," and "Death, Jail, or a Turnaround: Making the Decision to Disengage." There is a focus on attachment theory as a theory that can explain the drive toward gang membership, which was a key finding of the qualitative research. Participants' verbatim quotes were included to highlight the themes found. No identifying information was incorporated and pseudonyms protected the identities of participants.

The study themes showed that there were several major findings. Participants had a lack of consistency with their primary caregivers. Almost all of them identified the gang and gang members as being either a family or replacement family. Some felt as if it was an extension of their family because they had family members that were in the gang as well. Additional participants felt as if they had no other options available to them but to join a gang because of their environment, socioeconomic status, or upbringing. Some of the gang members interviewed decided to disengage from gang membership because they wanted to turn their lives around and wanted something better for themselves and their families. The participants in this study all were able to walk away from gang membership without consequences by moving out of the area and by disassociating with gang members.

> Many risk factors that were seen in the literature were also seen with participants such as: residing in a neighborhood with a gang presence, experiencing childhood maltreatment such as abuse and neglect, lack of parental supervision, poor school performance, not being invested in school, low family income, desire to make money, having friends who are involved in crime or gangs, history of family criminal or gang involvement, living in disadvantaged communities, lacking a stable or intact family, lack of a stable father figure, and weak attachment to family and school. (Alleyne & Wood, 2014; O'Brien et al., 2013; McNulty & Bellair, 2003; Del Carmen et al., 2009; Gover, 2002) (De Vito, 2020)

De Vito (2020) stated that psychological factors can have an impact on social factors. All of the primary caregivers of the study participants lived in a low socioeconomic area and struggled with poverty. Communities that have a lack of opportunities and resources due to poverty, racism, and inequality may have a higher incidence of gang membership in their area. Having a lack of opportunities and resources along with inequality can be driving forces behind inner-city gang membership. Children coming from an area of higher socioeconomic status may lack a stable attachment figure but may not turn to a gang. Instead, they may turn to drugs, for example.

2.12 Seeking a Secure Base: Gangs as Attachment Figures

However, they have more resources and a better safety net, which may decrease the likelihood of jail, if they do get into legal trouble.

> Reasons participants left gangs were reflected in the literature including: getting tired of the gang lifestyle, being a victim of violence, witnessing violence, gang disillusionment, stable employment and relationships, moving away, and aging and maturing, which will promote marriage, having children, and family responsibilities (Berger et al., 2016; O'Brien et al., 2013; Pyrooz & Decker, 2011). Former gang members may have been searching for an attachment figure initially in gangs, but realized that this lifestyle could not continue forever. All participants wanted a life where they were not in danger of getting killed or incarcerated. All had been incarcerated for crimes and suffered abandonment by fellow gang members, creating a sense of disillusionment. Their search for a more stable attachment figure did not end positively. In leaving, all participants wanted a better life and to bring something positive to the world. (De Vito, 2020)

Methodology*
Participants

Eligibility Sampling criteria for this study included being 18 years of age or older, being able to speak conversational English, and being a former member of a street gang.

Recruitment A flyer and recruitment e-mail describing the study were used to recruit participants. Nominations sampling was a recruitment strategy (Padgett, 2017). Gatekeepers who worked with former gang members selected potential participants based on study criteria. The gatekeepers included school professionals and an organization that rehabilitates former gang members. Interested participants were prescreened prior to interviewing. For the informed consent process, a consent form was given ahead of the interview, and verbal consent was obtained to protect confidentiality. No identifying information was gathered. The consent form explained the study purpose. Each respondent was given a $25 gift card for participating. The Institutional Review Board (IRB) at Rutgers University approved this study and all protocols.

Respondents The fourteen former gang member participants were between the ages of 19–56. Two participants were female and twelve were male. Ten participants identified as African American and four identified as Latino/Hispanic. This sample included minorities, which is typically representative of the racial makeup of an inner city. Overrepresentation of minorities living in inner cities is a contemporary social problem. Ten participants resided in a city, while four resided in a suburb. The highest education received was some college for five participants, high school diploma for five participants, a GED for two participants, one completed school up until 10th grade, and another completed school up until 12th grade but did not finish. Nine participants were employed, and five were unemployed. Five participants were married, and nine were single. Nine participants identified as Christian, three identified as Catholic, and two did not have a religion. Ten participants had children, while the rest did not. Four participants lived alone, and ten lived with family. The participants joined a gang between the ages of 12 and 15, with five joining at age 12, providing average and standard deviation.

Data Collection A semistructured interview guide was prepared. All interviews were done over the telephone. The participants felt more comfortable keeping their anonymity by doing telephone interviews, as opposed to in-person interviews. Some were also living a great distance away. The pro is that telephone interviews provided comfort, so participants may have felt more at ease and open. The con is that the face-to-face interaction is missing, which can give interviews a more personal and comfortable feel. Interviews were done in April and June 2018. Demographic questions included age, gender, race/ethnicity, religion, marital status, children, employment, area of residence, household residents, and age of gang initiation. Questions were asked surrounding positive and negative experiences in childhood and relationships with family and primary caregivers while growing up. Experiences with school and school staff members were explored. Participants were asked about gang initiation and involvement, including what factors drew them to membership. Several questions about whether gang members were considered family were asked, including whether the gang took the place of family. Reasons for leaving a gang were discussed, as well as positive and negative experiences of gang membership. All participants were assured that their responses would be confidential. All interviews were audio recorded and transcribed verbatim for analysis.

Data Analysis Qualitative method prefers interviewing and observing in a natural setting (Padgett, 2017). When one does a qualitative study, one is speaking directly to those involved, which can capture a more intense experience rather than a quantitative report (Padgett, 2017). It was important to give a voice to this population. The form of data analysis that was used in this study was the six steps of thematic analysis (Braun and Clarke, 2006). According to Boyatzis (1998), thematic analysis is a way of seeing. It is a way of looking through qualitative data and discerning observable patterns, which are themes (Boyatzis, 1998). The themes are networks that epitomize the main themes in a section of data (Attride-Stirling, 2001). During the first step, the author interviewed the participants and audio recorded the interviews. The interviews were transcribed verbatim and then read closely for ideas while taking notes. The second step involved generating initial codes from the data and organizing it into meaningful groups. The author identified codes and sorted the data, creating a spreadsheet of codes. During step three, the coded data was searched and analyzed to see what themes emerged. Step four included refining themes, which included reviewing the coded data to discern patterns, seeing if themes were valid in relation to the data, and seeing how everything fit together. The data was examined to see what fit and what did not with the themes. Step five involved defining and naming the themes. Step six was producing the report, including all findings, which told a story about the data.

Qualitative research needs to be conducted in a way that is rigorous and meticulous to reach results that can be helpful and purposeful (Nowell et al., 2017). Strategies for producing rigor and trustworthiness were built into the study plan (Barusch et al., 2011; Padgett, 2017). Peer debriefing was used with members of faculty and cohort at Rutgers University Doctor of Social Work Program (Padgett, 2017). This method can reduce researcher bias and could help with coding. Memos were written during the analytic process that acknowledged any internal reactions or biases that might hinder an objective analysis. Another method used was member checking, where this author went over interview data with respondents to ensure accuracy (Padgett, 2017). An audit trail, which tracked the steps of the project from start to finish, was used, which is useful because it highlights accountability and transparency in research (Barusch et al., 2011).

Limitations and Conclusions*
Limitations include mostly male respondents, with only two females. Participants were mostly African American and Latino/Hispanic. This population is hidden as they can be unwilling or untrusting of sharing their stories, which made recruitment challenging. This sample is not representative of all former gang members because some may have had different life experiences, leading to different outcomes. While the participants did not endure consequences for leaving gangs, there are those who cannot get out and some who pay serious consequences, such as injury or death. Also, attachment theory may not be generalizable to everyone. While attachment may figure prominently with these participants, it may not with others. More research must be done in this area. Further studies must obtain a larger and more diverse sample size.

*Taken from "Seeking a Secure Base: Gangs as Attachment Figures," by K. De Vito, 2020, *Qualitative Social Work*, 19(4), p. 754–769. Reproduced with permission.

References

Alleyne, E., & Wood, J. (2014). Gang involvement: Social and environmental factors. *Crime & Delinquency, 60*(4), 547–568.

Berger, R., Abu-Raiya, H., Heineberg, Y., & Zimbardo, P. (2016). The process of desistance among core ex-gang members. *American Journal of Orthopsychiatry, 87*(4), 487–502.

Brownfield, D. (2010). Social control, self-control, and gang membership. *Journal of Gang Research, 17*(4), 1–12.

Del Carmen, A., Rodriguez, J., Dobbs, R., Smith, R., Butler, R., & Sarver, R. (2009). In their own words: A study of gang members through their own perspective. *Journal of Gang Research, 16*(2), 57–76.

De Vito, K. (2020). Seeking a secure base: Gangs as attachment figures. *Qualitative Social Work, 19*(4), 754–769.

Dickson-Gomez, J., Pacella, M., Broaddus, M., Quinn, K., Galletly, C., & Rivas, J. (2017). Convention versus deviance: Moral agency in adolescent gang members' decision making. *Substance Use & Misuse, 52*(5), 562–573.

Gover, A. (2002). The effects of child maltreatment on violent offending among institutionalized youth. *Violence and Victims, 17*(6), 655–670.

Hill, K. G., Howell, J. C., Hawkins, J. D., & Battin-Pearson, S. R. (1999). Childhood risk factors for adolescent gang membership: Results from the Seattle Social Development Project. *Journal of Research in Crime and Delinquency, 36*, 300–322.

Howell, J. C., & Egley, A. (2005). Moving risk factors into developmental theories of gang membership. *Youth Violence and Juvenile Justice, 3*(4), 334–354.

McNulty, T., & Bellair, P. (2003). Explaining racial and ethnic differences in serious adolescent violent behavior. *Criminology, 41*(3), 709–748.

Kubrin, C. E., & Weitzer, R. (2003). New directions in social disorganization theory. *Journal of Research in Crime and Delinquency, 40*(4), 374–402.

O'Brien, K., Daffern, M., Chu, C., & Thomas, S. (2013). Youth gang affiliation, violence, and criminal activities: A review of motivational, risk, and protective factors. *Aggression and Violent Behavior, 18*(4), 417–425.

Pyrooz, D., & Decker, S. (2011). Motives and methods for leaving the gang: Understanding the process of gang desistance. *Journal of Criminal Justice, 39*, 417–425.

Sampson, R., & Groves, W. (1989). Community structure and crime: Testing social disorganization theory. *American Journal of Sociology, 94*, 774–802.

Santiago, C., Wadsworth, M., & Stump, J. (2011). Socioeconomic status, neighborhood disadvantage, and poverty-related stress: Prospective effects on psychological syndromes among diverse low-income families. *Journal of Economic Psychology, 32*(2), 218–230.

Sharkey, J. D., Shekhtmeyster, Z., Chavez-Lopez, Norris, E., & Sass, L. (2010). The protective influence of gangs: Can schools compensate? *Aggression and Violent Behavior, 16*, 45–54.

Thornberry, T. P. (1987). Toward an interactional theory of delinquency. *Criminology, 25*(4), 863–891.

Thornberry, T. P., Krohn, M. D., Lizotte, A. J., Smith, C. A., & Tobin, K. (2003). *Gangs and delinquency in developmental perspective*. New York: Cambridge University Press.

Vigil, J. D. (2004). In M. A. Gibson, P. Gandara, & J. Peterson Koyama (Eds.), *School connections: U.S. Mexican youth, peers, and school achievement*. New York: Teachers College Press, Columbia University.

Chapter 3
Lack of Family Consistency: Relating Attachment Theory with Gang Involvement

> *The number one thing is consistency. How consistent is anybody really to helping? I mean, you got a coach, you got a teacher, you got a mentor. You got a mother, you got a father, you got a brother, but how consistent are they? Nobody's consistent. But your homeboys are out there every single day. They're the ones that are consistent. So, it's easy to go down that path....(De Vito, 2020)*
>
> – Former Gang Member Josue

3.1 Classical Attachment Theory

The relationship between children and their primary caregivers forms a foundation from which all future relationships follow (Bowlby, 1998; Parrigon et al., 2015). The first primary relationships are the most important relationships to a child. Primary caregivers are the guides who provide a road map on how to navigate and respond to relationships in life. How an infant attaches to the primary caregiver is key. Our first lessons in self-care begin when we are cared for by our primary caregivers (van der Kolk, 2014). Children need to grow up having a sense of confidence and agency, which will develop if they have caregivers who cherish them and support them (van der Kolk, 2014). The attachment figure is a safe haven and a source of comfort in times of need and is the basis from which a sense of self-worth, the feeling of being worthy of love and care from people, and seeing others as available and responsive to their needs comes (Fearon et al., 2010). Children need to be able to feel safe enough to play and learn in their environment in order for there to be a society that is healthy (van der Kolk, 2014). Individuals who grow up feeling a sense of safety and having a connection with other people that is meaningful are less likely to turn to other things like drugs or violence (van der Kolk, 2014). Arthur Becker-Weidman, CSW-R, PhD, DABPS is the founder of the Center for Family Development, which is an attachment center that specializes in the treatment of

© The Author(s), under exclusive license to Springer Nature Switzerland AG 2021
K. De Vito, *Gang Prevention in Schools*,
https://doi.org/10.1007/978-3-030-82914-8_3

foster and adopted families experiencing attachment disorder and trauma. In speaking with him about attachment theory, he described the attachment system and what happens when it becomes activated and what is needed to calm it down:

> The attachment system is a biologically-based system. But it only gets activated when the person gets distressed. It's like your heating and cooling system. If it's 72 degrees out, you don't know if your air conditioner or furnace is working. It has to get hotter or colder to get in. The attachment system is kind of the same thing. It only kicks in when the person is distressed. Once it's activated, then attachment behavior gets exhibited. Very simply, attachment behavior is proximity-seeking behavior...getting closer to your preferred caregiver. Your preferred caregiver is the one who provides you with a sense of safety, security, and comfort. (Becker-Weidman, 2020, Unpublished)

When a child seeks and finds that sense of safety, security, and comfort, then he can internalize a sense of self-confidence when looking at and interacting with others in the world. Primary caregivers develop that attachment, which creates a secure base for children from which they can safely go out and experience the world (van der Kolk, 2014). Having that safe haven to return to can foster resilience in children and helps others to develop a desire to be helpful and sympathetic to others who are experiencing distress (van der Kolk, 2014). Self-confidence is developed when one has that support and comfort and has expectations that are positive, socialization of emotions and values that are moral, primary caregiver is modeling positive prosocial behavior, parental care is consistent and supportive, and there is good emotion regulation (Fearon et al., 2010).

3.2 Types of Attachments

Three types of attachments that can form between infant and primary caregiver are secure, insecure, or disorganized attachment. A secure attachment develops between primary caregiver and child if the primary caregiver is providing consistency and safety (Bowlby, 1998). The child can investigate his environment, knowing that the caregiver will be there to offer support and comfort (Bowlby, 1998). Children who have a secure attachment to their primary caregivers experience a caregiver who is responsive when needed and supportive, and they expect that their caregivers will be responsive when they need them (Fearon et al., 2010). An internal locus of control forms when one has a secure attachment and competency (van der Kolk, 2014). Children who form a secure attachment are able to develop a sense of agency and learn that their actions can change their feelings and can affect how others respond to them (van der Kolk, 2014). van der Kolk (2014) reported that children who are experiencing secure relationships learn from their parents the ability to communicate their distress as well as their interests, goals, and preferences. If adults respond appropriately, with sympathy, they will be less likely to experience high level of frightened arousal.

An insecure attachment will develop if there is no consistency with adequate care from the primary caregiver or there is neglect (Bowlby, 1998). If the primary

3.2 Types of Attachments

caregiver is not consistent and instead is inconsistent with care and support, the infant will not be able to trust that there is someone reliable or dependable. Children who have an insecure attachment to their primary caregiver have a different experience, where they are rejected or inconsistently responded to when they call upon their caregiver; therefore, they need to use different ways of coping to handle their stress or needs (Fearon et al., 2010). van der Kolk (2014) reported that children learn to expect rejection and withdrawal if their caregiver is not responding to their needs appropriately or resents them. Even if the child blocks out the negativity from the parent and pretends as if it does not affect them, their bodies will remain in a state of high alert to fend off abandonment, abuse, or neglect.

Dr. Becker-Weidman discussed the different attachment styles and their prevalence:

> In terms of secure, versus insecure…what the research shows…this is pretty much cross-cultural…about 60 percent of the population have a secure state of mind with respect to attachment. Meaning they value emotions and relationships and can have some degree of empathy toward others. Then there are two insecure patterns. For adults, the preoccupied and the dismissing…constitute about 35 percent of the general population. I like to make clear those are not mental health diagnoses. They don't represent impairment. They don't require treatment or intervention. They just reflect the way these people manage their relationships. They can have family, marriage, find careers, all kinds of things. The dismissing pattern, those individuals don't really value emotions that much. They tend not to talk about them. It's not high in their consciousness. They don't have many specific memories of the earliest childhood, but they still have families and relationships. They can be very good parents. If you want to think about stereotypes. Your engineer might exemplify a dismissing pattern, they are concerned about facts and figures, not so much feelings. And the preoccupied pattern, these are people who get overinvolved, they have trouble letting go. (Becker-Weidman, 2020, Unpublished)

In addition to the attachment styles mentioned, there is another one, disorganized attachment. "Fright without solution" is a way to describe disorganized attachment (van der Kolk, 2014). A disorganized attachment is usually found in children who are abused or neglected (Main & Solomon, 1990; Hesse & Main, 2000; Hill, 2015). Primary caregivers who abuse and neglect their children are a source of danger and fear (Hill, 2015). Insecurely attached children, such as those who are abused and neglected, have come to learn that nothing they say or do stops the abuse from the caregiver, and they then are taught essentially to give up on challenges in their lives (van der Kolk, 2014). Disorganized attachment is predictive of childhood externalizing disorders, PTSD during the middle childhood years, dissociation as teenagers, and adulthood borderline symptoms (Murphy et al., 2014). Children coming from a background of low socioeconomic status are more likely to have parents who are experiencing stress from family or economic instability; therefore, they are more likely to have a disorganized attachment (van der Kolk, 2014). Not only abused children experience disorganized attachment. Children who have parents who are dealing with their own trauma either due to the death of a parent or sibling or some kind of domestic violence or sexual assault can also not be emotionally stable enough to attune to their child's needs (van der Kolk, 2014). Dr. Becker-Weidman discussed disorganized attachment:

The other 5 percent of the population have what is called a disorganized pattern of attachment. And what that really means is that they don't have one consistent pattern. They don't exhibit across the board secure, dismissive, or preoccupied. They exhibit two or more patterns of attachment when you administer the adult attachment interview and that's why it's called disorganized. Typically, that pattern develops when they're raised in a family where the primary caregiver is either frightened or frightening. And the reason that causes attachment disorganization... the attachment system is hard-wired into the mammalian system. And so, the attachment system gets activated when you're distressed. What happens if the source of threat is your primary caregiver? The attachment system gets activated, so you want to get closer to your primary caregiver, but they're your source of threat, so you want to get away from them, and that's like driving your car with your foot on the break and the gas at the same time. Eventually systems break down and that's why you get this disorganized pattern. Disorganized pattern is most likely to produce children that also have a disorganized pattern and might develop psychiatric disorder, reactive attachment disorder, or some kind of overcontrolling pattern of personality. (Becker-Weidman, 2020, Unpublished)

Children with a disorganized attachment are stuck in a situation that is impossible for them as their primary caregiver is also a source of pain and fear (De Vito, 2017). They are in a no-win situation. Children who fall into this category are more likely to develop psychiatric disorders or other issues as mentioned above. Since this is the case, some type of intervention with children with a disorganized attachment pattern can be indicated.

3.3 Modern Attachment Theory: Affect Regulation

Attachment theory posits that the earliest relationships shape our lives and survival functions and are the focal point of emotions and how we interact with other humans (Schore & Schore, 2012). Early interactions between primary caregiver (attachment figure) and infant influence the brain systems' maturation and organization, causing affect and self-regulation (Schore & Schore, 2012; Hill, 2015). Affect is described as how emotions are communicated through facial expressions, body movements, and tone of voice (Hill, 2015). The primary caregiver helps to regulate an infant's emotions when the infant is hyper- or hypoaroused (Hill, 2015). These states are seen when an individual cannot handle the emotions and cannot tolerate them. For example, hypoarousal is a state achieved when an individual cannot tolerate the state of sadness (De Vito, 2017). Hyperarousal is achieved when an individual cannot tolerate the state of anger (De Vito, 2017).

Early attachment communications are crucial to neurobiological systems in the right brain, which is where stress regulation, emotional processing, and regulation of self are all found (Schore & Schore, 2012). The primary attachment figure, in being that secure attachment figure and responding appropriately to an infant's needs, can soothe and regulate his internal system, thereby teaching emotional regulation at an early age. The back-and-forth reciprocal interaction between primary caregiver and infant teach the infant how to regulate its system and how to soothe itself. When the infant learns to self-regulate and soothe himself at an early age, it carries on throughout his lifetime.

Our ability to self-regulate depends on interactions with primary caregivers (van der Kolk, 2014). If we have a good relationship with our primary caregivers, we are better equipped to handle life's stressors (van der Kolk, 2014). Emotional attunement is important in a child developing a secure attachment (van der Kolk, 2014). Children are in tune with their caregiver's tone of voice, posture, expressions, movements, changes in the body, and actions (van der Kolk, 2014). Children are also programmed to form a natural communication system with one primary caregiver, sometimes a few, forming a primary attachment bond (van der Kolk, 2014). The attachment between adult and child will be closer, the more responsive the adult is to the child, which helps teach the child how to respond to others (van der Kolk, 2014). A child may have difficulty throughout the life span with affect and emotion regulation if a secure attachment is not formed early on in life (Bowlby, 1998; Pistole, 1989).

3.4 How Insecure Attachment Has a Lifelong Impact

Brain development is impacted by trauma. An insecure attachment can impact a person over the course of a lifetime. Children who are insecurely attached will develop behavioral problems more often than securely attached children (Kim & Page, 2013). Insecure attachment is associated with externalizing behaviors and a higher level of behavior problems (Fearon et al., 2010). Securely attached children are able to regulate their emotions more easily, thus having fewer behavioral problems, including in school (Kim & Page, 2013). Many behavioral problems in school come from attachment issues, such as acting out, aggression, and bullying (Parker & Forrest, 1993). Inability to handle anger can lead to problems with mental and physical health, including dating violence, low academic performance, peer rejection, substance abuse, bullying, and gang involvement (Konishi & Hymel, 2014). During middle school, peer difficulty arises from children who have difficulty with affect and emotion regulation (Kim & Page, 2013). One might see opposite spectrum of behaviors such as helplessness and withdrawal on one end and aggression and dominance on the other (Hollidge & Hollidge, 2016). The anger could be displaced anger that is being taken out on others in the youth's environment.

3.5 Gangs and Attachment Theory

Attachment theory[3] has the ability to add to the existing knowledge about gang membership (De Vito, 2020). If an adolescent with an insecure attachment is looking outside the family unit, they may find that comfort and security of an attachment figure in a peer group or in a larger group of peers, a gang, if it is available in their environment and neighborhood. Insecurely attached children may turn to gangs as a way of coping with the lack of having a consistent attachment figure (De Vito, 2017). They may have been looking for a secure base in the gang membership, so they would have a replacement family, searching for that stability (De Vito, 2017). If a child feels a sense of abandonment, or worthlessness, or feels invisible to others, then nothing will matter in life (van der Kolk, 2014). If nothing they do makes a difference, children may grow up feeling as if there is no way out and join a gang or turn to drugs, religious extremists, or political movements that are violent, looking for a way out and to feel relief (van der Kolk, 2014). Gangs can show a sense of stability at first, for youth who are lost and looking to escape something else, or looking for a sense of love or belonging, but they may find that that is not the case once they join the gang. Dr. Arthur Becker-Weidman talked about what the gang provides that is missing in the youth's life:

> The gang provides them with that sense of safety, security, and comfort that is not present with their primary caregiver, whether it's a mother, father, aunt, uncle, grandparent, whoever. Gangs provide safety, security, and comfort. I think that's really why kids gravitate toward them when they don't have that in other areas of their life and that's why they stick with it. You see gangs aren't just for teenagers. You see people in gangs who are in their 20s, 30s, 40s, 50s, 60s for the same reason. (Becker-Weidman, 2020, Unpublished)

The gang is providing members with something they are missing in other areas of their lives, including within the family and peer group. In terms of security and safety, they may provide protection from other peers or rival gang members. They may feel the sense of someone always having their back. But is that really the case? Father Greg Boyle, Founder of Homeboy Industries, the world's largest gang intervention and rehab/re-entry program based in California, talked about how gang members represent themselves as being a substitute family, but members will come to find out that that is not really the case:

> When people say it's a substitute for family, it's again another proliferated notion. When people say it's my second family, it comes from gang members self-presenting. They are representing this view. But that's only because they're strangers to their pain. And they haven't welcomed their own wound. So, they're going to talk in those terms. Join a gang and see the world, wine, women, and song, and this is my second family. Well, that's only because they can't talk about what they've had to suffer in their own homes. (Boyle, 2020, Unpublished)

Gang members may represent the gang as having a lot to offer prospective members. Some represent it as a family, but those who are turning to a gang are often turning to a gang as a last resort because they feel they have no other option, or they are running from something else in their lives, often within the home. They feel the gang may be able to offer them something they are missing. Gerald Mallon, DSW, LCSW, Associate Dean of Scholarship and Research at Silberman School of Social Work at Hunter College and a Julia Lathrop Professor of Child Welfare, who has worked with many young people during his career, spoke to this same point and talked about youth having a gap and needing to have that gap filled by something important in their lives because they may not be getting that at home for various reasons:

> Some kids need to fill a gap in their lives. This is not just with kids who are in impoverished situations. There are kids that have parents that are either working too much because they have to support their family, or parents who are substance abusers, or parents who are just

not really paying any attention to them, so they don't have people who are on top of them saying, no you need to go to that practice today, or no you really need to do this, so you've got kids who are really looking to fill that gap that they have in their life and I would think that that's where the prevention piece could come in. (Mallon, 2020, Unpublished)

Having issues within the home such as absent parents due to various issues such as incarceration, substance abuse, or just not being available can cause a void in a child's life and is a huge reason why kids look outside of the home for something else. They look for support, an escape, or a replacement. Having a gang readily available in the area makes it more likely they will join. Figuring out how to fill these gaps and support the piece missing at home could be where prevention fits in.

Issues with attachment can be a reason youth look to gangs for the missing piece. Kirk "Jae" James, DSW, MSW, BA, AA, Clinical Assistant Professor at NYU Silver School of Social Work, has focused his work around mass incarceration. He consults with those working with youth to help them broaden their understanding. In linking attachment with gang involvement, he said:

I definitely think issues of attachment, most of those people have had multiple ACEs, most of those things are not factored into any clinical assessment or intervention of gang members or youth involved with crimes. I grew up in a neighborhood, that right now, is probably more gang-infested than ever, but there was this community center, Forrest Hills Community Center, and it wasn't even our community center, it was maybe a mile and a half away. We all went there because one of the people that ran it was our guidance counselor in junior high school and he was a guy who always showed up as a father figure no matter what happened. He organized the football games, the basketball games, and everyone had such a tremendous respect for him. It was that attachment piece…it was that someone that you were able to see who you believe saw you and created spaces for you in which you felt value, in which you felt you belonged, in which you felt supported. (James, 2020, Unpublished)

Being valued and having that sense of support, love, and acceptance are things that every child needs and should have when growing up. If that is not offered in the home, it is human nature to try to seek it elsewhere. Someone else can step up and be a supportive role and attachment figure that is missing in a youth's life and make a world of difference. Mentors, teachers, coaches, family friends, other relatives, religious figures, school counselors, and therapists are all examples of options of people who could take on the role of attachment figure. Someone needs to consistently be involved in that child's life in order to make an impact.

3.6 Clinicians Can Step In

The attachment relationship between social worker and client is of critical importance. The way we perceive reality, what is safe and not safe, how to get our needs met, and who we can depend upon and who we can't is shaped by our primary caregivers, and that information is retained in our brains and is relatively unchanging over time (van der Kolk, 2014). However, that map that is created in our brains can be changed by experiences in life such as a positive loving relationship or the birth of a child (van der Kolk, 2014). The core of attachment theory states that our lives are impacted both socially and emotionally by our early relationships in life (Bowlby, 1998; Schore & Shore, 2010). If a primary caregiver is absent for various reasons, another person can step in and fill that role or repair that attachment difficulty, such as a clinician. The relationship between client and therapist can be similar to early attachment relationships (De Vito, 2017). The therapist is an object of intense affect much like is seen in early attachment relationships (Farber et al., 1995). During the therapeutic relationship, the client relies on the therapist, which is similar to attachment relationships early on. Parts of the therapeutic relationship that show attachment includes feeling supported, proximity seeking, and looking toward the therapist as a role model (Obegi, 2008). van der Kolk (2014) reported that having a memory of feeling safe with another individual earlier in life can be reactivated again when you are an adult in relationships that are attuned, either in therapy or with other individuals. But the part of the brain that responds to kindness may not develop if one does not have that feeling of safety and love.

Schore and Schore (2012) discussed how attachment theory is a theory of regulation, and developing an attachment to a therapist can assist in internal affect regulation. The therapist can become a secure base (Ainsworth, 1989). The therapist takes on that attachment role and can help the client regulate emotions internally by becoming that secure base and creating a sense of safety and security. Once that secure relationship is established, the therapist has access to help with other relationships in the client's life (Hollidge & Hollidge, 2016). When the counselor takes on the role of attachment figure, they can have access to the client's internal working model (Pistole, 1989). The counselor then can work on fixing current relationships and problems that arose earlier in the youth's life (De Vito, 2017). The clinical relationship can repair damage done previously and can help create a new way of coping (Schore & Schore, 2012). A client can develop a resilient self through a secure attachment that can then have meaningful relationships (Schore & Schore, 2012). The client can reconstruct the lived past and form healthier relationships (De Vito, 2017). The therapeutic relationship can repair damage from other relationships by helping the client to form healthier relationships and to help them handle daily life and life's inevitable stressors (Bowlby, 1988; Mallinckrodt et al., 1995; Schore & Schore, 2012).

Attachment theory can show some clues as to how children who survive childhood adversity can move toward healthier lives by breaking the cycle (Murphy et al., 2014). A way to do this is by forming positive supportive relationships with another positive person, such as a spouse or therapist, which can aid with emotional regulation, psychological coherence, and attentional processes (Murphy et al., 2014). Having family members or friends who one can go to talk about emotional problems or feelings are less likely to report a depressed affect and are more likely to report good health (Murphy et al., 2014). Since gang members may be seeking attachment figures that were not present in childhood, as youth develop meaningful relationships with therapists or school counselors, that counselor can take on a role of an attachment figure, thus helping to repair some of that damage and possibly intervening in the way of gang prevention. School counselors and staff members are present and consistent on a daily basis in the lives of youth, making them accessible and prime people to aid in prevention. Dr. Mallon talked about how another adult can step in and fill that missing void in a youth's life, especially as they get older, when there is no parental figure:

> I worked in group homes and ran this Green Chimneys program for 20 years and a lot of my kids are now adults. The nice thing is that I see some of them still…and talk to them. Traditional social work, you terminate with them and you never see them again and hope the work you did with them sustains them through life. One of them just called me the other day about a business idea and asked my opinion. So, then I asked questions like how much is the rent and what is the start-up cost and have you spoken with an attorney. He said, oh yeah, I didn't think about that, that's why I'm calling you because I knew you would help me think about these things. That's really what they would do with a good parent if they had one. But they don't. That's why if they're lucky enough to have a connection with somebody…the ones I had great connections with still utilize me like that and it's a great thing. I think it's a sustaining thing throughout their lives if that's what they need. The ones who keep in touch with me the most are probably the ones who had absolutely no connection to a parent or parental figure in their life. Having that relationship and an adult who cares for you is so important. They are longing for a connection with somebody. (Mallon, 2020, Unpublished)

I see this with my work with students as well. Sometimes, the ones who have the strongest connection have been the ones who are longing for that connection with another person or are in need of a mentor or role model. They do not feel like they have anyone at home that they can talk to or rely or depend on for support. Some of these students will still check in once they graduate from time to time as well. It is always great to hear from them or see them and to know that the work that I did with them has been helpful. They also know that I am always there if they needed something.

3.7 Lack of Family Consistency

Having a lack of consistency with the primary attachment figures in the core family unit can cause a sense of mistrust and a feeling of a lack of support. Without that consistent love, attention, support, and sense of belonging, there can be a disruption in the key secure attachment developing as an infant and child, which can impact that child for a lifetime. In De Vito (2020), hearing former gang members speak about their upbringing and the disruption, loss, and lack of consistency illustrated this point:

> All participants reported a lack of secure, consistent primary care givers/attachment figures during childhood for various reasons, including death, divorce, substance abuse, and being absent. In the first theme, "Lack of Family Consistency," all of the participants had some disruption in their attachment with their primary caregivers. The participants lost one or both parents to death, divorce, jail, substance abuse, or just not being around due to working struggling to make ends meet. Many were left without supervision. Some felt as though they could not depend on their parents in times of need, which creates a sense of loss and mistrust. Some participants experienced abuse and wound up in foster care. (De Vito, 2020)

Some of the former gang members who were study participants looked outside of the family for sources of consistency and love, due to not having it at home. Some of those sources were peers and gangs. They provided what was missing at home for the youth at the time. Josue discussed this issue:

> Looking back on it, if I could have it all over again, I would never [have] joined a gang… "The number one thing is consistency. How consistent is anybody really to helping? I mean, you got a coach, you got a teacher, you got a mentor. You got a mother, you got a father, you got a brother, but how consistent are they? Nobody's consistent. But your homeboys are out there every single day. They're the ones that are consistent. So, it's easy to go down that path…" (De Vito, 2020). I think it's more of like a seed of hope. And I think like that's where it starts. I mean, I think a lot of people that grow up in the lifestyle you gotta look at them and you think, like damn, how many of them are already broken? How many of them in their life are already depressed because every single day is the same? Nothing changes. And it's like well what would give hope is opportunities you know? What would that look like? …Consistency would have definitely changed my life. It may have changed a lot of things in my life… "I really feel like [consistency] would have prevented me from joining…" (De Vito, 2020). You don't know you're hurt; all you know is I love where I come from but you don't know why? "But like if you were to think about it and most of the people from our area like to get initiated you stand in a circle and they beat you. And then you get up and say thank you for letting me be a part of it. I mean tell me that's somebody that's not broken for willing to do that? To get beat by your friends just to be a part of it and then go to prison, you know?" (De Vito, 2020). There's something already that's there. So, I think like with consistency and that right there will begin to start to put somebody's walls down and they can start to see that maybe that's not so much love that you feel there, maybe it's love that you need, you know? (Josue, 2019, Unpublished)

Having that sense of consistency is extremely important. By being a consistent figure in a young person's life, one can change that young person's life. Working in a school, I am privileged to work with some awesome students. It is an honor for them to let me into their lives and put their trust in me and allow me to help. If you can make a connection with a student, that may be the only connection they have with anyone that is positive. That one connection may just be what makes a difference in their lives. Someone showing and providing opportunities could change things. Looking at Josue's situation, he was longing for that sense of connection. Since he didn't have it at home, he looked for it outside in a gang. The gang was providing that sense of consistency for him, even if the consistency involved paying the price of having to accept violence into his life. If he had had a person showing him that there are different opportunities and that things could be different, perhaps he would have chosen a different path.

Another former gang member, Antonio, also spoke about looking outside of his home for love. He talked about cultural differences between how children are raised. He spoke about how if the parents are not offering love at home, or if they are not around due to work circumstances, they go looking outside of the home, perhaps with youth and gangs:

> I think one of the main reasons is because some of us—I think it's because they don't get as much love from their parents. Especially Hispanic because Hispanic parents are always working, working… they probably worry more about the material stuff or the money and stuff or the bills. They would leave the kids at home by themselves…I guess they don't

receive as much love, so they probably go and look for it somewhere else like with friends, or they feel good smoking or getting drunk. I think that's the reason I did because I didn't have any brothers or anything growing up, so I kind of went and looked for my own kind of like brothers that I could hang out with. We always had fun especially when we were playing soccer, but then after that, everybody just started smoking. Everybody just started doing their own thing. So, I think that's one of the main reasons why young people join gangs is because they don't feel that—I guess they don't get as much as love from either their family members or they get abused at home or something. (Antonio, 2019, Unpublished).

Antonio brought up the point about children not getting enough love at home and seeking it elsewhere. Many of the children that I worked with over the years have hardworking parents who are in tough situations. They often have to work multiple jobs just to make ends meet and get basic needs met. Sometimes, that is not even enough. But in doing so, that makes them absent from the home, which leaves the children open to idle time and lack of supervision. At that point, they may be drawn into being with their peers more, which could include gangs.

3.7.1 Being Raised in a Single Mother Home, Absent Father

Some participants described a childhood where their primary caregivers, for various reasons, were not in a position to provide that caring, consistent relationship. Many of the participants did not have both parents in the household. Many were missing father figures. Archie said, "It was just mom in the house…I met him [dad] years later and all of that, but I wasn't raised with him" (Archie, 2019, Unpublished). Another participant, Hector, had a similar experience, and he said, "I grew up in a broken home, no father, that type of thing, you know what I mean? No father. I didn't meet him until like I was like a full-fledged gang member. Like I was probably 19" (Hector, 2019, Unpublished). Joey had a similar experience too: "It was hard. [Dad] was away. I seen him sometimes every now and then, but yeah it was hard because he was away though" (Joey, 2019, Unpublished).

Not having consistent support from a father figure within the home can be difficult. Some participants felt as if fathers would know more about street life and gang life, which could have dissuaded them from joining, as Jamie discussed:

"I didn't really have the best childhood life because my father was in and out of jail since I was two, so it was kinda hard…just being raised with a single parent like my mom" (De Vito, 2020)… She tried…but it was hard for her to understand me as a teenager…there's certain things you can't do and certain things you could do. "I kinda had to figure things out on my own. I didn't have that father figure in my life…I say if my father was home, I wouldn't have took that route…you cannot raise boys into men as a single mom. There's no discussion on that…" (De Vito, 2020). So my mother, she could tell me, "Oh don't join no gang." So, you think I'm gonna listen to a female like my mom? I need to hear from a father figure standpoint because he could kinda weigh the options out to me. My mother don't know the streets like my father knew the streets. (Jamie, 2019, Unpublished).

Jamie felt that absence from his father and felt that if his father had been around, he would not have taken that path. He also felt that if his mother had tried to intervene, it would not have had as much of an impact because he felt she did not understand what he was going through.

Another former gang member, Jamie felt similarly. He described how difficult it was for his mother to intervene in his life because she was not able to provide the type of support he needed at that time in his life:

> Okay let me tell you then to keep kids from doing the same things I did…or the same thing that my son is doing…There's a lot of parents… "in the single parent homes… where the mom is raising a son that's a gang member… It's hard when she knows not an inch about gang banging…" (De Vito, 2020). She don't know anything about being a gang member, but "she has a son that's already rebelling because he's in a gang" (De Vito, 2020). He's rebelling already and "he's looking for some kind of support or some kind of love from somewhere that's opposite of what she is giving him." (De Vito, 2020; Jamie, 2019, Unpublished)

Jamie felt as if his mother could not relate to what he was going through. Since she did not have knowledge about being in a gang, he felt she could not understand. He was looking for the kind of support, attention, and knowledge that she just could not provide for him.

Youth are often influenced by their peers and their environment. Without supervision and consistent support at home, youth may be more influenced by people outside of the home more easily. Sometimes, that influence is negative. Jay described how hard it is for single mothers to raise boys. They need to support their families alone and are often out of the home working long hours, so the streets become a negative influence:

> Well, I was raised…with a single mother who had to work two jobs to take care of two kids. So…it was tough living. And living with a single mom you know, we bounced from place to place, lived with people, lived with families, seen a lot of things, I mean seen a lot of things…It's just "when you grow up with a single parent and she's working two jobs…[so] you're influenced by the street [and] the negativity you see, because you don't have that father figure…or a positive environment. [You only have] gang members." (De Vito, 2020; Jay, 2019, Unpublished)

Living in a single parent household can have difficulties. Some of the participants mentioned some of the challenges they personally faced, such as their mothers needing to be at work in order to provide for them or feeling as though their mothers did not understand some of the issues they were facing as teenagers. All of these participants felt impacted by the loss of a father figure in their lives. While this can prove to be a challenge, it is something that can be helped in some ways if proper supports are in place, such as mentors or other family stepping in to provide a male figure in their lives or additional support.

3.7 Lack of Family Consistency

3.7.2 Parents Absent Due to Drug Addiction or Death

In some situations, participants did not have either parent in the home and were raised by other relatives. One participant, Luis, talked about his experience of losing both parents as a child, his anger as a result, and believes that if his mother had been alive, he would have made different choices:

> For me [childhood] was a little difficult at first. But I had to get through it. I had lost my father on my birthday. I had my mom until I was about six…so I had to grow up earlier than most kids and had to do more things than most children would have to do at seven. "Their passing built up a lot of anger in me…" (De Vito, 2020). I had to bottle it up till I was maybe in the third or fourth grade. That's when the anger really kicked in…I was in fights every other day. Got suspended as a kid…I was basically like acting out with anger… "When you lose your parents when you in school, you sort of stick out like a sore thumb when holidays come around like Mother's Day and Father's Day, and stuff like that, parent teacher conferences…" (De Vito, 2020) people look at you a little weird. My sister would come and people would be like, you don't look alike, that's not your mom… "I mean, my mother was my heart. If she was alive, you know, I wouldn't say I wouldn't have joined. But I wouldn't have joined as early as I did." (De Vito, 2020; Luis, 2019, Unpublished)

Losing both parents at a young age can have a lifelong impact on a child. In Luis's situation, it caused a lot of anger. If not dealt with properly, grief and anger can cause problems. But having support, especially within school, could have helped him. Had some counseling been put into place early on, perhaps there could have been a difference in his life.

Some participants, such as Johanna, had parents who were physically present but absent mentally due to drug addiction. Having no stability at home and having to be a parent to siblings and to not have parents to depend on meant an inability to experience a typical childhood, absence of freedom, and the ability to rely upon and trust adults. There is no consistent attachment and trust. She said:

> "I didn't have too much of a childhood because growing up I had to kind of parent my parents" (De Vito, 2020). My mom and dad have always been together…however my dad has been basically addicted to prescription painkillers for all of my life and longer, and my mom is addicted to prescription pain pills as well. So, my father would drink, as well as smoke cigarettes and do whatever drugs he was on… "I pretty much raised myself…They've always been there, but they've been absent…" (De Vito, 2020). I remember when I was younger, around 12, I remember losing housing, losing cars, things of that nature…Having to grow up early…I had other siblings that I had to practically be a parent to…so instead of me having a childhood, "it was plagued with me having to, you know, parent those other siblings…I had to wake up early in the morning, clean, comb hair, bathe, and dress them, and get them ready for school…" (De Vito, 2020) so I didn't have much of a childhood. I didn't get much of going outside, playing with Barbie dolls, things like that. I didn't have that type of lifestyle at all…I pretty much raised myself just based on trial and error…I did a lot of learning and teaching to myself on my own… It was hard for me to trust anyone… "I emancipated myself in my mind" (De Vito, 2020) because that's who I came accustomed to being, someone older, someone more understanding, when it came to understanding the dynamic of life. When other kids in junior high and high school are basically just living with oh…I got to go to school and grades and stuff, when I was thinking of bigger things, you know like jobs, cars, stuff that at my age, I shouldn't even have been worrying about. (Johanna, 2019, Unpublished)

Johanna felt she had to grow up on her own. With her parents being absent due to addiction, she had to raise her siblings by herself. She missed out on having a childhood. In addition, she also felt as though she could not trust anyone based on her experience within the home. When children are left to handle life themselves, without supervision, they may gravitate toward other things, such as a gang.

Having absent parents can take a toll on the entire family. Evelyn talked about being raised by her parents but having an absent father due to employment and a mother who suffered with addiction. She was removed from her home and placed into foster care which caused trauma for her:

> [I was raised by] my mom and dad. Mostly my mom. My dad was never home. He was in and out. [It] was just because of employment. There was never no communication…we never had that relationship…A lot of friends passed away…my mom, after a while, she started drinking, so she started drinking heavily. So, there was a lot of trauma with that alone with her…My mom had an issue she shared…some stuff that she was going through, and they came in and removed us all from the home for a minute. So, we were in foster care…It was kind of hard…the foster parents that we ended up having were…way older…she ended up kicking me out from her home…I left, and then…ended up somewhere else with my brother, my little brothers…that's how my journey came – I dropped out of school and then getting jumped, getting into too many fights. It was…a struggle. (Evelyn, 2019, Unpublished)

When drug addiction is present, it can feel like parents are not really present. There are many children who grow up in this kind of environment where they need to care for themselves and siblings without help from parents. That absence can cause them to look outside of the family for some other kind of support. If a gang is in the area, then that could be an option for them.

If a child does not have primary caregivers that are reliable or dependable, it can cause feelings of despair, hopelessness, and just feeling alone. Not having a consistent home and caregivers that are struggling with addiction can lead to a constant state of uncertainty and feeling like one cannot depend on anyone. Leo described this experience:

> I never met my father and my mother was…hooked on drugs…so I always lived with my grandparents… "Growing up, you know, there was alcoholism in the house. Everybody drank. My house was kind of like the hangout spot. So, there was, um, drug abuse…" (De Vito, 2020) my grandparents drank a lot. They kicked it a lot…They [gang members] were always in my house, so all my uncles and cousins, they were all from the same gang…homies would be at the house, from the neighborhood…we moved around a lot. We got evicted from our house…My grandmother lost the house and then we were just moving. Like every year we would move…we wouldn't stay at one school for more than a year… It wasn't like enticing to be a gang member. It was kind of like more "I was in a hopeless state…There was nobody at home" (De Vito, 2020). My mom was gone. My grandma was at the bar. My grandfather had passed away already, so it was kind of like me and my grandmother and my brothers and sisters. And so, there was really nobody at the house…and if there was, they were always arguing and fighting. (Leo, 2019, Unpublished)

Having a feeling of hopelessness and being in that kind of state can drive people to do different things. If there is no one in the home for support and youth are living in an area where gangs are prevalent, youth may decide to join a gang. In this particular case, Leo was also moving a lot, so he was changing schools often, not being

3.7 Lack of Family Consistency 33

able to find a consistent support system or friend group. A combination of all of those things factored into his decision.

Leo also talked about how the lack of consistent support at home was a driving reason behind his decision to turn to the homies for support and join a gang and discussed that fateful night when he made that decision. He said:

> When I was like thirteen years old, my cousin got murdered. He was fourteen. He was like a brother to me, so…that was pretty hard to deal with…So as soon as I went to junior high school, things started to change for me…so I got jumped into my gang…the summer right before junior high school…So, I had said no for a long time. So, my cousin, the one that got killed, we had like this – we had a pact when we were younger like we were never going to get in. And then he got in, he got in like, you know, like a few months before I got in, and then once he got in, I was kind of like, damn, you know, we don't know no more, and he started hanging out with homies. And then it was kind of like spur of the moment, to be honest with you. Like, I still had said no. They had asked me a few times; do you want to get in? I'm like, no, I'm good. And then I had like a bad situation kind of happen, so I went to the homies. I had another friend that I would go over his house all the time, but his mom used to like kind of get annoyed with me being there…I went to her house and knocked on the door and they acted like they weren't home, and they like turned off the living room lights, turned off the TV. And so, then I walked back to the town where like the homies were kicking it, and then I got jumped in… "My mom was on methamphetamine at that time…She was gone. She was out of the picture. My grandma was going to the bars a lot" (De Vito, 2020). So, that night is the night I got jumped in. (Leo, 2019, Unpublished)

Feeling alone, without support from family or friends can impact a person greatly. Losing a family member that is close to you is also difficult, especially when it was because of gang violence. Leo was left in a place where he did not feel as though he had support or any other options really but to join a gang at that point. He felt alone. So he joined a gang. Having someone, even a mentor at school, may have made a huge difference in his life.

3.7.3 Victims of Abuse

Some participants described experiencing abuse at the hands of their caregivers with some winding up being removed and placed into foster care. Johanna described some traumatic events that occurred during her childhood, including being abused by her mom, witnessing the death of a younger sibling, and being placed into foster care:

> I had a younger sibling and his heart stopped and he stopped breathing in my arms. He pretty much died there in my arms because he was born with a birth defect…he was like 6 months when he passed. So, we rushed him to the hospital…then they took him out of my arms and rushed him to the back and when they came back, they basically pronounced him dead. And we didn't have any grieving periods or anything…They informed us and [told us to] go ahead and go home and somebody would contact us. However, the contact that we got was from [child protective services] and they removed us from my mom. They picked up two of my siblings from the school they were going to and they took my brother and I from the house. In the beginning, they placed us all together. About a week or two out, "they actually split us all up and we all went to different foster homes. So as a child, that was the

most traumatic experience…beside being verbally and physically abused by my mom." (De Vito, 2020; Johanna, 2019, Unpublished)

Johanna had lived through a lot of trauma growing up including having parents who were struggling with addiction, being physically and verbally abused, losing a sibling, and being placed in foster care. Experiencing that trauma impacted her in many different ways. It also may have affected her decision to join a gang.

Lamar also talked about growing up with both parents in the home but having an abusive father: "I grew up in a two-parent household. My mom was a very nurturing mother, a loving mother. My father was kind of…tough, hardcore…abusive in terms of his way of disciplining me and my brothers. But I remember one time he punched me…I had a broken blood vessel in my eyes" (Lamar, 2019, Unpublished).

Losing a loved can be a trauma. Suffering from abuse at the hands of a parent or caregiver is a trauma. Being removed from the home and being placed in foster care can also be a trauma as well. If these traumas are not dealt with properly and support is not given, it can cause lifelong problems for youth.

3.7.4 Lack of Supervision at Home

Not having supervision in the home or absent parents is a risk factor for gang involvement. Hector talked about not having a lot of supervision, which gave him a lot of leeway and he expressed how issues originate in the home:

> I think I felt a lot of pressure to be perfect…there was more expectation than anything. Because people were like, "Oh, like you're smart." …It's more like they feel like they know you can do this and you can do that. So, you know, why worry about him? You know, which ultimately gave me a lot of leeway to do other things… It'd be the same thing that's happening in environments with blacks and Hispanics that happens but with whites, too. Like in the suburban areas where they got skinheads there. People go through the same social issues. "Mom and Dad at work…Maybe they didn't have Mom and Dad around. And they're causing them to hang out with the kids" (De Vito, 2020) and then…they get into it…start messing around. And the ultimate thing is that it all starts from the home. It always starts from the home, the homelife. (Hector, 2019, Unpublished)

Hector spoke about how there are social issues that are similar across neighborhoods, cultures, and races. He felt the issues always start in the home with parents being absent or hanging out with peers that are a negative influence. The big similarity is that these issues always start with the homelife.

Antonio also talked about not having his parents around at home because of them working and coming home late, so he was left without supervision, so he went outside of the home:

> Well, I'm an only child, so maybe I was lonely at home and my parents used to work…I always wanted a little brother or something or an older brother. I mean I had a lot of cousins, but it wasn't the same because they used to live outside of the city. I would still go over there and sleep over at their house, but sometimes, I would lie to my parents that I was going to go sleep over there, and I would still like come out of their house and just go hang out with

my friends all night and then come back to my cousin's house at like 5:00 in the morning or 6:00 in the morning. Even though I had my cousins I would still choose to hang out with my friends…I felt accepted…My parents, they always used to work and come in late… I guess I used to like the adrenalin…like just being on the street…like making trouble and stuff like that or seeing fights and smoking and stuff. (Antonio, 2019, Unpublished)

A lack of supervision can cause many problems. One of which could be youth getting into trouble with peers, like a gang. Having supervision at home is key. If parents have to work, getting their children involved in after-school clubs, sports, or programs can be helpful. If they are busy and involved in something, they have less time on their hands to get into trouble.

3.7.5 Influenced by Family Members in Gangs

When a youth has family members who are already involved in a gang, it can be difficult to not go down that same path. Some families have parents who are not around because they need to work so often to make ends meet so they may become influenced by people outside the immediate family. Jerry talked about how he had excellent parents, but his parents spent so much time at work and school that he was left to be influenced by other family members, who were gang involved. He said:

I didn't grow up like with a messed-up household. Like I had excellent parents. Like my dad and my mom, they both worked…We had a good upbringing towards home, but it was like my uncles, cousins, everybody else was in gangs….my mom spent so much time at school and trying to further her education. My dad spent so much time at work that it was like my time was really with my grandparents, my uncles, my cousins, and everybody else that's older than me that was gang bangers. So, it got to the point where my dad was no longer my role model. It was one of my uncles. My uncle…he is the one that is real serious…where you know he was just killed two years ago…at 51 years old…He was really heavy involved, real heavy involved…It kind of started with an infatuation of seeing the money and the stuff that my uncles and them had, towards cars, towards you know the high-end clothes, at the time the young ladies, you know. It was all that. It was all that that made you, made me kind of infatuated with the gang life. So that's how I said I kind of came up different than the average person that came here. My infatuation drove me to be the best that I could be in that world. You know what I mean. It wasn't by force or anything like that. A lot of these guys is born kind of forced into it. But me, it was an infatuation I had that kept me like full throttle… I wanted to be someone like my uncles. My uncles wouldn't let me be from the gang from where they were from. You know, they kept me away from their gang. So, it was like okay you know what, I'm going to go over here and do it then. You know what I mean. You can't stop me over here. You got no say so over here. So, I turned the attitude that I was seeing them have and the stuff they were doing, and I started doing it over here with these guys. (Jerry, 2019, Unpublished)

Having that influence from family members being in gangs can make it hard to say no. In Jerry's case, he came from a household with parents who were giving him what he needed, but he was drawn to the gang lifestyle by seeing his extended family involved. Being around that lifestyle can be appealing to some youth, and they may think that it is going to be something other than what it really turns out to be.

Some families have generations and generations of gangs. Josue also talked about how families can influence the decision to join a gang. Some children are born into generations of gang membership if their family members are already gang members:

> My father was murdered before I was born. I was raised by my mom… My whole family was involved [in a gang]. Yeah, my uncle already had life without [parole], both of my other uncles went…to prison for violence. I mean my other uncle, all my aunts, my mom, they're all from the neighborhood…So you know "we grew up" (De Vito, 2020) my mom, my dad, my aunts, my uncles, my cousins, my brothers, everybody… "in the same neighborhood, we're all from the same gang. It was generation after generation of gang. You know from one generation to the next generation. So, I grew up I guess you could say, like you know, at the house where you couldn't sleep on your bed, you had to sleep on the floor because of the drive by shootings…" (De Vito, 2020). At the end of the day gangs is worse than drugs or anything else and the reason why is that there's so many that "gangs can influence: children" (De Vito, 2020) at the age of freaking 5 and 4 years old… "they're bred" (De Vito, 2020) and it's a breed of generations…everything that happens is based on those beliefs that are instilled in you and that you become hateful for… "You're a gang member way before you become involved in gangs" (De Vito, 2020). And you're instilled with these beliefs of what a man is: don't cry, don't tell, don't snitch, and all these things and the next thing you know by believing these things you turn into a monster. Well, what happens if someone hurts your family member and you're not supposed to tell, you're not supposed to cry you're not supposed to snitch. The only option you got is to be violent. It's like we turn around and we instill all these things and this poison inside generations…what happens is they pass it on…and next thing you know it's like "we're just killing generations to come…and we don't even know it" (De Vito, 2020). So, gangs is not just…in this moment. It destroys generations that are coming up. And you know "it all starts in the home and it's hard to stop." (De Vito, 2020; Josue, 2019, Unpublished)

Being born into a family that has generations of gang members makes joining the likely course. I have seen students who have become involved because they felt that they really did not have a choice. Their parents, uncles, cousins, and siblings were all involved. When a student is in that situation, it is very difficult to get out of it and choose a different path. That student would need help and some intervention from support outside of the family. Josue also talked about how youth are brought up to believe certain things about growing up as a man, where you cannot show emotion or ask for help. He felt his only option at that point was to turn violent as his outlet. He also felt everything starts within the home. Intervention to break this type of cycle is warranted.

All of these former gang members interviewed spoke about how issues within the core family unit influenced their individual decisions to join gangs. There was a crack in the family foundation that caused them to seek something outside of the family. Some had parents who were absent due to death or drug addiction, some had only single mother-headed households where there was no father, and some were placed in foster care or living with other relatives because of abusive situations or parental drug addiction. Some had parents who just had to work and were not around, and some were influenced by family members who were gang members. If these former gang members had had some preventative interventions in place, would it be possible that they would not have made the decision to join a gang?

Perhaps if the families had had some kind of intervention early on to assist, would these individuals have chosen to join a gang? If another role model had stepped in and been that missing attachment figure, providing that consistency, or if the school could provide some kind of consistency in that youth's life, would they have chosen a different path? These are all possible things that could be addressed in gang prevention.

References

Ainsworth, M. (1989). Attachment beyond infancy. *American Psychologist, 44*, 709–716.

Bowlby, J. (1998). *A secure base: Clinical applications of attachment theory*. New York: Routledge.

De Vito, K. (2017). Schools fall short: Lack of continuum of care in public schools. *Reflections Narratives of Professional Helping, 23*(4), 4–19.

De Vito, K. (2020). Seeking a secure base: Gangs as attachment figures. *Qualitative Social Work, 19*(4), 754–769.

Farber, B., Lippert, R., & Nevas, D. (1995). The therapist as attachment figure. *Psychotherapy: Theory, Research, Practice, and Training, 32*(2), 204–212.

Fearon, R. P., Bakermans-Kranenburg, M. J., Van Ijzendoorn, M. H., Lapsley, A. M., & Roisman, G. I. (2010). The significance of insecure attachment and disorganization in the development of children's externalizing behavior: A meta-analytic study. *Child Development, 81*, 435–456.

Hesse, E., & Main, M. (2000). Disorganized infant, child, and adult attachment: Collapse in behavioral and attentional strategies. *Journal of the American Psychoanalytic Association, 48*(4), 1097–1127.

Hill, D. (2015). *Affect regulation theory: A clinical model*. New York: W.W. Norton and Co..

Hollidge, C. F., & Hollidge, E. O. (2016). Seeking security in the face of fear: The disorganized dilemma. *Psychoanalytic Social Work, 21*(2), 130–144.

Kim, H., & Page, T. (2013). Emotional bonds with parents, emotion regulation, and school-related behavior problems among elementary school truants. *Journal of Child and Family Studies, 22*(6), 869–878.

Konishi, C., & Hymel, S. (2014). An attachment perspective on anger among adolescents. *Merrill-Palmer Quarterly, 60*(1), 53–79.

Main, M., & Solomon, J. (1990). Procedures for identifying infants as disorganized/disoriented during the Ainsworth Strange Situation. In M. Greenberg, D. Cicchetti, & E. Cummings (Eds.), *Attachment in the preschool years: Theory, research, and intervention* (pp. 121–130). Chicago and London: University of Chicago Press.

Mallinckrodt, B., Gantt, D., & Coble, H. (1995). Attachment patterns in the psychotherapy relationship: Development of the client attachment to therapist scale. *Journal of Counseling Psychology, 42*(3), 307–317.

Murphy, A., Steele, M., Dubic, S. R., Bate, J., Bonuck, K., Meissner, P., Goldman, P., & Steele, H. (2014). Adverse childhood experiences (ACEs) questionnaire and adult attachment interview (AAI): Implications for parent child relationships. *Child Abuse & Neglect, 38*, 224–233.

Obegi, J. (2008). The development of the client-therapist bond through the lens of attachment theory. *Psychotherapy: Theory, Research, Practice, Training, 45*(4), 431–446.

Parker, K. C., & Forrest, D. (1993). Attachment disorder: An emerging concern for school counselors. *Elementary School Guidance & Counseling, 27*(3), 209–215.

Parrigon, K., Kerns, K., Abtahi, M., & Koehn, A. (2015). Attachment and emotion in middle childhood and adolescence. *Psychological Topics, 24*(1), 27–50.

Pistole, M. C. (1989). Attachment: Implications for school counselors. *Journal of Counseling & Development, 68*, 190–193.

Schore, A., & Shore, J. (2010). Clinical social work and regulation theory: Implications of neurobiological models of attachment. In S. Bennett & J. K. Nelson (Eds.), *Adult attachment in clinical social work: Practice, research, and policy* (pp. 57–95). New York: Springer.

Schore, A., & Schore, J. (2012). Modern attachment theory: The central role of affect regulation in development and treatment. In *The science of the art of psychotherapy* (pp. 27–51). New York: W.W. Norton and.

van der Kolk, B. (2014). *The body keeps the score: Brain, mind, and body in the healing of trauma.* New York, NY: Penguin.

Chapter 4
"Brotherhood, Sisterhood, Unity:" Gang as Replacement Family

> *"They became my brothers" (De Vito, 2020). Those are my brothers. You know, like, a lot of people say, "Oh you know, those are not your brothers." Those are my brothers. "We had a different kind of connection..." (De Vito, 2020; Luis, 2019, Unpublished)*
>
> – Former Gang Member Luis

4.1 Gangs and Family Systems

Gang internal processes function like family systems. Similarities include feeling protected, receiving affection, and having a sense of belonging and loyalty (Ruble & Turner, 2000). Special Agent Edwin Torres, President of the East Coast Gang Investigators Association, an organization that aims to increase gang awareness in society and to assist law enforcement and agencies to combat gang activity, said:

> It always seems to boil down to family in one way, shape, or form. Whether they don't see or feel that they are getting the family that they want or that they don't get everything they believe they need from the family. So the family is always one of the critical issues when you look at a kid's involvement in a street gang. Most of the kids that I've dealt with refer to their gang as a family. It's one of the first ways they'd describe it. (Torres, 2019, Unpublished)

Youth can look to gangs to replace family. The gangs can become a "surrogate family," filling the void left behind from the family of origin (Ruble & Turner, 2000). The youth can look to find that brotherhood or sisterhood outside of the family of origin. Those without secure attachments with their primary caregivers will look elsewhere to fill that void (Ainsworth, 1989; Bowlby, 1998). Peer groups are a place that adolescents can form attachments (Ainsworth, 1989). One group of peers that they could look to is a gang, if it is available in their area. Gangs give youth a

© The Author(s), under exclusive license to Springer Nature Switzerland AG 2021
K. De Vito, *Gang Prevention in Schools*,
https://doi.org/10.1007/978-3-030-82914-8_4

sense of community with peers who can offer support, validation, and emotional fulfillment, all things they may be missing at home (Estrada et al., 2018). If there is nothing to attach the youth to the home, a youth can feel that he needs to search for something else to replace what is missing within the family, sometimes a replacement family, a sense of brotherhood and sisterhood.

The absence of a positive consistent family role model within the home would be a major risk factor for gang involvement (Higgins et al., 2010; Alleyne & Wood, 2014; Walters, 2016). Interest in crime can rise if there is no strong family attachment in the home because youth will not care about the effect of their actions on their parents' opinions, school performance, or discipline, leaving them vulnerable to poor peer influences, crime, and gangs (McNulty & Bellair, 2003). Positive role models and attachment figures can be protective factors. Having that support and guidance within the home can be helpful in dissuading gang involvement or be a resource to pull youth out of the clutches of gangs by showing the youth that there are other options and resources available to them to help.

Gerald Mallon, LCSW, DSW, Associate Dean of Scholarship and Research at Silberman School of Social Work at Hunter College and a Julia Lathrop Professor of Child Welfare, worked with youth in foster care and in the streets for 45 years. He ran group homes for teenage LGBTQ+ youth, who were not involved in traditional gangs, for the most part. However, they were part of houses. He made an interesting comparison of gangs to houses, noting the similarities, with the common thread and theme of looking for a replacement family:

> These houses were kind of like gangs in some ways…Sometimes, there was initiation into the houses…they sign up and belong to this house where they have a house mother and a house father. You have young people who live in the foster care system, so they're estranged from their families, sometimes through no fault of their own, and they kind of always have this gap in their life for family. I think these houses create a sense of family for them in ways that they can't get in a group home… I think when you belong to a house or a gang, there's some comradery there around the way in which you engage with one another because you have a common bond. I think it fulfills some need for young people who might have a need for family, a different kind of family. And I think there's positive and negatives about that. There are some real sustaining qualities about being a part of a gang or a house. It provided them with this kind of family system and nurturing from people who weren't paid to take care of you and who you chose to be with…The houses provided them with structure that they didn't have with their own families or the group homes. And many of them had long-lasting and deep relationships with people in their house. (Mallon, 2020, Unpublished)

Comradery creates a sense of unity. That sense of unity can create a bond which keeps people together. Gangs can create that sense of unity, that sense of everyone being in this together. A gang, like a house, can provide that different sense of family, which can be missing at home. Dr. Mallon described the downside of being involved in a gang and a house:

> But then there's also, you know, these things you kind of get caught up in, the drama about what's going on socially in a gang, the drama of who's in charge, who's powerful and who's not powerful, and having to do things that you don't particularly want to do, because maybe your status in the group is not as high as maybe someone else's status in the group, and I would see that play itself out a lot. And sometimes kids joined up because they thought it

would be great and then once they were involved, they realized this is not so wonderful and they would try to get out of it. Sometimes, it wasn't so easy to get out of it as they thought it might be to get out. (Mallon, 2020, Unpublished)

While the houses also provided something that the members did not have at home, much like gangs, a sense of belonging and a sense of having someone there for them, it also came with a dark side, much like gangs. There could be violence, drama, and crime. Also once involved, it can become more difficult to extricate oneself from the group.

4.2 "Brotherhood, Sisterhood, Unity:" Gang as Replacement Family

In De Vito (2020), the theme "Brotherhood, Sisterhood, Unity:" Gang as Replacement Family showed examples of the consequences of absence of the primary attachment figures. The youth have looked outside of the family of origin for support. The majority of participants said that they considered the gang a family, including a replacement family, for their family of origin. A lack of secure attachment at home makes it more likely that the child will look for a replacement (Ainsworth, 1989; Bowlby, 1998). If there is no secure attachment to primary caregivers, and a difficult home situation, then youth could look outside the family to peers and a gang to fill the void. Gangs consistently provided unity, love, affection, and attention. The majority of participants felt they had to grow up early and raise themselves because of absent primary caregivers. Some participants said if their parents, especially fathers, had been present, they would not have joined.

4.2.1 Brotherhood, Sisterhood, Unity

Most of the participants described a bond and a unity among gang members and said they became brothers or sisters. They found love, protection, and unity among each other. Always having someone to look out for you and having your back was something they found to be invaluable, especially if one is not getting that same type of love or attention at home from family. For example, Luis described gang members becoming bonded brothers over a murder of one of their own friends:

We connected, a lot of people connect because they're in it and just because they wear the same flag you know, something like that. We connected because we all had that one connection, "we all had that brother that got his life taken from him at such a young age, so it was like we all had that one desire, that one feel, that one love" (De Vito, 2020), you know... You know, only my brothers and my brothers' keeper. "We vowed to keep each other safe, all that, you know... It was like a brotherhood and a unity..." (De Vito, 2020). Just having somebody you know like, a big brother in a situation and always have someone to call...You know, my big brother was always there for me. He's still always there for me to this day. He still texts me every day, every other day. Calls me every other week. Makes sure I'm good...Tellin' me every day, stay in school, keep grinding. [He] says I'm proud of you my boy. You doing you. You know like that that's the real positive. The negative is always you know losing a homie, losing a brother, you know? (Luis, 2019, Unpublished)

Having experienced this one trauma and tragedy formed a bond for these young people. The murder gave them a sense of purpose for joining the gang, so they would have each other's backs. That sense of comradery and unity, if it is missing at home, can be something that is extremely appealing. If a kid is feeling unsafe in the neighborhood or school, a gang can provide protection, which may feel needed in certain environments and situations. Having a big brother to look out for you, when you don't necessarily have that at home, can also be a draw.

Being in a gang can elicit a feeling of brotherhood. Josue talked about having that brotherhood feeling from being in a gang. He said they knew that there was violence involved, but they craved that love that they were willing to accept the violence in exchange for the feeling of being loved by the brothers:

"It's like a brotherhood. And you're willing to do whatever it takes for them because you know they're willing to do whatever it takes for you. And then next thing you know, one of them gets harmed and all of you guys get harmed behind gang violence" (De Vito, 2020) and next thing you know, it become you guys against them and that's on a bigger scale...you understand you still got people that fight and people that do this and that with each other you know. "But as long as you have somebody who loves you, it's worth staying." (De Vito, 2020; Josue, 2019, Unpublished)

Being involved in a gang was seen as a trade-off by some participants. In exchange for that love and brotherhood, they needed to do what was necessary to protect the gang, which included violence. That exchange was worth it to many of the participants, at least at first.

The gang often was a place the gang members went to look for an escape from home, which was described as being broken in some way. They were looking for an escape and trying to get away from a negative situation and seeking something else. Jamie said:

They was more like my brothers...I wouldn't even say it was a gang because they always had my back no matter what. "If I got into any type of trouble, I called them..." (De Vito, 2020) and I needed them at this location, or someone's about to jump over at the school, and someone wants to jump me, they there. "It was like a brother type of thing...it's a family..." (De Vito, 2020). The one thing that attracted me was you get a lot of love from it. For instance, I be walkin' around certain areas to this day right and...you get a lot of respect...No type of ego, no type of reputation, yeah, it's all a respect thing from the whole ghetto. (Jamie, 2019, Unpublished)

Having that respect and that love is something that is worth more than anything to some participants. If they needed protection, they could call up one of their fellow gang members and know that someone would be there for them. That sense of reliability and dependability may have been something that did not have at home. It was a brotherhood for them.

Participants described a sense of comradery and "sticking together" through the rough times and having each other's backs. That made the gang life attractive to have

4.2 "Brotherhood, Sisterhood, Unity:" Gang as Replacement Family

that comfort and support. Jay described a situation where he and his fellow gang members got into a situation where he became injured. The rest of his gang members rioted and caused so many problems in the school as retaliation. The school officials had to contact him and ask him to speak up and calm the situation down:

> And I had gotten so deep into it that I was stabbed in front of the high school. I was 18 when I got stabbed, and it was a pretty serious situation…tore up my insides, so it took them nine-hour surgery to repair my insides, so I was in the hospital for about 35 days… [the school] called me at the hospital and asked me if I could give a speech to my friends so they could stop rioting and tearing up the school and the town. So I did that and got everything quieted down. I had a lot of friends, I was a pretty popular person, I got along with everyone…We didn't believe in all that racial division and fighting and all that, so we all stuck together. We partied together, we ate together, we hung together. So I got in a situation I shouldn't have got into, and it almost cost me my life. (Jay, 2019, Unpublished)

Realizing that being involved in a gang could cost a person his life can be enough to cause that person to make a decision to choose another path other than the gang. Having a serious injury or near-death experience can be a catalyst for change.

Some participants were looking for a way to fill a void at home. What was missing was respect, love, validation, affection, and attention, which they looked for in a gang. Evelyn said:

> "Definitely a sisterhood… something that I was missing that I didn't have at home. Like I had created my own family. [I was missing] family, acknowledgment…just having that empowering one another" (De Vito, 2020). I mean, I knew everything was negative that we were doing, but it was still that empowerment… that I never received at home. (Evelyn, 2019, Unpublished)

Receiving that validation and empowerment was worth it to Evelyn in exchange for the negative gang activities. Gangs can provide that consistency and support that is not available at home. Evelyn felt as though she had created another family.

4.2.2 Gang as Replacement Family

Gangs can be seen as a family for youth. Youth may see gangs as a replacement for their family of origin or as an extension of their family. Participants felt validated and accepted by their brothers and sisters seeing it as a brotherhood and sisterhood. Being willing to die for them was something that was a trade-off, a huge cost, which was violence. But some of the participants felt it was worth it at the time because they were so starved for that love, validation, and acceptance at home. They were willing to do whatever for their homies. Josue described wanting that love, but it came with an exchange for a brotherhood filled with violence:

> How did I know I was an official member? …When I accepted it…when you would walk into a house or a party or wherever you would go and somebody 40 years old or 30 years old would come and give you a hug. People that are 15, and 13, and 12 years old…like everybody loved you. And that was the affection you got. "There's no better feeling than to be validated and appreciated and you feel a part of it, like you have meaning, it's a lot.

> Especially when you're broken and the only thing that validates you is your homies and you'd be willing to die or do whatever for them..." (De Vito, 2020). I loved the unity. At the end of the day, I mean, shoot, we didn't have a lot. So if we were hungry, shoot, we boiled both eggs and you had one and I had one. Like there was a love that people wouldn't get or understand...A lot of them were [like family] ...It doesn't take like the whole hundreds and hundreds of people like we're all a big family. All's it takes is two people that you're real close to that you love. And you know they love you. (Josue, 2019, Unpublished)

Love, affection, unity, and validation are needed in a family life. If those things are missing, then youth may seek outside the family for them. Feeling loved by your homies is something that is needed when one is not receiving that love at home. Jose identified as feeling broken and only having his homies available to validate him. His words say a lot about what his homelife must have been like, for him to be searching for that love and validation elsewhere and for him to have been willing to accept the violence in return.

Other participants talked about negative feelings they associated with having a home that was broken in some way, which caused them to seek validation and appreciation. Josue described his homelife as broken and said that the gang made him feel appreciated, needed, validated, respected, and loved. He looked for what he needed in a gang:

> I think "what the gang did... was give me things that I didn't have at home. It gave me affection. I didn't grow up with affection, so when I would be hugged out there by my homeboys, that meant something to me. You'd go to school, and in school you don't feel like you fit in, you don't know how to read... coming from a poverty community and then you go to the neighborhood and all of a sudden, you're good at fighting and you're loyal" (De Vito, 2020). And you won't back down and little things like that where we come from mean everything. On a bigger scale in the community and like regulars don't mean nothing for people, but for us, when you're solid and all you got is your heart, that right there means everything. "That's where I stood out. That's where I belonged." (De Vito, 2020; Josue, 2019, Unpublished)

Not feeling like one fit in at school can be a huge source of stress for children. This feeling can be felt by students who struggle with academics in particular. If there is no attachment to school, that can be a risk factor for gang involvement. If the youth does not feel acceptance at school, he may become influenced by a gang because that may be a place he does feel accepted, with his peers.

Continuing on with how youth see gangs as a replacement family, Jamie talked how his "brothers" replaced his family and talks about how they replace a lot of family for other people:

> They did [replace my family] because I spent more time hangin' outside with those knuckleheads more than I spent time with my own mother...so they kinda did replace the family thing. And my mother, she didn't really know that I was runnin' around with them until things kinda hit the fan... "Some people trust gang members more than they trust their own blood and family. It was more of a gang/family/brothers, you get what I'm sayin', because we always had each other's backs." (De Vito, 2020; Jamie, 2019, Unpublished)

4.2 "Brotherhood, Sisterhood, Unity:" Gang as Replacement Family

The gang being a replacement family is a common theme. Jamie illustrated it by saying that it was a replacement family and saying the gang members always had his back. Trusting gang members more than one's own family says a lot about the family life. Antonio felt the same and said that the gang was a family or extension of their family members. Antonio said, "Yeah, they were [like family]. I don't hang with them anymore, but at one point, we used to call each other like brothers and stuff you know" (Antonio, 2019, Unpublished). Hector felt similarly, but some of the gang members were actual family members, and said, "They were my family. You know, through marriage, they were all my step cousins. Because all my family lived in a different state" (Hector, 2019, Unpublished).

Some participants felt that there was a lack of something within the home that was causing them to look outside of the home for a replacement. Tony said that there is a lack of family values, trauma exposure, and absent parents, which cause youth to look outside of the home for something to replace what is missing:

> "I think the family values and structures in a certain environment are completely diminished. There's a lot of broken families and homes and broken people…" (De Vito, 2020) in the midst of these environments, that's where so many people have to come together. That's where you find, you know, these youth that are tore up… "when you see things that's tore up around you and you come together with other kids and things are tore up…shot up or people in jail that are in your family and ain't nothing to eat…" (De Vito, 2020). There's certain instincts that start to come out of you when you're around certain things, so you start selling drugs…in order to make a couple dollars there, bringing money in… not only that but "I think the traumatic issues that people go through within the homes... just stirs up in some of these environments." (De Vito, 2020; Tony, 2019, Unpublished)

Tony spoke of the environment contributing to gang involvement as well. Poverty, violence, incarceration, and trauma are all contributing factors of gang involvement. He spoke of lack of family values and structure also being diminished. Having a lack of support system and lack of structure at home is seen in youth that are gang-involved. Many of those youth from similar backgrounds come together and make their own family unit, which is a gang.

Other participants found that they could find what they were looking for outside of their family life. They did not need to be in a situation where they were in an environment at home that they did not want to be in any longer. They did not need their families anymore because they could support themselves by the money they were making in the gangs. Jerry explained:

> So then it got to be running away. I said I would go ahead and leave then. I said I need to go out on my own because anybody I dealt with was older than me. While I am 13, they were 17-, 18-year-old kids. So it was like I had a buddy that was 18 that had a girl that was 24. They already had an apartment. So it was like okay. I'm 13. I'm leaving, but I can go to this apartment and rest my head, eat, shower, you know, use the restroom, do what I need to do. So it was like what do I really need you for? Then I was selling drugs at an early age. So it was like I was already making money. What do I need you for? Not like that. I love my mom and dad to death, but I don't need you for nothing. I don't need no money from you. I don't need nothing. I don't need clothes. I bought my own clothes, my own shoes, you know. It became a lifestyle now. Now it's different. (Jerry, 2019, Unpublished)

In this situation, Jerry felt love for his parents but did not need them anymore. The gang provided shelter, money, resources, and basic necessities for him. He did not feel as though he needed to be home any longer because the gang was providing him with everything he felt that he needed.

4.2.3 Growing Up with Gang Members

Gang-involved youth often grow up in an environment with gang members. The gang members are friends, classmates, neighbors, or even members of their own family. Having that gang influence around can make joining a gang more likely and may even seem inevitable in some cases. Lamar talked about how gang members were always around because his brother was involved in a gang. He became friends with them by association through family. He saw joining the gang as following in his brother's footsteps and that it was an inevitable life course for him:

> Yes, [gang members were] always around…the biggest influence was my older brother who… ran away from home at an early age and going to see him…He left home early, and he kind of like adopted a new life for himself…the bond, connection I had with him exposed me to new friends and some of his homies, who became my friends. (Lamar, 2019, Unpublished)

Having family members involved in gangs makes it more difficult to say no to gang life. Lamar's biggest influence was his older brother, someone he looked up to in his life. He provided that influence for him.

Some youth become drawn to the street life because they are familiar with the people from their neighborhood, and that is who they grew up around. They may also want a sense of protection and knowing someone has their back. Having a lot of money and material things along with a sense of protection can seem appealing and draw youth into it. Archie talked about what drew him to a gang. He had a large family and love in the household. But he was drawn to the lifestyle and knowing that people had his back:

> I chose the streets to teach [instead of school]. I liked school, but it wasn't my favorite subject to go to school. I'd rather go on the streets and do what I did, which is probably the wrong lifestyle. That's why I'm sitting in this [wheel]chair and in the hospital today…Just the atmosphere and the environment [drew me to a gang], it was like a magnet. It just sucked me in… The recognition of people. Having you and your boys riding together knowing somebody has your back. And knowing if it goes down, I'm not going down by myself… I had friends that were involved, neighbors, the people you grew up with. They're like let's go do this… I had enough understanding as a child coming up and in a certain neighborhood that they knew me. And it was like I'm just part of the team. I was already a little kid that fought a lot when I was young… I just liked the flavor. I just liked the glamor of it… Most people come from a family broken up with mama and no brothers or sisters. I've got brothers and sisters that are schoolteachers and shit. I got love in the household. I chose what I chose because of the way I saw it. I liked the way it looked. (Archie, 2019, Unpublished)

4.2 "Brotherhood, Sisterhood, Unity:" Gang as Replacement Family

The gang lifestyle can seem appealing for youth. Archie found himself drawn to the gang lifestyle for various reasons, as many young people do, especially when they do not fully understand all that is involved. Having people who had his back was something that was alluring to him. People in his neighborhood and people he grew up with were also involved which made it more likely for him to become involved as well.

Some youth also have family members that are deeply involved in the gang already, so it is just something that they grew into. The gang is an extension of the family that they already have. Jay talked about the size of his gang and how a lot of his family were members. Everyone was very close and saw the gang as family, which offered love, protection, discipline, food, and life teaching. He saw the gang as an extension of his family:

> Where we grew up…at the time there probably was 200–300 of us [in the same gang]. So you become one big family and you migrate into it. In my neighborhood…I probably have about 20 cousins from my neighborhood where I grew up at [that were gang involved]. It was a brotherhood to me. You know, everybody was real close…you're a big help with your big brothers who guide you and – who told you what to do, you looked up to them… Family, it's a love, they discipline you, they protect you, they feed you, they teach you. They are teaching you – I've got a lot of moms. My friends taught me everything I know. Everything I know I learned from people from the streets. It was an extension of my family, 'cause I was – our family's real close. (Jay, 2019, Unpublished)

Gangs can appear like an extension of family. Jay said he learned everything from his gang members who were also family members. He even says he had a lot of moms and that his friends taught him everything he knows. Having big brothers who are looking out for you and teaching you things can become a family.

Jerry also described the gang as his family. These people were the people he grew up knowing in his neighborhood. They were already close and like family. There can be a comfort level and a seemingly natural progress or way of life into gang life. He said:

> A lot of people misjudge gang members. You know what I mean. They think just because a person is from a gang, they've got to have a messed-up attitude or they've got to be, you know, this way or that way, and they've got to be an evil person. No, that's not true. That's not true at all…Gangs were like family. That's your family. Like you walk outside, even if you are not from this gang…it's like you're five or six years old and you know who these guys is that's outside. So it's like it's you're growing into a family. (Jerry, 2019, Unpublished)

Living in an environment where one is growing up with gang members can make it seem like joining is the natural next step in life. It might not seem as though there is anything wrong with it if that is what everyone in the neighborhood does. It becomes a family.

4.2.4 Conditional Love

A few participants felt the gang was not a replacement for their family but was rather an extension. But they still considered the gang members as part of their extended family. There was one negative case. Johanna said she did not think the gang was a family at all. She could not trust them:

> "The gang I'm from, you're taught you don't love nobody and you don't trust nobody because anybody can be your friend one minute and be ready to kill you the next over money, or cars, or jewelry, so they wasn't my family members" (De Vito, 2020). I had family members. (Johanna, 2019, Unpublished)

In this case, the gang was not a family because there was no trust. Johanna realized that she could not trust the gang members, and it was not a family to her. She realized how conditional the situation was where one can turn on someone in a minute.

Others felt that the gang love was conditional. Another participant, Leo, felt as if there was love in the gang, but it was conditional. So there was not full trust because he knew that the gang could turn on him too:

> We were really like poor…the homies don't really help you out like when you can't pay your bills and stuff. So I got in…there was some homies that I was close with…I just felt like for me I was really kind of alone, and I was broke, and I'd kick it with the homies…but I really didn't connect with people because by that time, I was pretty much shut down. When you're from a gang, it's conditional love. So like it's very conditional. You always have to like put on a show…if you get locked up and you come back out, it's conditional. It's like, okay, well, you got locked up. You know, you were gone for a while, but now you're back out. What are you really doing, you know what I mean? It's just a really conditional type of feeling like you don't really feel like, like fully embraced. I think that you already know in the back of your head like these folks can turn on me too, you know? Just based off the rules and the way things are in the neighborhood, in the gang. (Leo, 2019, Unpublished)

Leo gave a good example of how conditional the love is in a gang. He did not get help when in need at times, and he felt that it was conditional. He could sense that they could turn on him. Leo did not have that experience of a gang being a true family.

Most participants felt as though the gang replaced their actual family of origin because there were different problems within the family. As a result, they sought a replacement family in the gang that offered that love, attention, affection, validation, and unity, whereas others felt as if the gang was an extension of their family, and some actually had family members involved in the gang already. There was one negative case where the former gang member felt as though the gang did not replace her family. There were others who felt that the love was conditional or found it was conditional as time went on.

References

Ainsworth, M. (1989). Attachment beyond infancy. *American Psychologist, 44*, 709–716.
Alleyne, E., & Wood, J. (2014). Gang involvement: Social and environmental factors. *Crime & Delinquency, 60*(4), 547–568.
Bowlby, J. (1998). *A secure base: Clinical applications of attachment theory*. New York: Routledge.
De Vito, K. (2020). Seeking a secure base: Gangs as attachment figures. *Qualitative Social Work, 19*(4), 754–769.
Estrada, J. N., Huerta, A. H., Hernandez, E., Hernandez, R. A., & Kim, S. W. (2018). In H. Shapiro (Ed.), *The Wiley handbook on violence in education: Forms, factors, and preventions*. Wiley.
Higgins, G., Wesley, J., & Mahoney, M. (2010). Developmental trajectories of maternal and paternal attachment and delinquency in adolescence. *Deviant Behavior, 31*(7), 655–677.
McNulty, T., & Bellair, P. (2003). Explaining racial and ethnic differences in serious adolescent violent behavior. *Criminology, 41*(3), 709–748.
Ruble, N., & Turner, W. (2000). A systematic analysis of the dynamics and organization of urban street gangs. *The American Journal of Family Therapy, 28*, 117–132.
Walters, G. (2016). Someone to look up to: Effect of role models on delinquent peer selection and influence. *Youth Violence and Juvenile Justice, 14*(3), 257–271.

Chapter 5
"No Other Option:" The Role of Social Environment

> *I was good in school…school was an outlet for me. And basketball and playing sports was an outlet. But "at the end of the day walking up and down the streets, I was going to have to pass by the gangs…And eventually, I did the one thing that I always said when I was a kid I wouldn't do, and it was to join the gang. 'Oh, I'm not going to join the gang. I'm not going to put them in charge of my life.' And bam." (De Vito, 2020; Lamar, 2019, Unpublished)*
>
> – Former Gang Member Lamar

5.1 "No Other Option"

Violence and threats of violence are inherent to gang life. As seen with the participants in De Vito (2020), some youth feel as if they have no other option but to join a gang because of the influence of having a heavy gang presence in the neighborhood, low socioeconomic status and need for making money, gang-involved friends or family members, and lack of attachment to parents or for a sense of protection if they feel threatened. The idea of perceived threat from another neighborhood gang drives organization of youth in another neighborhood and the need for protection, driving gang membership (Decker & Van Winkle, 1996). Threats of a gang in a certain area increase gang solidarity and also cause youth to join gangs, which will cause acts of violence that they may not otherwise have been engaged in (Decker & Van Winkle, 1996). If there are threats of physical violence, it will increase the bond within a gang within their neighborhoods (Decker & Van Winkle, 1996). Contagion causes gangs to become larger and to spread to surrounding neighborhoods and communities (Decker & Van Winkle, 1996).

Youth many times are seeking a sense of safety and protection when they join a gang. Gerald Mallon, LCSW, DSW, Associate Dean of Scholarship and Research at Silberman School of Social Work at Hunter College and a Julia Lathrop Professor of Child Welfare, talked about working with LGBTQ+ youth and the reasons they joined a gang:

> If I did see kids in gangs it was where their brother was in a gang, so they got involved in a gang. Or they joined for protection too. They weren't really out… so they would join a gang so people would leave them alone and not harass them. (Mallon, 2020, Unpublished)

Some of the LGBTQ+ youth that Dr. Mallon worked with joined a gang because they were seeking protection or because they had family members already in the gang. Both of these reasons are some of the reasons many young people turn to gangs across the board.

A sense of safety is important to youth. Kirk "Jae" James, DSW, MSW, BA, AA, Clinical Assistant Professor at NYU Silver School of Social Work, talked about how seeking safety, some as a result of the environment they grew up in, is one of the reasons youth join gangs:

> One of the things… this idea of safety. We're all seeking safety. You are seeing that the only time someone is afforded safety is when they are in a position of power, whether it's in numbers, or with guns, and that's again externally. Most of these folks have grown up in neighborhoods where they're targeted by police who function as a quasi-gang, and they have been shown that power and safety can only happen in numbers or with guns or with weapons. There's often this mirroring process that we often don't acknowledge in the formation of these gangs. I have my own history of incarceration. I was on Riker's Island in 1994, and the reason why this was significant is because the gangs in New York State prisons for years were only Latin Kings and Ñetas. Those were the pretty dominant gangs. Those gangs were Hispanic, but Ñetas were a bit more mixed. But they for a long time had supremacy, and a lot of the paps were down with them. Growing up in NYC, we didn't have Bloods, Crips, or maybe you have community crews, but not these gangs like there is now. Folks would come to places like Rikers and be assaulted by the paps or assaulted by Latin Kings or Ñetas. And then you started to see Bloods and Crips. And pretty soon, New York had all these gangs. These things didn't really start till 1993 and 1994 in terms of like in prison, and this was a direct result of the fear of folks coming in and the fear of being assaulted by people in power as well as other gangs that were there. (James, 2020, Unpublished)

Seeking safety is a reason youth join gangs. Dr. James talked about seeing that need for safety in the prison system as well with inmates being fearful of people in power such as the police or gang members, thus forming new gangs for protection. Some of the former gang members that I spoke to also talked about joining gangs because of feeling the need for safety. Needing to feel safe is a basic human need. Some feel they need to turn to a gang to achieve that sense of safety and protection given the circumstances in their living situation. Dr. James also talked about visiting an area that had gangs and finding out why they joined, and it was the lack of feeling like they had a safe space or feeling supported and feeling they needed to organize in numbers for safety:

> I was in Cape Town a few years ago and visited the Cape Town flats where there's this community gang disruption organization. It's so real because Cape Town is probably only a few miles. But there's 50 gangs in this really tight-knit area. And it was so interesting to have conversations with them. We went in and they were telling us about their experiences of how they got involved with gangs. And it's all the same stories, feeling unsupported, feeling like they're a threat to harm by the system if they weren't in numbers, feeling the lack of social access, and feeling like they need to rob and steal. So if you don't create spaces where people can feel, like I can feel supported, I can be seen, I can have access… This is always

going to be an issue. You look at the issue of America. And there's always been gangs. Some get labeled gangs, and some get labeled differently. But there's been Irish gangs and Italian gangs. Whenever people have come to this country and they haven't had an opportunity to access assistance and they feel harmed by the system, there will always be some kind of mobilization and unity against the system. (James, 2020, Unpublished)

Dr. James talked about meeting with gang members in Cape Town and hearing about the reasons they joined a gang. Feeling as if there may not be any other options available, lack of social access, feeling unsupported, feeling like they may be in danger of being harmed by the system if they were not in numbers, and feeling like they needed to steal are some of the same reasons that are seen in other areas of the world as reasons for gang joining. Dr. James illustrated how if people do not have access, they will feel like they are being harmed by the system and will organize against the system. A gang can be seen as such a rebellion against the system. Youth in these situations need to see that there are other options and resources to help them so that they choose another path.

In De Vito (2020), the theme "No Other Option" showed how various social factors contributed to participants choosing the gang lifestyle. Most participants felt as if there was no other option for them. Many grew up in a neighborhood with a heavy gang presence. Many had gang-involved family members or friends. Joining a gang appeared to be inevitable for them. Participants also grew up in areas with a low socioeconomic status where there were fewer opportunities available to them, and gangs were a way to make money. Some also joined because they had lost a close friend or family member due to gang violence. Most participants did not have secure present attachment figures in the household, which may have caused them to look outside of the family, and gangs were readily available in their environment. The participants felt as if they did not have any other option and that joining a gang was their path in life.

5.2 It Is Just the Environment We Grew Up In

Living in a neighborhood with a low socioeconomic status and less opportunities, along with a large gang presence, led many participants to join a gang. Having that steady influence can be very persuasive and overwhelming. Lamar talked about not having a choice of where he grew up and that having an impact:

> A lot of times…people tend to judge…gang members or criminals…Drug addicts, prostitutes, whatever the case may be…we're in a society and a community where we tend to judge and point fingers. And what I've come to learn is that sometimes…some people are just playing the cards they've been dealt. So what does that mean? Well, obviously if I grew up in Sherman Oaks, or Tarzana, or Belair…I wouldn't even be talking to you, right? There's no telling because those communities don't have…economic problems. You know what I mean? Those cities don't have gang problems. So these areas [are] very successful and the families that are living there are very successful, so they provide for their family members and afford them opportunities to be successful. So for those of us who were born in South Central LA, Compton, Watts, Inglewood, one thing's for sure…they grow up

where they grew up. So...my parents did the best they could, and God bless them for that...But "I didn't choose to grow up [where I did]" (De Vito, 2020) in South Central LA. (Lamar, 2019, Unpublished)

Sometimes, you're just playing the cards you've been dealt. Lamar talked about his neighborhood specifically being of low socioeconomic status and how higher socioeconomic status neighborhoods do not have gangs because of those neighborhoods having more opportunities available to them. Living in a community with less opportunity and less options may lead youth to make decisions based on what is available and right in front of them. If gangs are readily available in the area, that is what they may gravitate toward.

Some youth adapt to the gang lifestyle because it is what is going on around them. They grew up in that same environment with them. Luis talked about being around gang members in his neighborhood and growing up around them. It was who he adapted to in his environment:

> It was like, they [gang members] were always around me. I was always around older people. Me and my brother...and his friends were all...around the gangs and stuff like that...I always wanted to be around them because they wise, they know what it was. I always wanted to listen and go with the street mentality instead of the book mentality... As I got older, like 12, I started to go outside more. I was really an outside kid. I really was never one to want to be in the house all the time...When I went outside, I experienced it for myself. It was just the people I adapted to. (Luis, 2019, Unpublished)

Luis said that he gravitated toward gangs for two reasons: It was what was around him, and he gravitated toward the street mentality because he was not as into the book mentality. Having that gang influence in the area, especially if it's peers or family members, makes joining more likely. If there is a lack of connection to school, that can also be a risk factor for gang involvement.

Based on the area they lived in, some participants talked about how there was no other option for them but to join a gang. Jamie said that growing up, gangs were what was in his environment, and his friends were also involved. He was just affiliated right from the start. He had no other option:

> [I joined a gang at age] 12. I grew up with gang members. That's all I knew...I got exposed... [and did] what I had to to keep my friends. If they fight, I gotta fight with them every day on a daily. It was probably like after school. I wouldn't even go straight home. I'd go straight on the block... I'm always on the porch...we just out there chillin'. And if something happens, it happens. There was times that I got into situations and they had my back. It was more of a gang/family/brothers...because we always had each other's back. And that's a normal thing as far as gang members, you always gotta have their backs. If one fights, we all gotta fight...One is in trouble, we all gotta get in trouble. One person got beef with somebody, we all got beef with that person...That's how it was when I was comin' up... "It wasn't somethin' that I thought about because I grew up with them when I was young. So, it wasn't even an option...it came naturally...When you live in that type of environment, [there is no] option or no discussion...you just affiliated...You just in because you just grew up into that so I wouldn't say that I was pushed into that or anything it was just normal to me." (De Vito, 2020; Jamie, 2019, Unpublished)

If growing up with gang members is what all young people are exposed to and what is in the area around them, it makes joining more likely. Many of the former gang members said joining a gang was a way of life for them. In Jamie's case, he mentioned that growing up in that area meant that one is associated with the gang from the beginning. Joining was something that was expected and a natural progression.

Growing up with violence in the neighborhood seemed normal for some youth. Jay talked about how joining a gang was a natural thing due to his family environment which was also full of a lot of violence and witnessing trauma, which impacted him early on in life:

> It something you grow into, so it just happened naturally, in this game…You're used to fighting, you're used to seeing the violence all the time… at the age of seven…[I] seen my mother's boyfriend murdered…the old man walk behind him with a shotgun…he turns and looks at him and says ah, he ain't going to do nothing, and [he] shot him. It's something that will never, ever, ever go away, but you learn to deal with it. Growing up in the environment where we had to grow up in, it became the norm. (Jamie, 2019, Unpublished)

Witnessing trauma early on in life can impact a child for a lifetime. In some neighborhoods, violence is more prevalent, including gang violence. In these instances, following along that violent pathway may seem like the next step for young people living in that environment.

The promise of protection is something that gangs offer to youth. Jerry spoke about getting involved in a gang because he was protected by them after he was attacked by a rival gang. They offered him protection, so everyone assumed he was in the gang, so he felt he had no other choice at that point but to join:

> As you get older, it's like something would go wrong with you out here… Some kids jump you because you are going to a school way over on the other end of town or something. So you get jumped or some guys do something to you. These guys right here, without you even being from their gang yet, they feel obligated to take care of you. Like, "Oh man, they did what?" Like this happened to you… and now you're starting to get a tag on you. You know what I mean. You're not necessarily from that gang yet, but just because your back-up gang was looking out for you, and they from this gang, now you're getting stereotyped. Oh, he's from over there. He's from over there, you know what I mean. So now it's kind of like you're almost getting pushed to the corner to where, hey man, you're getting treated like you're from over there anyway. You might as well make it official. (Jerry, 2019, Unpublished)

If a youth is living in an area where he feels as though he needs protection, a gang might become a viable option. In Jerry's case, he was jumped by a gang, then the rival gang started looking out for him, so he felt as if he was pushed into joining. He felt he was being treated like he was from that gang, so he might as well officially join. It may seem like the only option if one feels threatened and fears for one's safety.

Sometimes, the environment can make the choice for you. Archie talked about growing up in a gang-influenced area. He said that is the lifestyle that is given to you, and violence and trauma also came with it:

> I've been shot twice…I've been stabbed…hit in the head with a hammer, and you know it's because of the lifestyle you lived in [my area]. You make these decisions, and these are the consequences that come with it…Coming up, it wasn't easy. It was you made choices and then you deal with it. Because the environment you were in made the choice for you within itself. We did a lot of things that I felt was survival tactics. But I shouldn't have had to do it because I still had a choice. I just wasn't in a clear state of mind. We shouldn't have had to bring the bullet rides in houses and robbing people and doing stuff to that degree. Robbing

> stores and it was rough. I got stabbed at the age of seven. I grew up in the projects... I made choices that were not the best choices. But they were survival choices, and then once I got to high school, it really started jumping off then. Because that's when everybody wanted to make sure they knew what place you were from, what gang you were from, and who did you represent. And I was still young, but I was like I come from the rough side...so I can deal with this. (Archie, 2019, Unpublished)

Living in certain environments, youth need to figure out ways to survive. As Archie said, some choices he made were because he had to figure out a way to survive. For him, that meant joining a gang. He lived a life of violence, and he felt as if he had no choice. Many young people are in similar situations and make similar choices.

Having gang members around you daily can become an influence. Antonio was born in Florida but moved to Mexico for several years for family reasons. When he came back, he was placed in a bilingual class and did not know anyone, nor did he speak English well. That class was filled with gang members who became an influence on him, and he then gravitated toward that lifestyle:

> I had met new friends who were already influenced by the gang members through either their family members or they had friends or older brothers. So slowly, they started introducing me to that lifestyle. Over the summer, I started hanging out with them. I had never smoked or anything like that. I had never drunk or anything, so when I started my freshman year in high school, that's when I started experiencing new stuff. I used to hear of them getting high and this and that, so I asked one of my close friends that I wanted to smoke with him. And then, that's where it all started. They were already in a gang, so as soon as I started hanging out with a certain type of friends like another, rival gang already started seeing me with them like a lot. So they started talking to me as like I was already with them. I mean they were close friends. Like I treated them kind of [like] family because we kind of grew up together like in our high school years and stuff like that. So I was never, you know how they call it, getting baptized. You have to get baptized before you even get into the gang, but I never really got initiated. (Archie, 2019, Unpublished)

For Antonio, due to the peer influence around him, gangs became the next logical step to him. He became involved due to who he was hanging around with in his class. Gang joining starts this way for many young people, including students I have worked with in the past.

Environment can play a big role in the decision to join. George said joining a gang was like an inevitable life course for him because of who he was hanging around and his family:

> ... [I joined a gang] Well actually in 6th grade. It wasn't like a real big gang. It was a little gang we made up ourselves... When I got older, that's when it became more serious. I would say that was maybe around 10th grade. It happened naturally. Because the people I was hanging around, they all did stuff like that...It really came from my social class basically. That's the people I was hanging around...basically, my uncle was in it, and my cousin's dad was in it. Basically, they just let us join it. (George, 2019, Unpublished)

Having family and friends in a gang makes joining more likely and easier to do because the avenue is right there. Saying no can be really hard for youth when in that situation. In that case, outside intervention may be indicated.

5.3 Idolizing Gang Members and Lifestyle

Growing up in a community with poverty, joining a gang can be seen as an opportunity to make money. Children may grow up idolizing gang members or the gang lifestyle and see it as a way out to a better life. Jay described how he grew up idolizing gang members and the material things they had:

> No, you just have to understand that a lot of times it's the persona that they – the gang members put on. If I see this guy walking around, he's got nice gold chains, he's driving a fancy lowrider car. When he goes and parks that car, he pulls back up in a $70,000–$80,000 car and he's man of the hood, and everybody respects him, you want to be that. You want to do what you can do to become that…When you are that gang member that's cool and you know how to get money, you know how to party, you lead people in the right direction, but if somebody cross you, they will get dealt with, that's the person everybody wants to be… Man, those gang members, those hood dudes, they got swag, they got style, and that's who I want to be. Growing on up in the neighborhood and you see that…that's what you want to be. That's how I was from a kid. My first time in a nice lowrider car, I'm going to have me one of those. My friends were making cocaine traffickers, "I'm going to be a drug dealer. I'm going to get money like them. And those are the kind of gang members I hung around…influenced by…I seen my first million dollars cash in a filthy, broken down, raggedy apartment infested with gang members. Not many kids are seeing that kind of money in that area…" (De Vito, 2020) and the gang members had it…And you're getting that tax-free money, you want that. Who had that? "The gang members had that, so a lot of people they seen that, that's who they wanted to be." (De Vito, 2020; Jay, 2019, Unpublished)

Growing up in a community with low socioeconomic status, gang members can be idolized for the material things they have which are immediately evident, such as cars, clothing, and jewelry. Youth may look up to them and think they want to be a part of that because they want to have all the material things that they have. They think that joining a gang is the key to that kind of lifestyle. They just do not realize everything else that will come along with paying the price to have those things, such as violence and criminal activity. Sometimes they do not realize until they are a part of the gang. They need to be shown other ways and other opportunities.

Living in poverty can have a direct effect on the decision to join a gang. Jay spoke about having bills to pay in the family and needing a way to make money quickly:

> And yeah some were good and some were bad influences. I happened to migrate to the ones who were bad influences, pimps, drug dealers, gangsters, drug addicts. I migrated to that side, but we had a lot of bills in my family… it was just the influence that you follow. And at a young age, when you see stuff like that and you glorify it, that's what you become. (Jay, 2019, Unpublished)

Glorifying gang members can be easier to do when one is in a dire economic situation. It might seem like it is an easier way out and a faster way to get money for your family. Since gangs were in his area, that was the path he chose.

Young people may idolize people who have a lot of money and have things that they want. Youth see the gang members in the area bringing in a lot of money and having a lot of things. They think by joining that gang, they can get the lifestyle that they want. Jerry said:

> You find somebody that catches interest in people for different reasons...Like they look at NBA stars. They dream about it over here. They feel like that's a dream like they will never have that kind of money. They will never be able to do this, never be able to do that, but that's because [they don't] see that and that's why they start looking at the people like that just like in the streets. So people starting find them reachable goals and like maybe reachable goals can be through selling drugs. You are like okay, you know what, I've been to jail so much. Everybody's getting summer jobs. I am not going to get no summer job. I already know that. So you know what. I'm going to go pick up this stack. Now I'm making more money than you guys while you guys are at work and doing all this. I'm making way more money than you guys...People start substituting things. Like I started substituting a lot of things in life, like okay...I'm going to do it in the streets. People start saying, "You know you can get a job." I say, "Hey, I make more money than you in the streets than you do at work, so leave me alone." I'm talking to people like that when I was like 15. (Jerry, 2019, Unpublished)

Jerry talked about having reachable goals. Reachable goals for someone living in a low-income community that has a large gang presence may be different than someone living in a higher socioeconomic status community. Having someone be able to step in and show youth that there are other options and opportunities is needed.

5.4 It's Just a Way of Life

Gang membership is a way of life for some. Growing up in a family where there have been several generations of gang members, there can be an expectation for membership within families and peer groups. There can be police labels and assumptions about gang membership just based on the neighborhood you come from. Josue talked about this issue growing up:

> "If the cops see me... Oh, you're from such and such gang just by the area we lived in... since we were kids riding our bikes, the cops had already put us in a gang" (De Vito, 2020). Oh, you're from such and such gang. Your uncle...that's who you are that's where you're gonna be from...we had already been labeled that. When you at school people say your whole family is from there [then] that's where you're from. You've claimed that. You just automatically...put in that area, whether you're committed or not. You're already placed there. (Josue, 2019, Unpublished)

Based on whatever neighborhood you come from, you may be pinpointed as a gang member. If you have gang members in your family, you may be assumed to be affiliated already. What impression does this leave on young people if they are already assumed in a gang just from the area they live in or who they are related to? How does that impact their goals in life?

Participants said gang members are often bred from a young age. Gangs are often comprised of their childhood friends and family members. Many of them spoke about having no other options or opportunities available to them, and they had to just accept their destiny or fate. Josue gave an example:

> "It was more of an acceptance that this is a way of life, you know?... You can't run from it. Before that I always used to play sports and stay at the park. Then I realized that's not the reality. This is my destiny, so stop running from it, you know?" (De Vito, 2020)

Feeling as though this is a way of life and you cannot escape a predetermined destiny is sad. Feeling as if there is no way out and no other options can be a hopeless feeling. Youth need to be shown different options and opportunities outside of gang life.

Growing up in a neighborhood where violence is the norm can cause desensitization toward violence. Youth may just accept that this is what is normal for their area. Josue talked about there being a lot of violence and death where he grew up, and it was just a way of life for them:

> I mean, I think I've always been around them [gang members] my whole life… "This was just a way of life growing up for us" (De Vito, 2020). That's how I grew up. Good? There was a lot of good. I escaped from everything so that was cool. I mean, I don't know, one thing that even in the bad the one good thing was there was unity. But I mean, from the bad we experienced a lot of death in our family, so that was kinda the trauma. We lost a lot of people. People were killed and stuff…Like it was a way of life for us, you know. You know my aunt was murdered, like my uncle was sentenced to life, you know that was the kind of life…that's kind of where we grew up at. It wasn't about the gang. It was just the environment that we grew up in. (Josue, 2019, Unpublished)

Watching people get injured and witnessing death is traumatic. Accepting that this is a way of life based on the environment can cause a sense of hopelessness and despair. Youth need to be shown hope that there is something else outside of their neighborhood filled with violence.

5.5 Playing the Cards They've Been Dealt

Having fewer opportunities due to the environment means less options. Lamar talked about people growing up in poverty communities just being played the cards they've been dealt:

> And the question, "Well, how did that happen?" I mean, "Shoot, how does that happen?" "Uh, well, economic opportunity." Well, I, for one, hanging out with my brother. Secondly, the lure of trying to make some money. And once I decided that I wanted to make some money to take care of myself or to provide a living for myself, everything else was like a snowball effect. Bam, bam, bam, bam, bam. I'm selling, I'm getting guns, I'm doing, I'm getting, I'm getting harassed by police. And it went from there. So my message…is that sometimes people will just play the cards they've been dealt. And I think it's important that people know that some people [are] doing the best they can. And the only way you can kind of bridge the gap and help people do better is through awareness and to also help provide opportunities to underserved communities. (Lamar, 2019, Unpublished)

Showing youth that there are other opportunities out there other than gangs is key. Making them aware of the dangers of gangs and assisting youth in getting involved in other areas and interests will also help them to be more successful.

Needing the ability to find other opportunities is important. Jay spoke about not having many options and opportunities to make money in his area and how difficult it is to find a decent-paying job outside of prison. As a result, he wound up going back to the gang lifestyle:

> Life after 18, I learned there's things in the world called drugs. You can make tax-free money off of them. So I became this gang-banging drug dealer. Drug dealing, gang-banging popularity, it all goes together. And with all the friends and people that I use, I was able to make a lot of money. So I started doing that, in and out of jail, in and out, in and out, in and out. Finally, I kept going to one courtroom, and the judge he's like, I see you back in my courtroom one more time, you are going to prison. I kind of laughed it off. A week later, I was back in his courtroom. So after I got out, you know, I learned a lot, but I didn't learn nothing because once you become a felon, you have kids, they got this stuff called child support, and you can't get a job. And with the felony, it was tough to get a job. Luckily, I had a friend who worked in a warehouse, so he was able to get me a job. But that only lasted so long because after you start working and they start taking child support, you leave every morning at five o'clock in the morning traveling…to work in the hot warehouse, and you get a check, it's for $300 or $400 bucks, and you worked 72 hours. You don't want to go back to that. You know that there's an easier way to get money, and that easier way is like, it's in a cold air-conditioned house, and you can make ten times more amount of money than you can by getting up, going to work 12 hours a day for six days a week. So I started veering back into the old life… (Jay, 2019, Unpublished)

Once a person has a criminal record, such as with a felony like Jay had, finding a career path or higher-paying job becomes more difficult. After some time of trying, the person may feel as if he has no other option but to gravitate back to the same gang lifestyle just to be able to make a living. Places such as Homeboy Industries, the world's largest gang rehabilitation program based in California, can be monumental in getting former gang members acclimated back into society and giving them a place to land and get back on their feet again.

Having no direction and being unclear on opportunities, some youth may gravitate toward gangs if they are in the immediate area. Lamar talked about not having any idea of what to do after high school because his parents weren't very involved with him. His opportunity in the neighborhood was the drug trade, so that's what he gravitated toward:

> The biggest problem I had out of high school is I didn't really have a sense of direction. My parents weren't really hands-on and kind of involved in…promoting certain ideas or different things that I could look into after high school…I remember wanting to work in aviation…I was interested in working at an airport or working around airplanes. And I remember applying for those positions and never getting a call back. The only employment opportunity that was…available to me was the drug trade…Once I made the decision to sell drugs, it kind of was like no looking back. And once I became good at it, you know, like why, why even consider anything else when…I can be successful in selling drugs? (Lamar, 2019, Unpublished)

School staff members can be instrumental in a situation such as the one described above. Lamar did not have any direction, and his parents were not involved or hands-on with him. Lamar said that nothing was available to him as an opportunity but the drug trade. If he had had another opportunity, perhaps he would not have joined a gang and got involved in the drug trade. School staff members could be helpful in directing him and mentoring him to other areas and showing him other options.

5.6 Joining Because They Lost a Friend to Gang Violence

Some youth join gangs because of violence they have witnessed. Luis talked about the moment he decided to join. It was when his friend was killed due to gang violence. That was the moment he decided to join to avenge his friend's death:

> What really put it over the edge was [when his friend was killed]. He was like a big brother to me…He got killed at a party… that is what really put it over the edge for me. Seeing my brother, someone who was like my brother in that casket just lying there. You know, it opened a different animal in me, you know. That's what really put it over the edge. That's all I could say…when I got the call, it was like, it broke my heart. I'm like, oh man. I didn't want to believe it at first, you know, until we had the candle lighting. Then it started to become a little more believable…Then when the day came, and I seen him in the casket, then I knew it was real, so… It was more like, I started coming around more. I started being around them more. They see the look in my eyes. They seen it. You know, you might as well, you know. And it was like we'll take it from there then. (Luis, 2019, Unpublished)

The motivation to join for some can be the trauma of losing a friend or family member due to gang violence. The desire to avenge the death or right a wrong can be overwhelming. For someone like Luis, losing his friend is what pushed him over the edge and caused him to join the gang.

When Josue lost his brother due to gang violence, he made a similar decision to join a gang:

> I was turning 12 so when my brother passed away, that's when I just shaved my head and I became a follower… "there was a lot of violence…" (De Vito, 2020). My brother was killed by gang violence. He was only 15 years old. (Josue, 2019, Unpublished)

Growing up in an area that has a heavy gang presence may make joining a gang more inevitable. Having gang members in your community, within your family, and as your friends may make joining seem like it's a natural progression in life. Living in a disadvantaged or poverty community may make gang joining more likely because it is a readily available way to make money and there may seem like no other options. These are all reasons that youth may feel that there is "no other option" other than to join a gang. Prevention methods can and should intervene at an early age to show that there is another path in life and other options other than joining a gang.

References

Decker, S., & Van Winkle, B. (1996). *Life in the gang: Family friends and violence*. United Kingdom: University of Cambridge Press.

De Vito, K. (2020). Seeking a secure base: Gangs as attachment figures. *Qualitative Social Work, 19*(4), 754–769.

Chapter 6
"Death, Jail, or a Turnaround:" Making the Decision to Disengage

> *'It's only two things when it comes to that street life, either death or jail. But luckily, I didn't have those two options. I had death, jail, or a turnaround' (De Vito, 2020). That's the positive. But the negative thing, it kinda put a hold on a lot of open doors for me. (Jamie, 2019, Unpublished)*
>
> – Former Gang Member Jamie

6.1 Push and Pull Factors: Reasons Why They Leave

A combination of push and pull factors are usually involved when a gang member makes the decision to leave a gang. Push factors are things that are negative that would push a youth away from gang involvement, including gang disillusionment, being a victim of violence, witnessing violence, tiring of the gang lifestyle, and aging (Pyrooz & Decker, 2011; O'Brien et al., 2013; Berger et al., 2017). When gang members feel as though they were betrayed by their fellow members, that is when disillusionment happens (Berger et al., 2017). Gang members can betray their fellow members by abandoning them when they are in trouble, forgetting about them while they're in prison, and turning on them. What they thought was a family turns out to be something totally different. Sometimes, there is violent victimization of themselves, friends, or family, which is linked to leaving a gang, with some youth saying that is the reason why they left (Taylor, 2008). Being a victim of violence themselves and realizing they could easily die or watching a friend become a victim of violence, or die, may make the youth decide to leave a gang as well. Sometimes, just getting older and having more adult responsibilities makes one want something different than the gang lifestyle.

Pull factors are positive things that pull a gang member away from the gang including religious beliefs, moving away, aging, maturing, relationships, employment, and family responsibilities, like marriage and children (Pyrooz & Decker, 2011; O'Brien et al., 2013; Berger et al., 2017). When children are younger, things such as having children or being in a stable relationship or having stable employment are not important. As one gets older, priorities change and these things become more important. Some other important things can include going to college or trade school or having good stable employment. Having children and a stable relationship also means that there are responsibilities which would require more stable employment and a need to leave the gang. Gang members may recognize the dangers and not want that to be around their children. They may realize that they want to also be around for their spouse and for their children to watch them grow up and not be incarcerated or dead. Just simply moving out of the area would automatically create distance and a lack of involvement in the gang. Father Greg Boyle, Founder of Homeboy Industries, talked about leaving a gang and about Homeboy Industries, a gang intervention and rehab/re-entry program in Los Angeles, California:

> It takes what it takes. So it's a little like recovery from drugs and alcohol. It can take the death of a friend, the birth of a son, a long stretch in prison. Unfortunately, there's no way to accelerate this or to speed it up except to have places where they can go when they're ready, when they are ready to transform their life and turn things around. So those are usually the factors. You can't manufacture it. You just have to wait and hope that there are enough places that these souls can go to reimagine their lives and redirect them.
>
> Homeboy Industries is the largest gang intervention and rehab/re-entry program on the planet. 15,000 folks come through our doors each year trying to reimagine their lives. And so, we have training and nine social enterprises. Free tattoo removal therapy, case management, and the like. We have four paid therapists and 47 volunteer therapists. Including 3 psychiatrists. Everybody is in therapy. We have a place because they need a safe place where they can land. Then the healing can begin. And you need a sanctuary for them. And pretty soon, they become the sanctuary they sought. And then they go home to their kids, and they present for them this sanctuary to their children. And suddenly, you've broken a cycle, and that's kind of how it works. (Boyle, 2020, Unpublished)

Former gang members can have a place like Homeboy Industries where they can get back on their feet again. When someone has made the decision to change his or her life and get out of a gang, having Homeboy Industries there to assist in that process can help that decision become a reality. They offer so much to these individuals to help get their lives back on track and moving in a better more positive direction. Many of the former gang members who entered this facility seeking help are also giving back to new entries into Homeboy. It is a fantastic way to give back to the community in a positive way.

Places like Homeboy Industries offer a place of safety, security, and comfort, which is something that the gang may have provided initially. Arthur Becker-Weidman, CSW-R, PhD, DABPS, Founder of the Center for Family Development, talked about reasons why youth leave gangs:

> People leave because they're able to develop a sense of safety, security, and comfort elsewhere. Could be with a therapist, could be with a mentor, could be going through a gang prevention or avoidance treatment program. But it's connecting with another person who provides that anchor when the attachment system is activated that they can go to, which then reduces their level of distress. (Becker-Weidman, 2020, Unpublished)

If youth are able to develop that sense of safety, comfort, and security elsewhere, then the gang will no longer be needed. Other individuals can offer that attachment elsewhere and that could be a driving force behind leaving. Therapists, school counselors, teachers, school staff, coaches, religious figures, and mentors are all people who can provide that catalyst for leaving.

Many young people are looking to gangs for a sense of safety and security, especially if they are not getting it at home or they also feel they need protection in their environment. Kirk "Jae" James, DSW, MSW, BA, AA, Clinical Assistant Professor at NYU Silver School of Social Work, talked about reasons why youth leave gangs:

> They see that what they desire is not being served. Most folks irrespective of what they do in a gang are there to seek some type of safety. They're under the presumption they will be somehow safer and have more validity and be more seen in gangs. And I think that starts to diminish. And the perception starts to diminish. The fear and reprise of leaving is real for people. With growth and the belief that they can somehow leave and have minimal harm or maybe if they leave the harm may be perceived is greater than the harm of staying. (James, 2020, Unpublished)

There are many factors that are involved in the choice to leave a gang. One can be that what they thought they were getting from the gang, that safety and protection and validity, is not the reality of what they are actually getting. Perhaps they are not really as safe as they thought they would be because gangs also invite a world filled with violence. Perhaps that was not expected. One of the fears of leaving can be that they will have to incur even more violence with the decision to leave than if they were to just stay in it.

6.2 Consequences for Leaving?

The myth about being in a gang for life and not being able to get out is false. Taylor (2008) discussed the findings from several longitudinal studies of adolescents living in high-risk areas, and finding that gang membership usually is only 1 year or less. A pattern of gang membership seems to be that most gang members cycle in and out quickly, with membership being only for a short period of time (Ezell, 2018). Some studies report that 50–70% of gang members are only members for a year or less (Ezell, 2018). This gives hope to those that are in gangs looking for a way out because there is always a way out and people to help along the way.

Some gang members leave without any consequences and just walk away or slowly leave over time. The more "embedded" or the more "enduring ties" you have to the gang, the more difficult it will be to leave (Ezell, 2018). But most youth leave by just withdrawing slowly, moving out of the neighborhood, severing ties to gang associates, by getting involved with other things like employment and family (Taylor, 2008; Pyrooz & Decker, 2011). If youth suddenly have things that are taking up time, such as a good stable job, that will mean they are not around as much and have other things taking them away. Moving out of the area is a good way to distance oneself, becoming out of sight and out of mind. However, sometimes, having left a gang can present with some additional obstacles as well in the aftermath. Gang members are seen as threatening in the community because of the violence they engage in; therefore, they become isolated from prosocial institutions, like school and the workforce (Decker & Van Winkle, 1996). This isolation and marginalization make it difficult for gang members to engage in activities and with people that may draw them away from the gang life and reintegrate into society (Decker & Van Winkle, 1996). Reintegration may be difficult for them. Special Agent Edwin Torres, President of the East Coast Gang Investigators Association, talked about leaving a gang:

> I think it's very hard for kids to leave a gang. The longer you're in, the much more difficult it is to get out. It complicates the matters the longer you're in. Because now you're a liability. You're involved in things. You know things. If you leave, they're afraid you're going to turn and have information that's going to damage the organization. So when I do see kids that leave a gang or walk away from a gang, it's because their circumstances have changed. Maybe they've done a long time or been incarcerated. They've moved on. There are children or other factors like that. They've become ill. There are lots of reasons why kids leave a gang. Statistically, we hear that 7 out of 10 kids leave a gang within the first year…but most of the time, it follows some sort of incident. (Torres, 2019, Unpublished)

Once in a gang, young people may become afraid to leave. They're afraid of the consequences from their fellow gang members if they decide to leave. However, often, the drive to leave, which is aligned with certain circumstances or following an incident, becomes greater. It is possible to leave a gang, but sometimes, youth will need support with navigating their decision to get out.

6.3 Making the Decision to Disengage

In De Vito (2020), there were several factors leading gang members to want to disengage from gang membership. Some of the reasons were wanting a better outcome, other than death or jail. Some had started a family and wanted a better life for their kids and also wanted to be there for their kids and not in jail or dead. Some had been in jail and did not want to go back there again after their experiences. Participants felt their gang had betrayed them and some of their fellow gang members had turned their backs on them. Some felt abandoned. The participants spoke about how they got out of the gang. All of them just walked away and dissociated themselves from the gang and associates. None had any consequences.

6.3.1 Wanting a Better Life Outcome for Themselves and Their Families

Participants realized that gang activity was not going to be a lifelong decision for them and so they decided to disengage, realizing there was not going to be a positive outcome for them or a future. Many of the participants marveled at the fact that they had not experienced much of the world outside of the few blocks around their home.

6.3 Making the Decision to Disengage

Their area did not have many opportunities to give them a better life, being from a disadvantaged community area. Being in that environment influenced their decision to join a gang. However, they decided that they wanted something better for themselves and their family members. Luis said his fellow gang members understood when he decided to make a change for himself. He explained:

> What changed you know was that I grew up… One of the reasons that I decided to get out [is] because you do the same thing every single day. I'm talkin' about you do the same thing…every single day 24 hours nonstop. You wake up, yo, wake up, wash your face, brush your teeth, go right on the block. You go on the block, you hang around, joke around, you go back to eat…You gonna sit here and be able to do this all day, 24/7 every day of your life? No… I really did have to have a long talk with myself… you gotta do better… "The street stuff is not gonna take you nowhere really…You can't be in this forever. It was an eye opener, you know, once my brother got locked up. I don't want to be another statistic. I had to grow up and change my mentality…" (De Vito, 2020). You know you still got the love and respect from the homies, but you want to move on and be different. Everybody always trying to be the same at the end of the day, you know. But sometimes you know you gotta change. The majority of the people I really looked up to, the majority of the people were by my side, and they saluted me and understood what I'm doing. They always say you still got love, you still got respect, you still got help, whatever you need. We still here…They know that you can't be in this forever. I mean not forever. You can't be in this for that long, your whole life… "You want to do big and better things…You can't wake up street. Go to sleep street. Live the day street." (De Vito, 2020; Luis, 2019, Unpublished)

Many young people decide that they want something better for themselves. They realize that they cannot live this lifestyle long term. Sometimes, that thought starts after seeing something negative happen to a friend or family member that is tied to being in the gang, such as incarceration, physical injury, or death. Once that seed of hope starts, it can start some real change.

Having a family can change one's viewpoint as well. Joey said that he wanted a better outcome for himself and his family: "The negative would be taking me away from my kids, spending the time with my friends instead of my family…the decisions I made and the life that it gave me… [I left because of] my kids. My real family" (Joey, 2019, Unpublished). Jay talked about choosing a job because having kids made him want something different and better for himself and his family:

> And the whole lifestyle, it's just – "when you have kids and they're looking right at you, you're going to make a choice. If I get killed, who is going to raise my kids" (De Vito, 2020), or do I want another man raising my kids. So for me, it was my kids getting older and it's just – it got boring… [He got a call from someone offering him a job]. He's like man, you want to work, I'm like, you know I want to work. So he helped me out… and I've been there ever since. (Jay, 2019, Unpublished)

Major life events, such as having children, can be a driving force to pull individuals out of gangs. Not wanting to be in jail and unable to raise children is a moving factor. Gang members start to have families of their own and then want something different than what they may have had growing up. Sometimes, that helping hand may be all they need to get out.

Wanting better things for their families is a huge motivator. Josue also talked about feeling broken and accepting these things for himself, but not wanting better for himself, but wanting better for his family:

> I did [not] identify as feeling broken back then, until later on in my life. Until I started looking at things like, damn, like what was going on? Why was I willing to do that? Why was I willing to accept that? Why was I willing to lose my life over this? I think it's when you start asking, why? Why do I want better for my kids and my little brother, but why didn't I want better for myself? You know? For me it wasn't so much…like deciding to leave, as much as it was like going through…everything I went through. (Josue, 2019, Unpublished)

Josue talked about not being able to identify wanting better things for himself at the time. However, later in life, he began to think back and reflect on wanting to know why he felt that way at the time. He could identify wanting better for his kids or his brother. His frame of thinking began changing once he decided he wanted better for his family members.

Sometimes, being in a gang can cause disastrous results, and those results or even near misses could be what motivates someone to leave. Jay talked about a night where he almost got into serious trouble. Had he been with his gang members, he could have gotten a hefty prison sentence. He realized that that is not the type of lifestyle he wanted to be in anymore and wanted something better for himself:

> You know…we all went together one night, and for some reason, I go home and they go out and riot. They all got arrested, and they were sentenced to 106 years with two life sentences. [One guy] just got out after doing 26 years. You know, one moment of me saying you know what, hey, I'm going to stay with you guys and hang with you guys, I could have been gone for the last 26 years. Some of those guys are still trying to get out on appeals and stuff… Life can be ruined when you're in the wrong environment. I just can't do that anymore. So I really regret that. I regret the influence, the street influence…wanting to be something that I shouldn't of…cost me dearly. (Jay, 2019, Unpublished)

Jay talked about how in one moment, he could have lost everything. Thankfully, he made a different choice. But seeing what happened to his fellow gang members made him realize that he needed to make a change. The decision to leave followed one incident. But that one incident and that one positive choice was the catalyst for him to make more positive choices for himself.

Some participants saw their own children being drawn to the gang lifestyle because it is what is around them in their environment, but they did not want that for them. Jerry brought up a very good point when he talked about the reasons why he decided to get out of the gang lifestyle, and it had to do with his son getting involved in gangs and wanting something better for him and asking the real question, what about those who cannot afford to get out:

> He started living with me actually… I didn't know how to be a dad at the time. So I was saying, "You can't be doing that." You know I started treating him like a little homie…Like okay, this is my kid. This is how you've got to do this… Then I started recognizing me. I started seeing me in him like all day. When I used to look like that, I was feeling like this. You know what I mean? So instead of me forcing it on him, I said pull your pants up and quit doing this. I started talking to him. Hey, man, look, you need to quit doing this. The reason why I'm telling you to quit is because…you've got to get out…Instead of them being a mess up…Okay, what are you infatuated with? I'm infatuated with this lifestyle. Okay…well let me show you something different. Let me show him that he can make just as much money being a doctor or being a lawyer. Let me start taking him to the museums. Like think about it, that ghettos don't have museums close by or have libraries close by like the suburbs got. Like my kids, [I took them] an hour and a half from my neighborhood so

6.3 Making the Decision to Disengage

they can get better schooling. They get better everything. Now, they have a better chance at life because they live in a better environment, you know what I mean? It's the gang violence where I'm living is short. It's very thin…I was able to get out, but what about the other people that can't afford to move? (Jerry, 2019, Unpublished)

Jerry talked about seeing his own child go down the same path. He was able to intervene and make some positive changes in his life to help him get out, such as moving to a different neighborhood and showing him that there are more opportunities and options other than the gang lifestyle. However, it can be more difficult for those individuals who cannot get out of their environment. For those that cannot leave their neighborhoods for various reasons, intervention and support would be helpful.

Showing youth that there are more options and opportunities available to them can make all the difference in the world. Hector talked about how some positive childhood experiences away from gang lifestyle helped him to want something different for his own children when he got older:

When you're a kid, you're broke unless you have shit. Going to friends' houses, they got shit. You know, it was years before I have even seen the water. I met a friend. I met him. He's like he's my brother. I call him my brother. He's a white dude. He's my brother. We've been friends since we were like ten, 11 years old. And the most beautiful thing from my childhood was that was the first time I ever seen the water, like the ocean. I lived like 20 minutes from the beach and never been there. I'm trying to figure out how the hell have they never let us go past that square radius of a block. You know, you got a car and all the jewelry, you got money, and you've never been to the beach before? Are you serious? You know what I mean? Like it's 20 minutes away. Like, "Man, you ain't never been to no beach?" You know, like it's crazy. You know, and I'm coming from way – as far as my friend's mom, you know, she used to take us there – every summer, she'd take us to the beach for a week, and we'd go to a different beach every day…So those type of experiences like that ultimately helped to shape something different within myself. It helped me to want my kids to have more, for them to see more, and maybe want to travel more, and things like that. So that's why I…say that my shit ain't as bad as other kids. Because I know that some of these dudes, they ain't never seen the beach, and they don't live far. (Hector, 2019, Unpublished)

For Hector, having those experiences really helped him to see that there is another world outside of his immediate neighborhood. He attributed those experiences of being able to see the beach and to see that there's something outside of his immediate surroundings as something that drove him to leave the gang. He wanted more for himself and more for his own children as well.

6.3.2 *Witnessing or Experiencing Violence*

Gang membership comes with the risk of violence, death, physical injury, or incarceration. Witnessing or experiencing violence can be the catalyst for a gang member to decide they want to make a change. Many of the former gang members that I spoke with had said getting seriously injured themselves or witnessing serious injury or death in a family member or friend is what prompted the decision to leave.

Leaving a gang can be difficult. Johanna talked about how being in the gang is like an addiction. Nothing could make her stop until she got seriously injured due to gang violence, and it made her make a change for herself and her family:

> I got pregnant and even the child, my son, didn't make me want to leave that lifestyle because I was so addicted to it. It was like a drug for me just being around it...Being around the homies in the hood and stuff was an addiction for me. What really made me change is when I got shot. I gradually started changing my life then. I realized that you know, I could lose my life at any time and be in the hospital and not even have my own mother or father there. Getting out the hospital and not even being able to wipe my own ass, it gave me a different outlook on life… The important thing is to know that it takes a lot of situations for a person to finally want to say I'm due…I ended up here at the bottom of the barrel almost losing my house and everything else. (Johanna, 2019, Unpublished)

Many of the gang members I spoke with referenced one particular incident that was the breaking point for them and caused them to want to leave. For Johanna, almost losing her life is what prompted the change. She felt the gang was an addiction for her, but being injured was enough to break the addiction for her. The thought that she could lose her life at any time was powerful. Many times, an incident like that can prompt one to make a change.

With age comes different responsibilities and maturity. Also, witnessing violence can trigger a turning point. Antonio talked about how he and his gang members just stopped being involved as much as they got older. It was as if they were drifting away from the lifestyle with maturity, but that when one of his friends was killed, that was a turning point for him:

> I'd always hang with them. I was part of it. I was in everything, you know, all the fights and all that stuff…We were like 16 and 17 years old, but then some friends…started becoming parents. They kind of slowed it down so they kind of like moved in with their girls and stuff…I guess we were a little bit more mature, you know. We weren't as much troublemakers as before when we were younger…Two years ago (Antonio, 2019, Unpublished), "one of my closest friends, well, he got stabbed and he died. So, that's kind of what drew me off and kind of like told me like I need to stop it, because that could have been me" (De Vito, 2020). One day before that, I was hanging out all day with him. We were playing soccer…and I dropped him off that night, and then we had already said we were going to see each other the next day. He was going to go to work, and then the next day, I got a call when I was at work that he was already dead. I never expected it. He was one of my closest friends. (Antonio, 2019, Unpublished)

The death of a close friend due to gang violence is often something that prompts self-reflection on choices. Realizing that could happen to you is often something that will cause a change. In Antonio's case, he saw his friend that day and then the next, heard he had passed away. Losing a close friend brings the violence closer to home.

6.3.3 *Experiencing Incarceration*

Some gang members decide after going away to prison that they want to make a change to their lives. The experience of being in prison changed them, and when they got out, they wanted something better. Jamie talked about his experience in jail and how he decided he wanted something better for himself and a way to make a turnaround:

> I was [in prison] for seven days and that like changed me. Imagine people doing 25-life in prison. I was talking about being in there with people who killed people and woke up the next day fine. They took somebody's life. What you in for, ya'll just shot somebody, ya'll just robbed somebody, ya'll just kidnapped somebody. It's only animals, livin' in cages. It's crazy. And the craziest thing about it is you gotta listen to somebody. You a grown man, gotta listen to another grown man. It's that crazy. The system is just crazy. They treat you like animals. You're locked up. You're actually in a cell with a whole metal cage. Once they close that door, you're not breaking out…I was learning about how to survive in a rough environment…It's always survival of the fittest in there. (Jamie, 2019, Unpublished)

Gang involvement comes with it the likely risk of incarceration since there is illegal activity involved. Being incarcerated for any length of time can be an awakening and can prompt individuals to want to change their lives around.

Not only does gang involvement involve incarceration but sometimes with hefty sentences based on the crime committed. Josue reflected on how being sentenced to life in prison when he was 17 years old affected him. He started to have a whole different outlook on his decisions and choices moving forward:

> "When I was 17 years old, I was sentenced to life in prison, so that had a lot to do with it. Spending half my life in prison and really reflecting, you start to look at things different" (De Vito, 2020). And you see how many people come in and once your enemies, you are more the same than different, and you guys have the same struggles. And you've lived on that side and I lived on this side, but the truth is like, we're similar, you know, and I think things like that meant a lot. And then you start to question, why did I hate this person? Why did I get involved? And little, by little, by little, by little, by little. That's how. (Josue, 2019, Unpublished)

Being sentenced to life in prison at the young age of 17 is heartbreaking. Once on the inside, Josue was able to reflect on his decisions and actions that led him to that point. The people who he was against for so long were similar, and what was it all for in the end? He, as well as many others, gain perspective. He began to see things differently.

Jay also talked about how being in prison changed his perspective. He wanted something better for himself as well. He said that the lifestyle started to make no sense to him after an experience in prison:

> Well, I actually got older. I got tired of looking over my shoulder wondering who was going to get me or who's the next enemy…I learned me a lesson going to jail. When you're in jail, your enemy on the street, they put you guys in the same area, and they become your friends, or you guys are cordial because you guys are in a controlled environment. But as soon as you get out of jail, you guys are right back at each other's throat. That makes no sense to me. (Jay, 2019, Unpublished)

Jay also learned a lot from being in prison. He became friends with people who used to be his enemies. The violence and disputes were all for nothing. Jay learned that the fighting all did not make any sense in the end.

Some participants came out of prison and had a family and decided they wanted to have a different life. Lamar talked about having a family now and after being in prison, not wanting the same type of lifestyle anymore:

> You know, I'm more goal-orientated and driven…I have a son now. You know, I want to be a father to my son and a lot of people in my neighborhood, they're doing the same thing they were doing 20 years ago. And to me, that's ridiculous. Like it…isn't going to make sense to me no more…I just don't, I don't feel the same way, you know? I'm a college student. (Lamar, 2019, Unpublished)

The experience of incarceration can have a profound effect on people. They are able to see things more clearly. The effects of having kids can be enough to make them more driven to having a different path.

Similarly, Hector talked about how being in prison made him realize that he did not want that lifestyle. So he decided to make a change:

> Being in prison is one of the most messed up experiences that I had to cope with…I was there long enough not to want to go back…Like three and a half [years]…I don't find going back and forth to jail like a, you know, it being a thing for me. I've always tried to be a chain breaker. One of my downfalls is that because I had an older brother who was one of the gang members and going back and forth to jail. And actually, my mom and pops, what they went through. (Hector, 2019, Unpublished)

Seeing what his brother put his parents through with going back and forth to jail and being incarcerated himself made him realize that he needed to do something to break that chain. Then he decided to make a change for himself and get himself out of the gang lifestyle.

6.3.4 Experiencing Gang Disillusionment

Gang disillusionment is finding out that the gang is not what you thought it was going to be. Many participants had a feeling of betrayal and felt as if the gang was not there for them. If one had attachment issues with primary caregivers, it can be devastating to have their new "family" turn away. Some participants experienced a feeling of betrayal by their gang members, when they turned their backs on them, betraying them. Jamie gave an example:

> "I got locked up at 19. Only one person from my block came to court with me. So that kinda made me realize like, dang, I thought these was my so-called brothers back in the day. And now when things really hit the fan, only one dude shows up outta my whole clique. That kinda showed me why it's best to take a few steps back from that type of lifestyle, because when things really hit, you start to see everybody's true colors…" (De Vito, 2020). When you come home, yo, everybody be like, "Yo welcome home, bro, what's good?" …everybody be like buddy buddy then, but when you in jail, everybody forgets about you. Everybody. That's not even up for debate. Everybody. They be sayin' oh free you for like a

6.3 Making the Decision to Disengage

week. After that week, yo, they won't even know you no more…I kinda felt left and let down at that time because I'm like, dang, like I remember the times my mom used to feed ya'll, like ya'll used to come to my crib and all. Yo, that's crazy, and ya'll couldn't show up to the court date? Only one person from my block, only one. And I still got much respect for him till this day. Much respect. (Jamie, 2019, Unpublished)

Jamie was clearly disappointed by the lack of support he received from his gang members. After that experience, he began to see things differently. Many former gang members that were interviewed spoke similarly. They felt as if the trust and support they had put into their gang were not returned.

Others had an experience of having their gang members turn on them. Johanna had a falling out with several of her fellow gang members. It was then that she realized that everything she had put into the gang really meant nothing because they turned on her so quickly:

Another one of the main reasons why I left was because a rivalry gang that had you know shot some of my homies or whatever, I wound up dating one of those guys, but I didn't know he shot one of my homies. I didn't know anything about him because he didn't introduce himself as a gang member, he just introduced himself to me as himself. And long story short, we started dating and one of my homies saw us… afterwards…he tried to make like an issue…so "I kinda felt like they turned on me, you know?" (De Vito, 2020). And that wasn't the case, like I never disrespected my hood, I never brought anybody to my hood, you know, and I didn't even know that the guy was the person that supposedly had, you know, did some things to my homies. I didn't know none of that so because I had already started to, get my life together, you know, I was working, taking care of my child with my foster son, getting my life in order, so when one of my homies called me on it, I told him…that's the life that you livin'…, [you want] to fight these people and kill these people, you go do it. You go jump in the bushes and kill that person, because at the end of the day, that's not the life I live anymore. The life I live is going to church, taking care of my son, going to work, that's the only thing that keeps me here today. When I had…that big ass…fall out, I kinda looked at it differently, you know? I looked at the whole hood differently. "Like man this shit is not nothing, like everything I put in the hood is like no love coming back out of it. And that's what really made me change." (De Vito, 2020; Johanna, 2019, Unpublished)

Johanna felt as if she wasn't getting anything back from her gang. She had put in so much, risked her life, and she was not getting anything in return. She, like so many others, had felt betrayed. Because of that feeling of betrayal, she decided that she needed to make a change in her life.

Archie felt a sense of betrayal and abandonment when his fellow gang members distanced themselves from him when he became permanently disabled, due to gang violence, and was confined to a wheelchair. He felt he was no longer a part of it because he was not seen as useful by them anymore:

They [gangs] are not sticking together… "It wasn't for the long run, it was for the short run… Once I got hurt, it was like I wasn't part of the main clique anymore. Even though I still hung out, we still did things together. They picked me up. You could just feel the difference, like I've got to go" (De Vito, 2020). Your gang rolls. You can't roll right now. I've got to go. "I'm like well, I put my life on the line for this shit and this is the thanks I get? It was like I felt betrayed." (De Vito, 2020; Archie, 2019, Unpublished)

A feeling of being betrayed by people who were supposed to be your brothers can be enough to spark a feeling of wanting to change. Archie became disabled, as a result of gang violence, and felt, because he was no longer useful, the gang had no use for him.

Going to prison can trigger abandonment. Josue talked about the experience of feeling abandoned by his fellow gang members while in prison for almost 20 years, and then when he came out, people suddenly cared about him again. He felt he did not belong anymore:

> It's not so much leaving the gang as [it is] disassociating…I'll give you a perfect example. When I came home, I went to see my grandma…they're coming in, hey we missed you, and you see all these people, and one of the moms comes out and she's crying, like I missed you so much! And I'm thinking, I ain't never got no letter from this lady, and it's been 20 years! But at the same time, one thing I realized…is that I didn't belong no more. I didn't fit in. My values and what was important to me wasn't important to them. And I think that is why like I didn't belong no more. So what I told them is if you guys ever want to come around or you need any help or anything that you need, come and see me…I think the intention is you always want better for people…We're able to instead of bring each other down. We're able to help each other get back on our feet. (Josue, 2019, Unpublished)

Josue felt as if his values changed when he was in prison. When he got out, he realized he did not fit into the same lifestyle anymore. He wanted a better life for himself, and he was willing to help others get a better life for themselves too.

Some participants found that gang members were not going to be trustworthy. George talked about getting himself on a different path by going to school and also realizing that people were not really going to be trustworthy after witnessing a friend's experience and betrayal:

> We were on separate paths. I was seeing stuff that was happening to certain people, like certain people were acting a certain way and all that. I just didn't have time for it no more. Then I ended up going to school too… Yeah, like basically I just stopped hanging around them. And stopped saying I was in a gang…One of my friends, he got into something when we were younger, and he told on somebody. And everybody started disowning him. I still trusted him because he was one of my childhood friends, and I grew up with him. So like that shows right there that it's not really a family. Once you do something like that, they'll just disown you. (George, 2019, Unpublished)

George was able to see how quickly gang members can turn on you from his experience. Seeing his friend get disowned made him realize the same thing could happen to him as well. Once that sense of trust was gone, he realized he needed to make a change.

Many former gang members felt a feeling of abandonment. Evelyn said that she felt betrayed and abandoned by her fellow gang members as well:

> The people that I thought that were going to be there for me, at the end, they weren't there for me. Yeah, and having my back. And I ended up in prison. I did six years, and I didn't have no one to be there for me…At the end, I felt like I was left alone. (Evelyn, 2019, Unpublished)

After putting all of herself into the gang, Evelyn felt as if she was abandoned and left alone by her fellow gang members. On top of that, she went to prison and did not have anyone there to support her.

With age comes the ability to look back and realize some things. Jerry said that as he got older, he was able to see that you are being misused. He felt that he was

6.3 Making the Decision to Disengage

not getting the same love that he was putting into it, and then he is now seeing issues with his son and gang life. He talked about how finding God was key for him also:

> I had the experience that kind of like did it...I got shot at. There was a guy waiting in the closet for me...a girlfriend...called me over her house. Once I got to her house, there was a guy in the closet waiting to get me. I got shot four times... You know as you get older, you start recognizing. You start recognizing the snakes, you know, the things like that. You start recognizing people that's misusing you...when you thought that a person actually loved you and you are doing things for them because you felt like that you're getting loved, like this is out of love. Then a person don't give you the same love, then it's like hey, man, what's going on? I would have did it for you, but you wouldn't do it for me. So then you start looking at it like, oh man, I'm constantly going to jail and you guys not. You guys are out here sending out the kids, living the good life, but every time I get out, it's like, hey, we've got to go do that shit. You've got to go do that shit. You've got to go do that. You know what I mean, or this is going on...You know, like we never got actually to having a good life because I stayed doing the stuff I was...doing...towards their life. Now, like I said, I started having problems with...my son. I started having real problems with him to where... he almost got killed six months ago. He got shot five times...in the same kind of violence. So...a lot of things happened to me...I found God...in finding God, God brought me home. He brought me back together. So yeah, so from the experience that I been through, you know it led me to God. (Jerry, 2019, Unpublished)

Jerry started to see and recognize the disillusionment in the gang world. He was not getting back everything he thought he would. Once his son started getting involved in the same kind of violence, he needed to make a change. Finding religion helped assist Jerry in getting his life back together. He felt his experience led him to God.

6.3.5 How They Got Out

When youth try to get out of a gang, there are different tactics they may use. Some may just distance themselves from the gang or disassociate from their gang members. Some may just get involved in other things, like family, school, and work. Evelyn talked about how she got out of the gang: "I just stopped going...I just don't talk to anyone. I don't try to hang out, like I just do me" (Evelyn, 2019, Unpublished). Johanna had a similar experience. She spoke about how you're never really out of a gang. You just stop frequenting the area and disassociate from it, which is how she got out:

> You never really get out of it. Still till this day, I'm still part of a hood. I just don't frequent it. I don't go there. If I was to go there and say I didn't want to be a part of it, I'm pretty sure they'd try to put me off, like they would try to beat me up so I would get put off. (Johanna, 2019, Unpublished)

In some instances, getting out of the gang means just distancing yourself from the gang and focusing on other things. Moving out of the area and distancing yourself from people who are in the gang may be all that needs to be done in order to leave.

Joey said that it was easy for him to get out of a gang: "I just didn't hang around as much from me being in prison. It was kind of easy for me to just get out and not be around it" (Joey, 2019, Unpublished). Jamie said that his former gang members supported him and had respect for him because he wanted something different for himself. But he mentioned how getting out and what he did to get out and stay out is a combination of politics:

> You out of sight…Out of sight out of mind…this is how I got out of the gang. They used to tell me they ain't no way out, you gotta get jumped out and all this, and you gotta get a job and a girlfriend…So sometimes they be like…where the hell you been, we ain't seen you in a minute? Yo, I got a job. And that would shut everybody up right there. They won't have nothin' to say, and then they respect that. I just stopped coming around. I just disappeared. Like I just left for a few weeks or a month… [and say] Bro, I'm workin' now, you know; yo, I'm doin' my own little thing; I'm just doin' me. That's respect; yo, we respect you; yo, keep doin' your thing. That's how it was for me… sometimes I go around there right and I buy the whole hood pizza… I pull up with a whole case of water. Everybody, ya'll good? Ya'll thirsty? I got some water. I pop the trunk from the car. Everybody all sweaty, they got their t-shirts on. They lookin' hungry. I get some food for everybody on the block. Ya'll take that. And I bought my way out. It's like a politic thing right now… Because at the end of the day, you gotta do that in order to gain respect in the long run as well so they won't come back and say…you didn't work your way out, you still with us. It wasn't like that. I had to pay my dues. I had to. (Jamie, 2019, Unpublished)

In Jamie's case, he said he still keeps good relations with the gang members by treating them well and gifting them with food and drink, but he was able to just do other things. By keeping good relations, he said they do not bother him anymore. Using these tactics helped him to get out and stay out without consequences on his end.

For others, getting out of a gang may not be as simple. Lamar talked about the reaction of some people when he chose not to return to the gang lifestyle and how sometimes that it is not easy for everyone to get out of a gang:

> I'm on parole… I think with a certain type of respect, some people will respect it and acknowledge it, and then, you have some people who aren't going to feel that type of way. Like, you know, they don't like it or don't like me because of that. But that's fine. You know, I'm not really worried about that…but obviously, some people in certain gangs don't have that luxury. Some people don't have the luxury of saying, "I'm done. I'm not, I'm not banging no more." They don't, you know. They're in there for life. (Lamar, 2019, Unpublished)

There are other people who find that they cannot easily find a way out of a gang and feel as though they are stuck in it for life. Those are the people who need the most intervention and help to find a way out.

All participants said there were no consequences for them for leaving. Jay said there were no consequences when he made the decision to disengage from gang membership. He referred to it as having mutual respect for one another and like having an honorable discharge:

> No consequences for me. Zero consequences for me. I was respectable, electable the whole time. To this day, I can ride to my neighborhood, and – I don't light the fire. You'd think the President just rolled up… I quit gangbanging, but I have so much respect in the street. There was a mini war going on between three neighborhoods. And nobody could get these people together, the leaders of these three areas…So I set up a meeting at my house. All these factors, these head people came to my house, and we had a meeting just to see what was going

6.3 Making the Decision to Disengage

on…I wasn't even in a gang…And we got the problem fixed. So – if you were in the military, it would be an honorable discharge. (Jay, 2019, Unpublished)

Hearing that many people are able to get out of gangs without any consequences should give youth hope. It is not always the case that once one joins, leaving is impossible.

It is a common myth that once one joins a gang, one cannot ever get out. Jerry talked about how there is a myth that once you're in a gang you can never get out. He said that's untrue. He got out and that there were no consequences for him either:

> A lot of people think…once you're in, you've got to stay in or live by the gang and die by the gang and all those different little sayings. No, that's all BS. That's baloney, you know what I mean. If you really is somebody, that was the whole point. If you were there with somebody and involved in it and people know what time it was with you, it's that easy for you to walk away. Because like hey man, check this out. Let's not forget that I was the same dude a little while ago, you know what I mean. I was the same guy that was kicking ass a little while ago…Don't get it twisted. I still can be that same dude if you start messing with me…So they understand that as well. So like hey man, check this out. I spent so much time in prison. They leave me alone. I've got a family. I've got seven kids. I've got a business now. Leave me alone. Stay out of my life, you know. You guys have been doing me long enough. [I spent] all my life in jail…I've got to get back to my kids now and give back to the kids. (Jerry, 2019, Unpublished)

Jerry was able to move on without any consequences. He references them having respect and fear toward him because of his reputation. He felt he had done his time and now was going to move on and give back to his own kids.

6.3.6 Moving On

Some former gang members are finding that even after they leave, they run into stereotypes and obstacles. Jerry talked about still being stereotyped as a gang member just by the way he looks even though he is trying to make a better life for himself. So that is something else he needed to overcome as well:

> The only…stuff that I…face still right now, to this day, is being stereotyped by everyone. It's not the gang members. It's the regular civilian, supposedly civilian stuff out on the street. They see me because I've got a tattoo. I'm still in shape. I've still got a fairly nice build, so they see me and they're just like, oh my god. You know you got people that just naturally get scared just from seeing me sometimes and I'm not a bad-looking guy like that…I don't look like no monster or anything like that…I have tattoos…You know how it is sometimes… you automatically get that stereotype oh he is a gang member. But not anymore. Hey, I've got a company now… I'm not with that. You know, I'm making money on this hand. I'm doing something different on this hand. You know that everybody is cool…I've been on parole for five years…everything is different… I go to church every Sunday. I go to Bible study. I help out with the church…people don't know that part. They just judge a book by its cover sometimes. (Jerry, 2019, Unpublished)

Being judged by others after leaving a gang can make moving on difficult. Criminal records and having visible gang tattoos can make getting employment more challenging. Homeboy Industries is a wonderful resource for getting former gang members back on their feet.

Leaving a gang can be a complex decision brought upon by different experiences, such as witnessing violence, being a victim of violence, going to prison, feeling betrayed by your gang members, or just wanting a better life for yourself or your family. They also got out in the same fashion, just by distancing themselves, moving away, and severing ties. Many went to prison and just never resumed activity once they got out. Many of the former gang members wanted a way to give back to their communities and to offer messages of hope or inspiration for youth, so they would not join a gang, or to offer help for those trying to get out and start a better life for themselves. There is always hope.

References

Berger, R., Abu-Raiya, H., Heineberg, Y., & Zimbardo, P. (2017). The process of desistance among core ex-gang members. *American Journal of Orthopsychiatry, 87*(4), 487–502.

Decker, S., & Van Winkle, B. (1996). *Life in the gang: Family friends and violence.* University of Cambridge Press.

De Vito, K. (2020). Seeking a secure base: Gangs as attachment figures. *Qualitative Social Work, 19*(4), 754–769.

Ezell, M. E. (2018). In H. Shapiro (Ed.), *The Wiley handbook on violence in education: Forms, factors, and preventions.* John Wiley & Sons.

O'Brien, K., Daffern, M., Chu, C., & Thomas, S. (2013). Youth gang affiliation, violence, and criminal activities: A review of motivational, risk, and protective factors. *Aggression and Violent Behavior, 18*(4), 417–425.

Pyrooz, D., & Decker, S. (2011). Motives and methods for leaving the gang: Understanding the process of gang desistance. *Journal of Criminal Justice, 39*, 417–425.

Taylor, T. (2008). The boulevard ain't safe for your kids youth gang membership and victimization. *Journal of Contemporary Justice, 24*, 125–136.

Chapter 7
Case Illustrations

In this chapter, two case studies are discussed that will highlight school social work interventions with two students with attachment issues and gang involvement. The cases involve two students, both in a Behavioral Disabilities Program at a middle school. The case studies show real-world cases and the importance of intervention with students who have risk factors for gang involvement. The case studies support the need for gang prevention in schools. All names and other personal identifiers in these cases have been changed to protect privacy and confidentiality.

7.1 Kyle Case Illustration

The first case illustration of Kyle is excerpted from my published article: De Vito, K. (2017).[1] Schools fall short: Lack of continuum of care in public schools. *Reflections Narratives of Professional Helping*, 23(4), 4–19. This article focused on the need for consistent therapeutic care within public school settings and uses a case study to illustrate that fact. However, what this case study also shows is an example of how a child who had attachment issues turned to a gang as a replacement family. It also is an example of how a school counselor can step into that role of secure base to potentially aid in gang prevention. This case study was disguised to protect confidentiality.

---

[1] Courtesy of *Reflections: Narratives of Professional Helping*, Cleveland State University (De Vito, 2017).

7.1.1 Kyle

I am a social worker working in a middle school in an urban school district. My new client, Kyle, a 13-year-old African American male, was due to come in for his first session. Kyle was a new student in the Behavioral Disabilities Program, a self-contained special education classroom. Kyle appeared at my door and looked hesitant as his teacher, Mr. S, accompanied him into my office. "He's refusing to come for counseling. He says he doesn't like or trust women. He said he does not want counseling and is not going to participate." As there were no male counselors in my school building, his only option was a female counselor. Kyle was dressed in his school uniform, a neatly pressed white shirt and pants. He sat down in the chair in front of me with his head hanging down between his legs, his eyes averting my gaze. I introduced myself as the school social worker and said, "That's okay if you do not want to talk right now. Perhaps we can just sit together for a few minutes while I explain what school-based counseling is and what it can do for you, if that is okay with you." Without looking up, Kyle slightly shrugged. The teacher gave me the thumbs up sign, along with an eye roll, and left my office, leaving us alone together. I explained that counseling is a place where students could discuss and receive help for problems that they have at home or in school. I said that it is also a place where students can feel comfortable to say anything because it will be kept confidential unless students are going to hurt themselves or others or if someone is hurting them. The silence was heavy as I continued talking; there was no response from Kyle.

I tried to think of a way that I could get Kyle talking, so I decided to bring up the reason he was placed in the Behavioral Disabilities Program. I leaned forward and quietly said, "So the reason you are in this new program and counseling is because you were involved in a pretty violent fight in the school building. The other student was hospitalized as a result. There have been numerous consequences for you as well. Can you tell me what caused you to attack this student?" Kyle shrugged, clenched his fists, and then looked up, finally making eye contact with me. I was startled because he suddenly seemed to have a fire in his eyes. He then said, "Because he said something about my mother. Nobody, and I mean nobody, says anything about my mother. He does not know what she did to me. No one here does." Those words sent chills down my spine as Kyle promptly got up, turned around, and left my office.

May: The study hall classroom was bustling with chatter as 25 sixth grade students were talking about the latest daily gossip of middle school. The classroom teacher recounted the events of that morning. The teacher was taking attendance with his focus on the computer screen and away from the students. Suddenly, there was a loud crash and the sound of desks sliding across the floor and bodies hitting the ground. Before anyone could intervene, a fight had broken out between two students, Kyle and Billy. Kyle jumped on top of Billy and punched him repeatedly in the face. There was blood everywhere. Students were screaming, but no one made a move because everyone stood paralyzed while they watched the gruesome scene unfold. The teacher first frantically pressed the buzzer for security and then attempted to intervene. Once security arrived, it took three adults to get Kyle off Billy. Billy's left side of his face was shattered and bloodied. Later, doctors assessed that he had a broken eye socket. After Billy was taken to the hospital via ambulance,

7.1 Kyle Case Illustration

Kyle was taken to the principal's office. The principal asked, "What made you so angry that you would do that to Billy?" Kyle shrugged his shoulders and said, "Because he called my mother a whore and said she should never have had me. He has no idea. I just lost it."

Because of the severity of the incident, Kyle had to attend a 45-day interim placement at an out-of-district school for students with severe behavioral disabilities. That placement was filled with students involved in gangs. During that time, he became involved in gang activity. His locker was searched, and he had gang paraphernalia and knives. He was fascinated by gang activity and the gang lifestyle, possibly trying to follow in his father's footsteps. His father had been heavily involved with gang activity and had been in and out of prison for 10 years. Because of the nature of the incident, a Superintendent Suspension Hearing took place. As a result of that hearing, Kyle had to undergo a Child Study Team evaluation. The result of that evaluation yielded a classification of Emotionally Disturbed, which made him eligible for Special Education and Related Services. Our consulting neuropsychiatrist also diagnosed him with Oppositional Defiant Disorder. He was placed in the Behavioral Disabilities Program, housed at the middle school. The Behavioral Disabilities Program is a special education program where students with behavioral disabilities are kept separate from the other students in the building by staying in one classroom all day. They are bused to and from school on a separate bus and leave slightly earlier than the rest of the school. They have one special education teacher all day, and their class size cannot go higher than six. They also receive weekly school-based counseling.

As a result of the fight, Billy's family brought charges against Kyle, and he received probation and court-ordered anger management counseling. His probation officer was very involved with his case. She said that he was classified as a high risk to reoffend because he refused to participate in the anger management counseling sessions. Reportedly, he sat with his head lowered, hanging between his legs, for the eight sessions, and he never uttered one word. When speaking with her one day, she said, "I had the father when he was on probation too. He was very involved with one of the more dangerous gangs in our area. He is out of prison now and, I would like to think, is trying to live life on the straight and narrow. I hope that you can help Kyle to stay on the right path and not choose the path that his father chose to take."

September: Kyle entered the Behavioral Disabilities Program and meets me, his school counselor, and case manager. Our first meeting was a quiet one as Kyle was mostly silent, sitting with his head lowered, hanging between his legs. Kyle lived with his guardians who were his paternal grandparents, Mr. and Mrs. M. I called Mrs. M, a sweet woman in her 70s, and explained that he was not enthusiastic on his placement or counseling. She said, "Listen, honey, Kyle is not a bad kid. But he is a tough kid. I am going to tell you his sad story." She gave me a summary of Kyle's background, which was filled with abuse, neglect, and repeated abandonment. His parents split up when he was a baby, and he lived in deplorable conditions with his mother. During this time, he experienced abuse and neglect at the hands of his mother, who was a drug abuser. His father was in and out of prison, heavily involved in a gang, so he was not around. He was removed by the Division of Child Protection and Permanency and placed with his paternal grandparents. His father was recently out of prison and living with them, but he was not involved. Kyle's mother had three other sons, 12, 10, and 7 years old, who all lived with their paternal grandmother in South Carolina. They had a different father than Kyle. She also had two daughters, 5 and 2 years old, with another man, who currently lived with her. Kyle had difficulty with the fact that he could not live with his mother, yet the daughters were able to live with her. He also had difficulty with the fact that she was not consistently in his life. Mrs. M spoke about how close Kyle was to his grandfather. Mrs. M said, "Kyle and his grandfather are like two peas in a pod. They are very close. However, he does not trust women because of his mother. Good luck with him. You're going to need it."

7.1.2 My Work with Kyle

October–June: Mrs. M. was right. It took about 2 months before Kyle finally picked his head up and began to open up with me. Those months seemed like they dragged on forever since most of those sessions were spent in silence. Kyle would come into my office and sit down in the chair with his head hanging down between his legs, in complete silence. I felt like I was doing nothing, but that is how the attachment bond began to grow. It grew because I was there with him, not giving up on him, even though we were sitting mostly in silence. My work with him took patience and persistence. But I never gave up on him. He saw that I was not going anywhere and that I was consistently there for him. During our sessions when he was silent, I said, "Kyle, you do not have to talk, but I need you to know that I am not going anywhere. I am going to be here for you in school every day." Eventually, over time, his walls began to come down. I remember the first day he finally began to speak to me. He just began talking about the bond with his grandfather and how much their relationship meant to him. He said, "My grandfather took me to church this weekend. Everyone loves him in the community. He's cool." Our therapeutic alliance began to build from there.

I modeled appropriate affect and a secure base for Kyle within the walls of the school. As a theory, classical attachment theory is concerned with the notion of a secure base. In the therapeutic relationship, the therapist can model and become a secure base (Ainsworth, 1989). It is important to create a sense of safety and security for the client. Establishing a safe and secure relationship with the therapist can affect other relationships in the person's life (Hollidge & Hollidge, 2016). Once the therapist gains the client's trust, a sense of safety and security will follow. Trust and a secure attachment will then enable the therapist to have access to the client's emotions, and then work can be done. A therapeutic relationship may help to repair the damage of insecure attachment and in turn help the client to cope with stressors of everyday life (Schore & Schore, 2012). The client can then begin to explore memories and to reconstruct the lived past and form a better future with better experiences and relationships.

Over time, Kyle developed a very close bond and attachment to me as his counselor in school. I also knew he was involved with a gang, but he would not admit to it. Whenever I asked, he would give me a knowing smirk and say, "Nah, I'm not into that stuff." I was very involved with his probation officer in reporting his behaviors in class and with schoolwork. We worked as a team. If he was not complying with something on my end, she could reinforce it as a part of his probation requirements. I also was involved with his child protective services worker and kept him informed of his progress in school. It was important that he develop more appropriate attachments, as opposed to turning to a gang, which could be used in the place of an attachment figure. Perhaps seeing me as an attachment figure, and maintaining that attachment, could potentially dissuade gang involvement because he would not be looking for another attachment figure. Seeing Kyle being attracted to the gang lifestyle already was frightening for me to witness. I had seen many students be lured into the false promises that the gangs offer. Those students wound up either in jail, permanently injured, or dead. It is very upsetting to hear of these students once they have graduated from the middle school. I always think, was there something more I could have done while they were under my care? These students had such promise, and it was wasted. I did not want that for Kyle. I wanted him to rise out of what had been a less than ideal upbringing with gang influence already and become successful.

In working with Kyle, I used Solution-Focused Therapy. Kyle's main goal was to get out of the Behavioral Disabilities Program. To achieve that goal, we worked on smaller goals along the way. Kyle needed to improve his behavior to get out of the program and back into mainstream classes. We worked on coping skills, anger management skills, and stress reduction techniques. He learned the skills taught to him and implemented them in an appropriate manner. For example, Kyle would have difficulty ignoring people who were trying to get a rise out of him. While being in the Behavioral Disabilities Program, it is difficult to ignore the other students, as they are all there for behavioral issues. In working with Kyle, I helped him identify triggers for anger. Kyle could identify that other students talking about his mother would set him off. One day, another classmate, Jeremy, started jumping up and down on the floor pretending to jump on Kyle's mother's face to antagonize him. He laughed the entire time he did it, taunting him, by saying, "Look at your momma, laying on the floor. That is her face I'm jumping on!" Normally, this would enrage Kyle, such as with the incident that got him into this program. However, I had been working very closely with Kyle on how to regulate his emotions and anger. So when this incident presented itself, Kyle employed the tactics that I taught him. Kyle was instructed that if he became annoyed or frustrated with the other students, to become aware of his body and his anger warning signals. Kyle's warning signals were his heart racing, sweaty palms, and clenching his fists. Once he could identify problem situations and physiological changes occurring in his body, he would then be able to begin implementing strategies to calm down. Some strategies included removing himself from the situation by asking for a safety officer to walk him around, asking to go to my office, deep breathing, and progressive muscle relaxation. Outside of school, he was participating in martial arts as a way of reducing stress. During this incident, he just calmly asked to see me and walked over to my office. He wound up punching the bookcase in my office to let out some frustration. However, he said, "It is better than punching Jeremy's face." He was right! He was praised for using the coping skills and strategies learned, as this was a huge step for him. It was also a step in the right direction to achieving his goal of getting out of the Behavioral Disabilities class and into mainstream classes again.

I also used Kyle's strengths and the strengths of his social support system. Great focus was placed on Kyle's paternal grandparents as they were a great source of strength, stability, and comfort for him. However, Kyle's grandparents were willing to work with him at home as well. Mrs. M and I would have weekly conversations about Kyle. I kept in very close contact with her. During one of our conversations, she mentioned to me that she and Mr. M were very involved in their church community. I suggested that perhaps it would be a positive thing to try to get Kyle involved in that community. I thought that perhaps he could be around some positive influences. Mrs. M said, "I am trying to get him more involved in our church community. Mr. M and I are active members of the church community, so I think that having him attend church and getting involved with good influences would help him." In working from a strength's perspective, Kyle's strengths are that he is very intelligent, and he has the capacity and love for learning. Kyle was working on or above grade level and had a high average Full-Scale IQ score. He learned the skills taught to him and implemented them in an appropriate manner.

Kyle did very well in the Behavioral Disabilities Program. There were no behavioral problems at all during his first year in the program during seventh grade. In the middle of the school year, I started to transition him to In-Class Resource classes as his academic ability was very good. In-Class Resource classes are classes taught by both a general and special education teacher, containing a mix of general and special education students. At the end of the school year, it was recommended that he transition fully out of the Behavioral Disabilities Program.

7.1.3 A Tragic and Unexpected Loss

June: One warm spring day, I received a phone call from Mrs. M. She was very somber and having a difficult time speaking and getting words out. She managed to tell me, "Mr. M died last night. He had a heart attack with no warning, and now he is gone. Kyle will not be in school for a while." I sat there, speechless for a minute, trying to find the words to say. I knew that the only thing that I could do was to offer my support. I offered to come to the house and do a home visit. His teacher, Mr. S, came with me. We sat in the car for a few minutes to compose ourselves, knowing this was going to be emotional. When we rang the doorbell, Mrs. M, looking disheveled with puffy eyes and a tear-streaked face, answered the door. We walked into the dark house, which had no lights on, and into the kitchen. When Mrs. M turned the light on, I was amazed by what I saw. Every surface in the kitchen, including most of the floor, was filled with food! Mrs. M took note of my reaction and said, "Our friends, family, and members of our church have been really good to us. We are very grateful." We sat at the kitchen table, while Mrs. M told us some stories about Mr. M, while waiting for Kyle to come downstairs. When he finally appeared, Mrs. M asked him what had taken him so long. He responded, "I was pressing my shirt." Mr. S said, "It's just us! You didn't have to get so dressed up just for us." He replied, "My grandpa always said to look your best. So that is what I was doing." We then went outside to sit on the porch with him, and he did not do much talking at all. He just sat there, head hanging down between his legs. After some time, we needed to leave. He gave each of us a hug and said, "Thank you for coming."

Several days later, the family held the viewing. Numerous staff members and students attended. During the viewing, Kyle became so emotionally upset that he ran out of the main area of the church and locked himself in the bathroom for a half hour. One of the students came running to find a staff member and stumbled upon Mr. S. Mr. S talked to him through the door. "Kyle, you need to come out, buddy. We're all here for you." After some time, he finally opened the door but pushed past the crowd of people who had gathered, including Mr. S and ran out into the night. Mr. S ran after him in hot pursuit and finally caught up to him at a local park. He collapsed on Mr. S's shoulder, his entire body uncontrollably shaking while he was sobbing, repeating over and over again, "Why?" Mr. S held onto him, hugging him, trying to console him. Mr. S said, "I know, buddy. I know. We're all here for you no matter what." He eventually got Kyle back to the church and with his grandmother.

The day of the funeral, Mr. S and I arranged a bus to take the entire Behavioral Disabilities class and staff to Mr. M's funeral. It was a beautiful sunny day that day. The sunlight streamed through the Baptist church, which was alive with life and joy. It was a beautiful service. The patrons were singing, dancing, and telling stories to celebrate the life of Mr. M. However, during this celebration of life, Kyle sat forward, hunched over, with his head hanging down between his legs, the entire time. We were not sure if he noticed that we were even there. At the end of the service, all of us went up to Kyle and the rest of the family to express our condolences. At that point, Kyle turned to each of us, shook each of our hands, and said quietly, "Thank you for coming." Kyle was part of our school family. When one of us was grieving, all of us were there to support him or her. After the funeral, it took a while for Kyle to come back to school. When he did come back, it was evident that something had changed in him.

7.1.4 The Aftermath

With the school year rapidly ending, there would be no counseling in place for Kyle over the summer during a very critical period of his life. I gave Mrs. M outside counseling referrals, asking her to please follow up in the summer, as I felt that Kyle would be at a high risk for choosing bad options to comfort him without having therapeutic support, such as gangs. She assured me she would get him a counselor. I thought about him every day that summer and worried about how he was doing with the loss.

September: The first day of school, I telephoned Mrs. M. She said that the summer break did not go well. She said, "I was feeling so overwhelmed with grief myself that I was never able to get that counseling for Kyle. I'm so sorry. I feel like what happened to Kyle this summer was my fault because I did not get him help." I asked her what had happened. She said, "Oh, he got involved with the wrong crowd, honey. He would come home late smelling like alcohol and marijuana, or sometimes, he would not come home at all. He was stealing money from me too." This was especially disappointing for me to hear as Kyle had said to me, "I will never touch drugs or alcohol because of what my mother did to me while she took that stuff." What Mrs. M said next caused me to feel a deep sadness. She said, "I am afraid that I just don't have the strength to care for him by myself. I cannot control him. As a last resort, I am thinking of sending him to live with his other grandmother in South Carolina." Since his probation had ended prior to summer break, the probation officer no longer had any say over consequences for his actions.

A few weeks into the school year, a student reported the smell of marijuana in the boys' bathroom. The video cameras were checked, and Kyle was seen leaving the bathroom. When Kyle was questioned by the principal, he denied smoking marijuana; however, due to our suspicion, he was sent out for a drug test, which came back positive. At that point, Mrs. M had had enough. Shortly after, Mrs. M sent Kyle to live with his half siblings and their paternal grandmother in South Carolina. She called me up that final day and said, "I just want to thank you for everything you have done for Kyle and our family. However, I just do not think that I can handle him anymore. I am sending him to live with his paternal grandmother. Kyle asked me to call you up and say goodbye for him, as he is too emotional to do it himself." I let her know that if I could ever do anything in the future to please let me know. After I hung up the phone, I sat there for a while with my own thoughts, wondering, what if he had had counseling with me throughout the summer? Would it have made a difference in the outcome for this child's life? I feel strongly that it would have made a huge difference in preventing this outcome.

7.2 Emily Case Illustration

The case illustration of Emily is a composite case, another example of a situation involving school-based counseling with a student who had attachment issues, who engaged in gang membership. It also is another example of how a school counselor can step into that role of secure base to potentially aid in gang prevention. This case study was disguised to protect confidentiality.

7.2.1 Emily

January: As a school social worker working at an urban middle school, I just received a referral for a new general education student to my caseload for counseling. Emily, a 12-year-old African-American student in the seventh grade, was being referred for counseling because of issues with insubordination toward staff and threatening other students physically. Her guidance counselor, Ms. T, came to my office and sat down, sharing some background information with me. She explained that Emily has been having a lot of difficulties in school this year. She appears to like being the center of attention, and she frequently finds herself in trouble because she is consistently getting involved in drama with peers. She tends to focus on that drama, and it distracts her from her classwork. As a result, she is failing several of her classes. Also, some of that drama winds up turning into physical fighting, which has resulted in numerous days of out-of-school suspensions. She then placed a large stack of copies of Emily's discipline referrals on my desk. Those referrals had accumulated during the first half of the school year. The most recent incident was a fight between Emily and a peer, a girl who was reported to be one of her closest friends, over a boy they both liked. The fight transpired on the way home from school. The fight wound up being videotaped by one of her friends, and placed on social media, which was then reported to school administration. It was a bad fight, where Emily had worn combat boots and had tried to stomp on the girl's head and neck while she was down on the ground. The girl sustained some injuries, but she was fortunate because the injuries could have been much worse given the circumstances. Emily received a 10-day suspension and a referral the Child Study Team for evaluation. Ms. T said, "She is a tough one, and no staff member has had much success in talking to her and affecting any change, so good luck!"

7.2.2 My Work with Emily

A few days later, when Emily came back from her suspension, I called her into my office to introduce myself to her and to explain to her what counseling was and what it can offer to her. When she entered my office, she did not say much but instead looked around at the brightly colored paintings of flowers on my walls and picked up a toy on my desk and started fiddling with it. I introduced myself to her and asked if she had ever received counseling before. She replied, "Nope. I don't have anything wrong with me. I'm just fine the way that I am." I brought up the most recent fight and asked her to tell me about it. "Nothin' to tell," she said. "We got into some beef, but now we're cool. I didn't like what she posted about me, but it's all good now. We hashed out our differences. That's what we do when you're from the streets." I asked her what "from the streets" meant to her, and she said, "You know, the hood, the ghetto, the projects where we're from. That's how we handle things there." I said, "Really? Why don't you tell me more about it?" She smiled and said, "Nah, I'm good. I'll tell you some other time. Depending on how cool you are." Then her bell rang, and she went on to her next class.

I spent some time later that day going over her discipline record and also looked at her family information. It stated that she lived with her paternal grandmother and aunt. Her father was listed as living in North Carolina, and her mother was listed as deceased. I decided to call her grandmother and set up a meeting to see if I could learn some background information on Emily and hear how she was functioning within the home. When Mrs. L came in the next day, she entered my office full of personality. She was wearing a big fur coat and enormous fur hat. Her southern accent was noticeable as she greeted me. She told me that Emily's parents divorced when she was just a baby. Her father, Mrs. L's son, moved back to North Carolina, for work shortly afterward and has been there ever since. Emily talks to him occasionally but only sees him here and there. She lived with her mother after the divorce until her mother passed away suddenly when Emily was 5 years old. That's when she came to live with Mrs. L. She now lives with Mrs. L and her daughter, her aunt. I asked how she is doing at home, and she said that she's always trying to get her attention. She often tries to sleep with her in her bed, and this has been going on since she moved in with her. I asked if she had received any counseling after her mother's death, and she said that they did not. She said that they chose to deal with it as a family. She said they go to church a lot and are involved in a large community there. They have helped them, but she described Emily as very difficult and very strong-willed. She said that she's always been very smart and capable in school, but she's always had trouble with her behavior and her mouth. This year in particular, since she entered middle school, she said she is constantly getting phone calls because of the problems she has with her friends. She's always getting into some kind of fight. She's very sensitive and has trouble dealing with anger. She said she is tired of getting all the phone calls home from school and having to leave work to have meetings with the principal and having her be suspended. She is seeking help for her. I assured her that I would get to know Emily and work with her and the family to try to get them some help.

At our next session, Emily and I sat down and tried to do a genogram together so I could get a family history. When Emily described her family, she said, "I am an only child, and I live at home with my grandmother, aunt, and mother. My mother does not work though." I was quite surprised because I knew her mother was deceased. She was obviously unaware that I knew her secret, so I kept quiet and listened to what else she had to say. She continued to describe a wonderful perfect mother/daughter relationship where they were best friends and did everything together. She also said she is into cosmetology and wants to own her own hair shop one day, so her mother lets her practice on her hair. My heart was breaking for her, thinking that this was probably the fantasy that she wished was reality, if her mother was not dead. I decided to wait a bit longer before saying anything so I could try to gain her trust a bit more. Knowing that she has a history of disrupted attachment with primary caregivers and loss of attachment figures, I knew that this was something we would need to work on. She has difficulty regulating her emotions. As a school counselor, there is an opportunity to become a secure base for the child, which was what I was going to work on with Emily in addition to working on behavioral changes in school.

7.2.3 Moving Forward from Grief

February: As the days went on, Emily began coming to my office more regularly, including in between her scheduled counseling sessions just to talk. She even began asking if she could do my hair and practice cosmetology on me. I would allow her to try some hairstyles, which seemed to bring her guard down and allow her to open up. This helped our bond to grow. One day, as she was braiding my hair, she was saying that she didn't really have very many friends. She said, "We always seem to get into petty fights and drama. Then no one wants to talk to me anymore. But I won't stand for anyone disrespecting me." Then, her friend, Peter, came into my office looking for her. They began to argue because Peter had seen some things on social media. Apparently, there was a disagreement with Emily and one of her friends. Now that girl group of friends wanted to jump Emily. He was trying to keep her out of trouble. The disagreement started to get heated with both sides yelling and Peter said, "If your mother were alive, maybe she could talk some sense into you!" Then there was immediate silence while Emily froze and stared at him. Emily became so upset that she picked up a chair and threw it against the wall. Then shouted, "My mother is alive. How dare you!" She then burst into tears. Peter then stormed out of the office. Then she sat down in a chair crying. I said gently to her, "Why didn't you tell me that your mother wasn't alive?" She was quiet for some time. Then she said, "I didn't say anything because I'm embarrassed about not having a mother. Everyone else has one except for me, and I don't want to seem weird. I don't normally tell people she's dead. I wish she was still alive." After that day, we were able to begin chipping away at that wall she built up to protect this secret and began to have real discussions about the loss of her mother. I also called her grandmother that day and explained what had happened. She was surprised and was unaware that Emily was having difficulty with her mother's death still. I let her know that I would be working with her individually at school but also gave her an agency that specifically specialized in grief counseling for individuals and whole families as well. However, even after that conversation, the family still did not follow through on the counseling.

7.2.4 A New Beginning

April: Emily's Child Study Team evaluation was completed, and she was found to be eligible for Special Education and Related Services under the classification of Emotionally Disturbed. This meant that her emotions were getting in the way and impacting her educational performance. The recommendation was placement in a self-contained Behavioral Disabilities Program. Her grandmother agreed and she switched classes. At first, Emily was happy about the change in placement because she said there was less classwork and no homework. She also liked her classmates, most of whom were male. She became close with one of her classmates, Cory, and they began to depend on each other for a lot of things. Cory had just transferred into the district and was a student with behavioral challenges and suspected gang ties.

May: During the spring, Emily's behavior within school became much better. She was not getting into any fights within the building or on the way home from school. There was no opportunity. She was in one class the entire day, and they were escorted to and from the bathroom and bused to and from school. This programming prevented her from getting involved in any drama while in school or on the way to or from school. Then Cory's father died suddenly in the spring. Cory was struggling with the death, and Emily became his rock. Eventually through their common loss of a parent, they became even closer and began dating. Things went well at first, and Emily never seemed happier. Her grades were good, she wasn't getting into any trouble, and things were great with Cory. However, Cory continued to spiral downward after the loss of his father and became even more heavily involved in a gang. One day, Emily came into school, and I saw her with Cory in the hallway, and they flashed some hand signs at each other. They noticed me looking. Emily said, "I bet you don't know what that means, do you?" I said, "I'm curious, why don't you tell me?" She just smiled and grabbed Cory's hand and went inside the classroom. I alerted administration and called home and let grandma know that I had seen her making what I recognized to be gang hand signs. She said she would talk to her about it when she came home. She was unhappy with the influence that Cory was having on her, and she was going to call his family at home and talk to them. In the meantime, I tried to talk to Emily about it, but she denied that she was involved in any gang, all while smiling. The school year was coming to a close, and I was worried about what might happen over the summer.

7.2.5 More Losses

September: Once Emily returned to school that fall, things were much different. Her best friend, Peter, had moved to a different school district, and they stopped talking as much over the summer, so she felt abandoned. She had also gotten involved in some illegal activities with Cory over the summer, as a result of gang activity, and was now on probation. That was one of the reasons Peter stopped talking to her. Her relationship with Cory had not gone well over the summer, and he had cheated on her and gotten involved in drugs. His mother had kicked him out of her house, and he was now living with another relative in another school district about an hour away. Emily was heartbroken. She said, "I thought he loved me. I did all of these things for him and got into trouble with the police too. But I got nothing out of it. I was left with nothing, and now I have a record." She was still holding out hope that they would get back together eventually.

October: Emily started to have more difficulty with controlling her behavior. She was getting more discipline referrals and had some suspensions. She was having difficulty coping with the new loss of losing her boyfriend. I knew that having disrupted attachments and loss of her primary attachment figures have been affecting her throughout her whole life. She was likely looking for some form of attachment and belonging, which made her at risk for following along with her boyfriend and joining a gang. Luckily, she was trying to walk away from it, and so far, there had not been any problems.

January: A tragic event happened later that year. Her best friend, Peter, committed suicide. I had found out the night before via a phone call because we knew that this death would have a huge effect on our student population. I knew that Emily had seen him like a brother, and they had had a falling out over the summer over her gang activity, so she was going to be very upset when I saw her the next day. The next day at school when her bus got there, she ran into my arms and just collapsed sobbing into the hug. It took two staff members to get her to a chair so she could sit down. She spent the rest of the day with me. She felt a sense of guilt that if she had just spent more time with her friend, he would not have killed himself. She leaned on me very heavily during this time period, as she felt she did not have anyone else to turn to for comfort, as she said her family at home did not understand. She felt like she truly had no one. She started talking about suicide herself and needed to go get an assessment and was referred for outside counseling as well. She was cleared and came back the next day, but the family still did not follow up on counseling.

7.2.6 *Transitioning*

June: The rest of the year, I spent working with Emily, she did not turn back to the gang, and she managed to turn herself around the rest of the year and finish out the school year strong. When she left the middle school, she was sad to leave and move onto the next level, but she knew that I was always just ever a phone call away.

November: Emily entered ninth grade in the fall, and began struggling in high school. Her grandmother wanted to give her a shot at the high school in general education classes, so that is what she did. However, she struggled in the large environment and got caught up in the peer drama again. I got a phone call one day from a counselor at the high school asking me to come up and visit with her. I came up later that day and helped talk her through a difficult situation with another student. She said, "I wish that you were here at the high school with me. I do not feel like I have anyone here I can trust or depend on. Not like you." I encouraged her to give the counselors at the high school a chance and that she could always call me if needed. She continued to call me during times of significant struggle, and I would either talk to her on the phone or come up to the high school to visit with her. She had difficulty at the high school and was frequently in trouble for the same things, peer drama, fighting, and failing grades. She got into a large fight in the cafeteria of the high school and was ultimately unable to attend regular high school and was transferred to an alternative high school as part of their Behavioral Disabilities Program. While she was in the alternative program, I would hear some things about her. She was not able to graduate on time because she continued to get into trouble including fights. She had poor attendance and grades and had gotten into trouble with the law for some minor offenses, such as stealing.

7.2.7 The Return of a Familiar Secure Base

June: Several years later, I was walking out of the middle school after working late one day, and when I left, the parking lot was nearly empty. It was the first day the ice shop across the street opened up, and it was flooded with kids from all over the district who were getting ice. Suddenly, a car pulled up in the parking lot, drove around, and stopped behind me. The car door opened, and a teenage girl jumped out, running across the parking lot, yelling my name, "Ms. De Vito!" I immediately recognized the voice. "Emily?" I called. She finally reached me and gave me such a giant hug and would not let go. It was in fact Emily, and I had not seen her in years. I let her know that I had just received word that I was transferring to the high school next year, and she asked if that meant that I would be able to be her counselor again, even though she was part of the alternative program. I said that I would definitely find out if that could be a possibility.

September: Once I got to the high school, I began going to the alternative high school to do counseling sessions with her. When she first saw me, she said, "Ms. De Vito! I don't know about counseling. I think I'm too old for this. I'm over 18 already." She said that she had not been coming to school consistently because she wasn't learning anything there and didn't see the point. She saw no value in it, but she also did not want to get her GED because she wanted to be able to tell her kids someday that she graduated high school. She was currently on probation for stealing. She stole from her grandmother and aunt at home, and she was thrown out as a result. She was forced to live in a shelter for some time but was now living with her boyfriend, who she said had a history of being abusive. We began working on setting goals for her future.

December: With the help of her probation officer, we got her into some counseling and different housing. We were also able to get her into a GED program so she could get her high school diploma and start taking cosmetology courses, which she had always wanted to do so she could work at a salon.

7.3 Tying it All Together: Attachment Theory

Both Kyle and Emily had difficult early childhoods and difficulties with attachment. Attachment theory states that a primary caregiver shows the infant the world (De Vito, 2017). An infant's relationship with primary caregivers result in either a secure, insecure, or disorganized attachment (De Vito, 2017). A secure attachment forms when the primary caregiver provides an environment that is safe, consistent, and secure for children, and they can go to them for comfort (Bowlby, 1998). Kyle likely did not have a secure attachment to his mother because of the abuse he suffered. Emily did not have a secure attachment with her father and her mother died when Emily was young, so her attachment was disrupted. If a secure attachment is not formed, then the child may have problems with regulating affect and be unable to manage emotions effectively (Bowlby, 1998). Kyle kept his feelings to himself because he did not have a secure person to rely upon or trust since his mother was not attentive to his needs because of her drug abuse and was physically abusive to him and his father was incarcerated. He also exhibited difficulty managing emotions and affect. He may have had a disorganized attachment. Disorganized attachment is seen in children who are abused or neglected (Main & Solomon, 1990; Hesse & Main, 2000; Hill, 2015). Children who are abused are stuck in a situation that may seem impossible because their primary caregiver is not only a source of caregiving but also a source of pain and fear (De Vito, 2017). Emily lost both of her parents at an early age, one to divorce and the other to death, so she also wound up not having anyone and needed to learn to trust a new set of people and difficulty managing her emotions and affect. Both needed to learn how to build relationships with people and find secure bases.

7.3.1 Anger, Behavioral Difficulties, and Attachment

Kyle and Emily had histories of behavioral management problems. Kim and Page (2013) talk about how children with an insecure attachment to their primary caregivers also have a greater chance of developing behavioral difficulties, especially within school. Many of the behavioral issues stem from attachment difficulties and may be seen as acting out, bullying, or being physically aggressive (Parker & Forrest, 1993). Those with a secure attachment can regulate their emotions better (Kim & Page, 2013). Hill (2015) talked about how primary caregivers help infants to develop the ability for affect regulation. Emily and Kyle both did not have consistent primary attachment figures around for much of their childhood. Both had difficulty regulating their emotions, and they often became dysregulated and lost their temper with peers and family members. Neither student had had an experience with counseling. A therapist was needed in both situations. Emily needed a therapist to help her manage her emotions, to process the loss of her mother, and to help manage her behavioral issues. Kyle needed a therapist to process the various losses in his life and abuse. Both had attachment issues as well. A therapist can become a secure base in both of these situations for the clients.

Anger can cause a lot of problems in the life of an adolescent, especially when one has difficulty managing it. Anger can cause mental health problems, physical problems, bullying, gang involvement, dating violence, substance abuse, peer rejection, and low academic performance (Konishi & Hymel, 2014). Anger can cause difficulty in relationships with family and peers. They may have issues such as aggression, helplessness, withdrawal, or peer dominance (Hollidge & Hollidge, 2016). Both Kyle and Emily both exhibited difficulties managing their anger, as was seen in the numerous fights that they had in school. They both could not process their feelings in an appropriate way.

The difficulty managing anger was a product of not being able to regulate affect. Hill (2015) talked about affect being how emotions are communicated, as through body movements, tone of voice, and facial expressions. The primary caregiver's job is to teach the infant how to regulate affect (Hill, 2015). Both Kyle and Emily had difficulties with affect regulation likely because of their insecure and disrupted attachments. Kyle and Emily were unable to regulate their emotions and control their anger, which often led to fights with peers. Neither had a counselor to assist in teaching new skills and helping with affect regulation.

7.3.2 Counselor Steps in as Secure Base

Ainsworth (1989) stated that if a primary caregiver is unable to provide a secure attachment or secure base, another adult can step in and fill that role. During the therapeutic relationship, a counselor can mimic that early attachment relationship and thus fulfill that role for a student (De Vito, 2017). As their counselor, I tried to step into that role for both Kyle and Emily and become a positive role model and a source of consistency, security, and resources. Being there for them on a daily basis for years helped to form that bond. A counselor can attempt to correct the difficult attachment formed when they were younger and help with future relationships (De Vito, 2017). I worked with both students to help them express their anger and other feelings in general in healthier ways. I also showed them ways to soothe themselves and better ways to handle their emotions. I also helped with the families as well, which both happened to include grandparents as the primary caregivers, to help provide them with skills and resources on how to help their grandchildren, who they were now raising at home.

Many young people turn to gangs in search of something they are missing at home. Both Emily and Kyle had risk factors for gang involvement. Gangs were readily available in their area, and their peers were involved. So as both Emily and Kyle got older, they became involved in gangs. Kyle and Emily both were looking for a place to belong and a source of consistency and comfort since they were lacking that consistent attachment figure. A gang can provide that source of belonging, comfort, safety, unity, consistency, and replacement family. The gang can replace what they are missing at home and give the illusion of being a secure base. As a counselor, I stepped in as a way to try to be that protective factor and provide that secure base, support, and consistency. These two cases illustrate how school counselors can step in and provide that role of secure base and replacement attachment figure, which can be a protective factor for gang involvement. Sometimes, it is that one person that can make a difference in a youth's life and can change their life path.

References

Ainsworth, M. (1989). Attachment beyond infancy. *American Psychologist, 44*, 709–716.
Bowlby, J. (1998). *A secure base: Clinical applications of attachment theory*. Routledge.
De Vito, K. (2017). Schools fall short: Lack of continuum of care in public schools. *Reflections: Narratives of Professional Helping, 23*(4), 4–19. Available at: https://reflectionsnarrativesofprofessionalhelping.org/index.php/Reflections/article/view/1544.
Hesse, E., & Main, M. (2000). Disorganized infant, child, and adult attachment: Collapse in behavioral and attentional strategies. *Journal of the American Psychoanalytic Association, 48*(4), 1097–1127.
Hill, D. (2015). *Affect regulation theory: A clinical model*. W.W. Norton and Co.
Hollidge, C. F., & Hollidge, E. O. (2016). Seeking security in the face of fear: The disorganized dilemma. *Psychoanalytic Social Work, 21*(2), 130–144.
Kim, H., & Page, T. (2013). Emotional bonds with parents, emotion regulation, and school-related behavior problems among elementary school truants. *Journal of Child and Family Studies, 22*(6), 869–878.
Konishi, C., & Hymel, S. (2014). An attachment perspective on anger among adolescents. *Merrill-Palmer Quarterly, 60*(1), 53–79.
Main, M., & Solomon, J. (1990). Procedures for identifying infants as disorganized/disoriented during the Ainsworth strange situation. In M. Greenberg, D. Cicchetti, & E. Cummings (Eds.), *Attachment in the preschool years: Theory, research, and intervention* (pp. 121–130). University of Chicago Press.
Parker, K. C., & Forrest, D. (1993). Attachment disorder: An emerging concern for school counselors. *Elementary School Guidance & Counseling, 27*(3), 209–215.
Schore, A., & Schore, J. (2012). Modern attachment theory: The central role of affect regulation in development and treatment. In *The science of the art of psychotherapy* (pp. 27–51). W.W. Norton and Co.

Chapter 8
Risk Factors and Protective Factors

> There is a 12-year-old kid...He joined a gang at 12, was shot and killed at 13. 12 to 13. The entire homicide, leading up to his homicide took place on Facebook, Instagram, and Twitter. Last post on Twitter was from a friend. "Don't meet that girl, yo. She's setting you up." "Nah, I'm alright." That was his last post. Within 24 hours they found him dead. A 38. Sixteen-year-old girl shot and killed him on the streets about 200 yards from his Momma's house. That girl...I'd known six of her relatives... Every last one of them were murderers...You start seeing that family dynamic. It breaks your heart. (Torres, 2019, Unpublished)
>
> – Special Agent Edwin Torres, President of the East Coast Gang Investigators Association, excerpted from a Gang Prevention presentation at an urban high school

8.1 Risk Factors

The young person mentioned in the epigraph died tragically due to gang violence. The girl that killed him came from a family riddled with incarceration and murder. What if someone had been able to identify risk factors and intervened at an earlier age? Gang membership usually surfaces during the middle of adolescence; however, the risk factors and influences have likely been in place since a young age and may be seen as steps on the way to gang involvement (Sharkey et al., 2010). The motivation to join a gang is a combination of push and pull factors working together. External factors push youth toward gangs, and internal factors pull youth into gangs (O'Brien et al., 2013).

Risk factors contribute to youth joining a gang. There is a cumulative effect for risk factors, meaning the more risk factors one has, the more likely that youth would be involved in a gang (Howell & Egley, 2005). Youth may have a resiliency to some of the disadvantages seen in the risk factors, but the cumulative effect of them may cause a greater effect and cause them to turn to delinquency (Ebsensen et al., 2009). Gang membership is more likely with accumulation of risk factors, rather than just one risk factor, and even more so through the various domains (Ezell, 2018). Risk factors will be broken down into five domains: individual, family, school, peer, and community/social environment (Howell & Egley, 2005).

Father Greg Boyle, Founder of Homeboy Industries, talked about why he feels youth join gangs. He takes a different stance on risk factors and believes it's about push factors only, fleeing as opposed to the gang offering something positive that draws them in:

> No hopeful kid has ever joined a gang. It's about a lethal absence of hope. No kid is seeking anything when he joins a gang, he is always fleeing something. Always fleeing. It's all about push factors, never about any pull factors. Once you address what kids are fleeing, you've really addressed something. It's about traumatized kids and damaged kids. So it's not like they choose to join a gang, like it's some kind of thought process; gangs choose them. And the most despondent kid gravitates to a gang, and next thing you know, quite thoughtlessly, he's been jumped in. Kids join a gang because they want to belong. No, because belonging is a good thing. Because everybody wants to belong. So once you frame it as belonging, then you frame the thing that there is some kind of positive urge that leads a kid into a gang, and then you stop looking at what the kid is fleeing, and there's the danger in that kind of thinking. (Boyle, 2020, Unpublished)

Looking at it from this perspective, there is more focus on what the youth is fleeing from within the home. It is about the trauma and the damage experienced within the home. Father Boyle talked about a lethal absence of hope being the reason kids seek something outside of the home. His organization, Homeboy Industries, gives them a safe place to land when fleeing a gang and helps them get their life together and set on a different path away from gang membership. If there was someone available to intervene at a young age to intercept and treat the trauma, perhaps joining a gang could be avoided. Please see Figs. 8.1 and 8.2 for risk factors.

8.1.1 Individual Risk Factors

Individual risk factors are limited to the person. Many of the individual risk factors are related to mental health issues, behavioral issues, or learning issues. Hyperactivity is a risk factor (Wolff et al., 2019), as are cognitive and learning problems, which increase due to living in a disadvantaged area (Guerra et al., 2013). The National Gang Center reported that mental health problems, medical or physical condition, and early and persistent noncompliant behavior are also risk factors (National Gang Center, n.d.-a). Starting at an early age, early aggression and acting out behavior are warning signs for later behavioral problems (Guerra et al., 2013; Wolff et al., 2019). Aggressive behavioral patterns emerge early in life and predict variation in adult aggression later on in life (Huesmann & Guerra, 1997). Children who are aggressive when they are younger are more likely to be aggressive when they are adults. Normative beliefs, defined as beliefs that are self-regulating, about what behavior is

8.1 Risk Factors

Risk Factors

School
- Low attachment or investment in school and teachers
- School failure
- Poor school performance
- Low achievement in elementary school
- Low academic aspirations
- Labeling by teachers
- Low parent college expectations
- Low degree of commitment to school
- School failure in first grade
- Frequent school transitions
- Truancy, absences, suspensions, expulsions
- Unsafe schools
- Bullying
- Schools with poorly defined rules and expectations for appropriate conduct
- Poor student and teacher relations
- Poorly organized schools
- Poor school climate: Increased levels of student and teacher victimization, poor quality academics, large student-teacher ratios, schools with a higher rate of disciplinary actions

Peer
- Marijuana availability
- Involvement with neighborhood antisocial youth
- Being victimized by peers
- Safety fear
- Wanting a sense of protection from peers
- Association with deviant and delinquent peers
- Lack of association with positive peers
- Association with aggressive peers
- Peer acceptance and rejection

Community/Social Environment
- Living in an area with a heavy gang presence
- Having drugs or firearms available in the community
- Community arrest rate
- Feeling unsafe in the neighborhood
- Drug usage in the neighborhood
- Neighborhood disorganization
- Community poverty
- High crime neighborhood
- Low neighborhood attachment
- Neighborhood antisocial environment
- Living in a disadvantaged community and wanting to make money
- Having a teenage mother
- Lack of structured and orderly activities within the family
- Poverty/low family income/financial stress
- Having an imprisoned household member
- No health insurance
- Being placed in foster care
- Having gang-involved family members
- Family history of criminal activity
- Sibling involved in problem behavior
- Having antisocial parents
- Experiencing child maltreatment

Sources:
Alleyne and Wood, 2014; Del Carmen et al., 2009; Gover, 2002; McNulty and Bellair, 2003; O'Brien et al., 2013; Howard & Egley, 2005; Ebsensen et al. 2009, Dishion, Nelson & Yasui, 2005; Estrada et al., 2018; Hill et al., 1999; Gottfredson, 2013; Dishion et al, 2005; National Gang Center;

Figs. 8.1 and 8.2 Risk factors for gang involvement

Risk Factors

Individual

- Hyperactivity
- Cognitive and learning problems
- Mental health problems
- Medical or physical conditions
- Early and persistent non compliant behavior
- Early aggression and acting out behavior
- Lack of social skills
- Poor refusal skills
- Early dating and sexual behavior
- Lack of empathy
- Few social ties
- Experiencing negative life events
- Experiencing abuse and neglect
- Stressors and violent victimization
- Exposure to firearm violence
- Illegal gun ownership/carrying
- Exposure to violence
- Having friends who are gang members or involved with drugs
- Being around gang members who are in class at school
- Being involved in violence or delinquency, fighting, and aggression
- Having conduct disordered or externalizing behaviors
- Alcohol or drug usage
- Having favorable views or beliefs of deviant behavior
- Making excuses for delinquent behavior and low perceived likelihood of getting caught

Family

- Lack of secure attachment to primary caregiver
- Lack of parental involvement
- Lack of parental discipline
- Lack of family bond and structure
- Poor management of children
- Poor parenting skills
- Low parental education
- Low attachment to parents and family
- Parent proviolent attitudes
- Family transitions
- Broken home/change in caretaker
- Delinquent siblings
- Witnessing domestic violence within the home
- Having a teenage mother
- Lack of structured and orderly activities within the family
- Poverty/low family income/financial stress
- Having an imprisoned household member
- No health insurance
- Being placed in foster care
- Having gang-involved family members
- Family history of criminal activity
- Sibling involved in problem behavior
- Having antisocial parents
- Experiencing child maltreatment

Sources:

Wolff et al., 2019; Guerra et al., 2019; National Gang Center; Baglivio, Klein, Piquero, DeLisi & Howell, 2019; Howell & Egley, 2005; Ebsensen, Peterson, Taylor, & Freng, 2009; Esbensen et al., 2009; De Vito, 2019; Alleyne & Wood, 2014; Estrada et al., 2018; Del Carmen et al., 2009; Dishion et al, 2005

Figs. 8.1 and 8.2 (continued)

8.1 Risk Factors

appropriate regarding social behavior, are developed early on during the elementary school years, with how their own behavior is reinforced, and from observing the behavior of others, and teaching they receive from their parents, peers, and others (Huesmann & Guerra, 1997). Once beliefs are formed, it's more difficult to change them and then their beliefs will predict future behavior (Huesmann & Guerra, 1997). Normative beliefs about aggressive behavior are affected by children's early social behaviors and then become more stable in elementary school and then affect later social behavior afterward (Huesmann & Guerra, 1997). Once these normative beliefs are formed, it is difficult to change them, so early intervention would be helpful.

Having a lack of social skills can also be a risk factor. Guerra et al. (2013) said that children learn peer interaction and problem-solving skills between the ages of 6 and 12 years, when they develop a sense of what is right and wrong. If they do not learn positive social skills, then that makes them more at risk for gang joining, as they may choose to do activities that are not prosocial. Having poor refusal skills and early dating and sexual activity are also risk factors (Howell & Egley, 2005). The National Gang Center reported that having a lack of guilt or empathy and few social ties are risk factors. Young people need positive prosocial influences in their lives so they can develop appropriate positive social skills and social networks (National Gang Center, n.d.-a).

Negative peer influences can affect young people growing up. If youth are around peers who support antisocial, criminal, and aggressive behavior, this could impact their development (Guerra et al., 2013). Negative peer influence can influence their own ideas about violence and aggressive behavior. Having low involvement with positive peers, being socialized to the street, having friends who are gang members or involved with drugs, and being around gang members in classes in school are all risk factors (Sharkey et al., 2010). The National Gang Center reported that making excuses for delinquent behavior and low perceived likelihood of getting caught are risk factors (National Gang Center, n.d.-a). In addition, having favorable attitudes or beliefs about deviant behavior is associated with violence in adolescence (Esbensen et al., 2009). Being involved in violence and delinquency, fighting and aggression, having conduct disordered and externalizing behaviors, and alcohol or drug usage (especially at an early age) are also all risk factors (Howell & Egley, 2005).

Negative life events can impact a young person's life in a major way. Having experienced negative life events like school suspension, illness, or loss of a positive relationship are risk factors (Esbensen et al., 2009) as are stressors and violent victimizations (Wolff et al., 2019). The National Gang Center reported that being a victim of childhood maltreatment, exposure to firearm violence, and illegal gun ownership/carrying are all individual risk factors as is exposure to violence (National Gang Center, n.d.-a). Negative and traumatic events can impact the youth in a negative way and can influence the decision to join a gang. Special Agent Torres talked about individual risk factors and how mental health plays into it as one of the risk factors he has seen:

> I think mental health also plays into it as well. I see a lot of kids involved in gangs who have mental health issues. A lot of kids who are representing themselves who are in trauma, who come from traumatic backgrounds. A sense of belonging. (Torres, 2019, Unpublished)

Along with Special Agent Torres, I have also worked with youth who have joined gangs. Many of them have had some mental health issues which were impacting their decision-making abilities at the time. Others had experienced traumatic events as well, such as the death of family members or friends due to gang violence. Those traumatic events were enough to push those young people into joining a gang. In addition, some of the young people that I worked with felt they needed protection from the gang or were just looking to belong to a peer group.

8.1.2 Family Risk Factors

Family risk factors are issues that arise within the family, which can be push factors pushing a youth toward gang involvement. Cracks in the family foundation, including having a lack of secure attachment to a primary caregiver, can be a risk factor for gang involvement (De Vito, 2020). Having a lack of parental involvement and discipline (Alleyne & Wood, 2014) as well as having poor management of children and poor parenting skills can also be risk factors (Esbensen et al., 2009). Low parental education, low attachment to parents or family, parent proviolent attitudes, and family transitions are all risk factors for gang involvement (Howell & Egley, 2005). The National Gang Center reported that a broken home/changes in caretaker, delinquent siblings, having a teenage mother, and lack of structured and orderly activities within the family are all risk factors (National Gang Center, n.d.-a). Arthur Becker-Weidman, CSW-R, PhD, DABPS, founder of the Center for Family Development, talked about risk factors for gang involvement in youth:

> The risk factors are not having a primary caregiver in their life who can provide a sense of safety, security, and comfort and living in an environment that exacerbates that…The lack of that then makes you particularly vulnerable when you're living in poverty, having difficulty making ends meet in an environment where there is ongoing danger. The reason they join the gang is because the gang provides safety, security, and comfort. (Becker-Weidman, 2020, Unpublished)

Not having a primary caregiver who can give them what they need the most, basic needs of safety, security, and comfort, can cause youth to seek it elsewhere. If a gang is available in that area, it then becomes a viable option.

Certain situations within the family can also be linked to a higher chance of youth joining a gang. Family circumstances such as poverty, low family income, and financial stress can be tied to gang involvement (Howell & Egley, 2005; Alleyne & Wood, 2014). Unemployment rates are usually high and families have fallen on hard economic times with many children living with single mothers (Gottfredson, 2013). If single mothers need to work to provide income for the family, that may mean less supervision in the home. When there is a lack of parental monitoring in

8.1 Risk Factors

the home because parents are working, not around, and do not have funds to provide for adequate after-school care, youth are left on their own more frequently and hang out more with their friends (Guerra et al., 2013). If those peers are involved in a gang, that could influence youth and make it more likely that they will also join a gang. Disadvantaged families may be unable to provide a supportive and safe environment because parents may have to work to provide shelter and food (Estrada et al., 2018). Having absent parents means weaker family bonds and structure and less parental supervision, all risk factors for gang involvement (Estrada et al., 2018). Single parents have less support and have a harder time in general with having to shoulder the burden of parenting alone, and financial strain can affect mental health (Gorman-Smith et al., 2013). Lack of good parental monitoring is associated with poverty, stressors, structural transitions in the family, and maternal depression (Robertson et al., 2008). Having an imprisoned household member, no health insurance, and being placed in foster care are also family circumstances that are related to a higher risk of gang involvement (Wolff et al., 2019). Youth could also turn to gangs as a way of making money to help out their families. If gangs are readily available in their area, it makes joining more likely for them to join to find a source of income, especially if friends and family are already involved.

If youth have family members that are already involved in gangs, it can be hard to refuse. Having gang-involved family members makes gang membership more likely (Alleyne & Wood, 2014; Estrada et al., 2018). Youth may feel like they do not have much of a choice if many family members are involved in a gang. Joining may feel like the natural progression and an inevitable next step. A family history of criminal activity is also a risk factor (Del Carmen et al., 2009; Howell & Egley, 2005). Having a sibling that is involved in problem behavior is also a predictor of issues, especially when the siblings work together to undermine parents' authority and management (Dishion et al., 2005). A youth will grow up with the influence of criminal mentality or influence within the home, which can have an impact. The National Gang Center reported that having antisocial parents is also a risk factor for gang involvement (National Gang Center, n.d.-a).

Experiencing violence can have far-reaching effects on children. Experiencing childhood maltreatment is a risk factor (Howell & Egley, 2005; Del Carmen et al., 2009). Youth may develop a hypervigilance to threat because of witnessing or being victims of violence (Guerra et al., 2013). Children growing up in an area filled with violence become accustomed to witnessing violent events and have a general awareness of violence in their environment (Guerra et al., 2013). If there is domestic violence in the home, or if youth are victims of child abuse, these children not only witness violence but are also victims (Guerra et al., 2013). Children who are victims of child abuse are more likely to engage in violent crime and delinquency (Guerra et al., 2013). A female's risk for being arrested due to a violent offense doubles if there is a history of child abuse and neglect (Wolff et al., 2019). Father Boyle weighed in on family risk factors:

> I think home has a lot to do with it. The poet writes, no one leaves home unless home is the mouth of a shark. If a child has to navigate some mentally ill parent, there's considerable

risk in that and the list is long. So the more you can relieve these pressures and factors, the better. (Boyle, 2020, Unpublished)

Having an unstable homelife filled with risk factors, particularly if the young person is experiencing traumatic events within the home, can make gang joining more likely. The young person will be fleeing the environment and, if a gang is in the area, might look to join. If another person can intervene in a youth's life, there is more of a chance of a successful outcome.

Jay Franklin, a Gang Specialist and Captain of Security and Safety Manager for Riverside County, California, who collaborates and works with schools on a daily basis on gang-related issues, talked about not having a positive male role model in the home:

> You can give other stuff to these kids at school, and they say it, you're not going home with us. What's at home is definitely more impactful in a negative way than the positive we try to give throughout the day. And one of the things we found out at school is dads being absent, or incarcerated, or dead, so we would get happy when a mother would come in with a dad. We would automatically tell the kid, you're lucky, you have a two-parent home. Over the years, we started seeing that it's not just what everyone says, that you need a positive male role model. But that positive is key. Just because there's a man…these dudes were coming home from jail, getting out of the car smoking weed, and the influence was totally negative. And the mothers, sad to say it, were better off by themselves. But for school staff, when two parents would come in, we automatically would give them the automatic respect, because there are two of them here. We would do the same old spiel, and the kid would look at us, like get out of here with that. This is just for the meeting. And once we started picking up on that…we stopped doing that. (Franklin, 2019, Unpublished)

Having a positive role model, especially within the home, is a protective factor. Not having someone to look up to who can model positive behavior is difficult for youth. As Mr. Franklin said, just because there are two parental figures in the household does not mean that it is a positive home situation.

One of the biggest risk factors for gang involvement starts within the home environment. If the home environment is negative in some way, that can be a risk factor. Special Agent Torres talked about family risk factors for gang involvement:

> The biggest risk factor is family in the home and the home [environment]. It seems to be the biggest factor I see. The lack of the core and family nucleus is one of the bigger issues…We see kids whose siblings are gang members. In some cases, their parents are gang members. Some of the older gangs, the gangs that come out of the Los Angeles area in California, those gangs have been around since the 1920s, so you have generational gang involvement. The biggest risk factors are definitely family, self-respect issues, and mental health issues. (Torres, 2019, Unpublished)

Having a family history of gang involvement is a huge risk factor for youth gang involvement. It can be difficult to say no and want something different if the whole family is gang-involved. Intervention is definitely helpful in this case if the young person has a chance of making it through without becoming involved in a gang.

8.1.3 School Risk Factors

School risk factors can be impactful in terms of gang involvement. Risk factors include having a weak attachment or investment in school and with teachers and having learning disabilities (Gover, 2002; McNulty & Bellair, 2003; Howell & Egley, 2005; Del Carmen et al., 2009; Esbensen et al. 2009; O'Brien et al., 2013; Alleyne & Wood, 2014). Dishion et al. (2005) found that school failure was a predictor of gang involvement. Academic failure and poor school performance (Esbensen et al., 2009), as well as low achievement in elementary school, low academic aspirations, labeling by teachers, low parent college expectations, and low degree of commitment to school are all risk factors for gang involvement (Howell & Egley, 2005). The National Gang Center reported that school failure in the first grade is also a risk factor (National Gang Center, n.d.-a).

Behavior problems and academic problems go hand in hand (Gorman-Smith et al., 2013). Feeling like they don't belong will cause students to act out in class and not be engaged academically (Estrada et al., 2018). Students may adopt an attitude of not caring about school, which then impacts performance leading to low school performance, which is also tied to gang involvement (Gover, 2002; McNulty & Bellair, 2003; Del Carmen et al., 2009; O'Brien et al., 2013; Alleyne & Wood, 2014). The National Gang Center reported that frequent school transitions, truancy, absences, and suspensions or expulsions from school are all risk factors (National Gang Center, n.d.-a).

Students who attend schools that are not functioning well with poor school climate, increased levels of student and teacher victimization, poor quality academics, large teacher-student ratios, and a higher rate of school disciplinary actions such as suspensions tend to have more youth gang involvement (Estrada et al., 2018). Racial tension within school, with students feeling marginalized in school, may contribute to students turning toward street socialization (Estrada et al., 2018). The National Gang Center reported that unsafe schools, bullying, schools with poorly defined rules and expectations for appropriate conduct, poor student and teacher relations, and poorly organized schools are all risk factors for gang involvement (National Gang Center, n.d.-a).

8.1.4 Peer Group Risk Factors

Pull factors for youth gang involvement in the peer domain include wanting friendship, protection, and a sense of belonging (O'Brien et al., 2013). Hill et al. (1999) reported that marijuana availability and involvement with antisocial youth in the neighborhood were the highest predictors of gang involvement. Being rejected and victimized by peers can be a risk factor (Guerra et al., 2013). If there is a fear of safety, that can also influence gang joining. Being a part of a gang can relieve that anxiety attached to fear of safety. If youth are being picked on or bullied or do not have any friends, they may look to a gang for friendship or protection. Gangs can also be a social problem, where youth may feel that they need to participate to keep them safe from harm (Gottfredson, 2013). They may join needing a sense of protection from people around them.

Dishion et al. (2005) found that youth exhibiting antisocial behavior was a predictor of being involved with deviant peers and gangs. When youth are involved with peers who are engaging in deviant behavior, the influence to follow is great (Dishion et al., 2005; Howell & Egley, 2005). Association with deviant or delinquent peers is one of the strongest predictors of a youth's delinquency, along with a lack of association with positive peers (Esbensen et al., 2009; Zeldin & Handler, 1993). Youth will often follow along with what their peer group is doing. Association with aggressive peers is also a risk factor (Howell & Egley, 2005). Aggressive kids are often quickly rejected by their peer group, and being rejected by your peer group can also increase aggression (Guerra et al., 2013). Both peer acceptance and rejection were found to be predictors of gang involvement (Dishion et al., 2005). Youth may look to a gang to gain acceptance from their peers and may also look to a gang if they are rejected from their peers.

Peer group may offer a sense of belonging, security, support, social connections, resources, and identity that they are not getting from anywhere else, including family, school, and their environment (Estrada et al., 2018). Loyalty becomes stronger when the group bonds through activities like drug and alcohol usage, partying, and delinquent acts (Estrada et al., 2018). Gangs are made up of youth from various age groups ranging from as young as seven or eight through their mid-twenties (Estrada et al., 2018). The elder group members become mentors, teachers, and parents in the absence of positive people to fill these roles (Estrada et al., 2018). The older gang members encourage youth to do risky things and engage in violence, regardless of consequences, and because of loyalty to the gang, they will do it (Estrada et al., 2018).

Mr. Franklin talked about the lure and draw of gang life for youth which includes wanting that sense of protection and sense of belonging with peers, but then the harsh reality of what a gang really involves creeps in:

> There is the draw of gang life and then the harsh truth or reality of gang life. Kids join gangs to be accepted…peers…family replacement. There's a lot of lures to be a part of something. Those are things that any kid would want…to feel accepted and all of the above. It feels good initially. But then the reality hits. This is a criminal organization at the end of the day. I'm not going to be able to reap all of these benefits. I'm not going to be able to hang out and have protection and all that other stuff at some point, the gang piece is going to kick in. (Franklin, 2019, Unpublished)

Youth that join a gang for reasons such as belonging or a family replacement realize at some point that there is criminal involvement attached to being in a gang. Youth will need to engage in criminal activities as a trade-off for having that protection and that sense of belonging to something.

Special Agent Torres talked about peer risk factors and youth wanting a way to stand out from the crowd. He said, "Peer pressure. In terms of kids wanting to stand out, if you look at today with societal pressures and social media, kids are begging to stand out. Gangs are a quick way for kids to stand out" (Torres, 2019, Unpublished).

Another reason young people may join is because they feel pressured into it if their friends are doing it too. They may feel like they will be abandoned by their friends if they don't join.

8.1.5 Community/Social Environment Risk Factors

The social environment and the community can weigh heavily in gang involvement as a risk factor. Youth living in a neighborhood with a heavy gang presence makes gang involvement more likely (Del Carmen et al., 2009; O'Brien et al., 2013; Alleyne & Wood, 2014). Having that gang presence in the environment creates such a prominent influence that it makes joining seem natural or inevitable. Having drugs and firearms available in the neighborhood, community arrest rate, feeling unsafe in the neighborhood, drug usage in the neighborhood, neighborhood disorganization, and poverty are all risk factors (Howell & Egley, 2005; Esbensen et al., 2009). The National Gang Center reported living in a high-crime neighborhood, low neighborhood attachment, and having a neighborhood antisocial environment are all risk factors for gang involvement (National Gang Center, n.d.-a).

Gang problems are more likely to occur in areas that have poverty and experience social disorganization (Gottfredson, 2013). Living in a disadvantaged community and wanting to make money are all tied to gang involvement (O'Brien et al., 2013; Alleyne & Wood, 2014). Low socioeconomic status can impact parenting and make it more difficult (Robertson et al., 2008). Poverty is a big influencer and a concern. Poverty and economic hardship can cause much stress in individuals and families. Living in an area that is disadvantaged can mean fewer resources and an area that has a higher crime rate (Santiago et al., 2011). Poverty affects housing, nutrition, medical attention, and safe areas for children (Estrada et al., 2018). These families have much different daily threats, challenges, and demands than more affluent families (Estrada et al., 2018). People who are living in poverty are more likely to have more stressful events in life, compared to those in more affluent communities (Santiago et al., 2011). Some negative life events include violence, discrimination, traumas, family conflict, lack of basic necessities for living, and moving around frequently (Santiago et al., 2011). All of these events can cause much stress, feeling demoralized, and having a lack of hope (Santiago et al., 2011).

People living in poverty also have limited social networks from which to gain access to needs (Estrada et al., 2018). Impoverished communities cannot fully meet the needs of their families with poverty and social disorganization contributing to gang involvement within the communities (Estrada et al., 2018). Living in a disadvantaged neighborhood means not having as many opportunities, lack of attachment to neighborhood, hopelessness, poverty, safety concerns, lack of successful role models, and less recreational and employment opportunities (Zeldin & Handler, 1993). Youth will turn to gangs as a way of making money to meet their basic needs when there are no other opportunities available to them (Estrada et al., 2018).

Living in a low-income inner-city neighborhood, teen boys can become "street socialized" to violent social norms, as a perpetrator or victim (Guerra et al., 2013). However, youth make choices and not every child coming from a poor community will choose to become a gang member. Six to 30 percent of youth coming from poor communities will join a gang (Guerra et al., 2013). Racial profiling, systematic oppression, and discrimination in communities of color also contribute to the trauma and stress which then contributes to street socialization and violence (Estrada et al., 2018).

Special Agent Torres talked about youth looking to gangs as a way of making money, especially if they come from a poverty community. He said, "Gangs are a way for kids to make money, which is another way for kids to stand out. It's a quick way for them to get the reputation and a quick way to get the power" (Torres, 2019, Unpublished). Joining a gang may seem like a way of getting immediate power and money. Youth may see that as appealing based on where they are coming from and the opportunities they think are available to them. Gerald Mallon, DSW, LCSW, Associate Dean of Scholarship and Research at Silberman School of Social Work at Hunter College and a Julia Lathrop Professor of Child Welfare, talked about why gangs might be a draw for some at-risk youth, seeing the influence that the gang members have in their community and wanting to make money:

> What happens in the absence of having some structure, and I see it here, I live in East Harlem, is people who are drug dealers start to engage younger kids. And the younger kids look up to them because they have jewelry and they have big cars and they have money and everybody knows their name. It's not like any ethical or moral issue like, oh they're a drug dealer. They have money and I come from a family where nobody has money. If they want me to hang with them and do a little favor for them or deliver something for them, I'm going to do that and then they start being part of that gang which is pretty serious to be involved in dealing and participating in the drug world when you're 12, 13, 14 years old. (Mallon, 2020, Unpublished)

Without having the structure at home, youth may gravitate to seeking things outside of the home. If a drug dealer who is involved in a gang has things that they want, they may start to look up to them and idolize them because they want to have the same things. Then they start doing favors for them and getting paid for it, and then suddenly they are involved in a gang.

8.1.6 Tying Risk Factors Together

All of these risk factors taken together point to much larger scale issues within the world and in history, such as racism, oppression, trauma, and lack of access to basic necessities in life. These issues impact families and quality of homelife, which then impacts children for generations to come. The roots of the problems needs to be addressed before consistent change can follow suit. Kirk "Jae" James, DSW, MSW, BA, AA, Clinical Assistant Professor at NYU Silver School of Social Work, talked about the intersection of these larger scale issues in the world and in history and the impact on families and children and calls for change:

When we talk about risk factors, we have to really talk about the climate, the culture, and the history that we live under. And I think that really has to be a starting point. When you look at the majority of folks who end up in gangs... they are people who come from backgrounds that have been impacted significantly by racism, by oppression, by trauma, by lack of social access, by lack of economic access, medical access, so I feel if you look at the idea of who ends up in gangs and you look at that on a broad scale, there's going to be certain demographic features that you see across the board irrespective of where they're at. A lot of those again are going to tie to poverty and issues of oppression. Even if you look at South and Central America, where gang violence is probably even more prevalent than even in the United States, you see the same kind of markers. If you have this larger scale macro dysfunction and history of harm and dysfunction and oppression...these are the things that drive dysfunction in the home. It's going to impact the quality of life in the home. You then see the ACEs start to play out. You see parents with histories of trauma and their own history of abuse that are unrecognized and are unsupported. And this is further exacerbated because of whatever conditions they're living in now. That's being passed down to the children, in oftentimes abusive ways. But we can't have a conversation around the prevalence of gang violence or harm without looking at some of those deep-rooted things, and those are often drivers for community dysfunction of serious types and home dysfunction, which creates adverse experiences for kids in the household. And I think in most of the research, you have these parental disruptions, whether you have father in prison, and now we have women as the fastest growing prison population. So mothers are going to prison at high rates now, and again these disruptions are going to create these attachment voids which are now being sought out in gangs or in spaces that are often not healthy for lack of a better word. (James, 2020, Unpublished)

Dr. James brought up many good points. Dysfunction in the home is often caused by issues within the family, which can be caused by these larger scale issues mentioned, such as lack of economic access, social access, and medical access. Many of those problems are caused by a long history of racism, poverty, and oppression. Gangs often thrive in areas of lower socioeconomic status. Intervention needs to occur on multiple levels.

Risk factors are broken down into several domains including individual, family, school, peer, and community/social environment.

8.2 Protective Factors

Protective factors (see Fig. 8.3) are positive things in a youth's life that can dissuade them from joining a gang. Many of the protective factors are opposite of the risk factors. There is not a wealth of information in the literature regarding protective factors, calling for more extensive study. There needs to be more research (Ezell, 2018).

Protective Factors

Family

- Strong attachment to family
- High level of parental supervision and monitoring
- Having role models including parental and nonparental
- Having a positive relationship with parent who is of same sex
- Strong family relationships with caring and support
- Stable family

School

- High investment in school
- High attachment to school and staff members
- Teaching youth coping and social skills
- Creating an environment where students feel a sense of belonging and acceptance by peer and staff

Peer/Community/Social Environment

- Having positive peer influences
- Having a high involvement within the community and attachment to the community
- Having activities to be involved with after school

Sources: McNulty & Bellair, 2003; O'Brien, Daffern, Chu & Thomas, 2013; Gover, 2002; Walters, 2016; Higgins, Wesley & Mahoney, 2010;; Robertson, Baird-Thomas & Stein, 2008; Li, Stanton, Pack, Harris, Cottrell & Burns, 2002; Guerra et al., 2019

Fig. 8.3 Protective factors

8.2 Protective Factors

8.2.1 Family Protective Factors

Having a strong attachment to family and a high level of parental supervision are protective factors related to the family domain (Gover, 2002; McNulty & Bellair, 2003; O'Brien et al., 2013; Walters, 2016). Role models are also important including having both nonparental and parental role models (McNulty & Bellair, 2003; Higgins et al., 2010; Walters, 2016). Having a positive relationship with the parent who is of the same sex is also important (Walters, 2016). Strong family relationships with caring and support are protective factors against high-risk activity involvement (Li et al., 2002). In addition, parental support may reduce the negative effects of additional risk factors in a youth's life (Li et al., 2002). A stable family, supervision, and monitoring by the parents are protective factors against delinquency (Robertson et al., 2008).

Father Boyle talked about protective factors: "Having loving, caring adults, who pay attention, are the highest protective factors" (Boyle, 2020, Unpublished). Dr. Becker-Weidman said, "If you have a secure pattern of attachment, even living in a dangerous area where there is gang violence, where there is general violence, where there are robberies and shootings, the protective factor is a secure attachment with your primary caregiver" (Becker-Weidman, 2020, Unpublished). Having that loving, caring, supportive adult who is offering supervision and being a good role model is one of the most important things if not the most important thing in a child's life. Having one or more adults in that role can really make the difference.

8.2.2 School Protective Factors

Protective factors within the school domain include having a high investment in school and a high attachment to school and staff members (Gover, 2002; McNulty & Bellair, 2003; O'Brien et al., 2013; Walters, 2016). Teaching youth social skills and coping skills is teaching them important protective skills (Gover, 2002; McNulty & Bellair, 2003; O'Brien et al., 2013; Walters, 2016). Creating an environment where students feel a sense of belonging and acceptance by peers and staff can be protective factors because students will want to come to school, enjoy it, and want to participate in activities and academic challenges, including graduating and going on to college (Estrada et al., 2018).

8.2.3 Peer and Community/Social Environment Protective Factors

In the social environment domain, having positive peer influences is a protective factor (Gover, 2002; McNulty & Bellair, 2003; O'Brien et al., 2013; Walters, 2016). Also, having a high involvement within the community and attachment to community are also protective factors (McNulty & Bellair, 2003; Higgins et al., 2010;

Walters, 2016). Having activities to be involved with after school are protective factors (Guerra et al., 2013). Communities can unite to advocate for themselves to get more resources and change the social system that is marginalizing the youth in their communities (Estrada et al., 2018). Community kinship support and compassion need to be strengthened, which can then humanize the gang member and can transform positivity and hope in an area that was previously hopeless and marginalized (Estrada et al., 2018).

Special Agent Torres commented on what he feels are good protective factors that could dissuade youth from getting involved in gangs:

> Protective factors are I think a strong sense of family, community. I think having done a lot of trainings, why does a gang pick a community? What is it in the community that is lacking that allows gangs to exist? When you look at some communities and how they're structured, it doesn't really allow gangs to exist. So maybe a tighter sense of community, a better and stronger education system. I think education plays a key role as well. I think the stronger the education system, it can prevent or insulate kids from joining street gangs. I think that schools have a really good opportunity to create a good community. When you create a really good community and foster good communication within the school, you can create a dialogue where schools can be seen as an oasis, a nice territory, where kids are there for a good reason, a reason to learn. Education is key. For some kids that I've dealt with, they only see the four blocks in which they live. Schools have that opportunity to expose kids to something they'll never see in those four blocks in which they live. So with that opportunity, you can expose a kid to a world that's outside of those four blocks and outside of that gang mentality. So by exposing kids to that, exposing kids to a community that's not based on fear, schools can change the dynamic that kids are exposed on a day to day in the community in which they live in. (Torres, 2019, Unpublished)

Protective factors include a strong attachment to family and school. In terms of school, if the environment is positive and the staff support an environment of safety, it can be incredibly valuable to students. Schools can become an oasis for youth, when they may not feel safe anywhere else. Showing students that there is a world outside of their neighborhood and showing them there are other opportunities available to them and guidance on how to get more options and opportunities in life can make a difference in a young person's life. It could make the difference between walking down the path toward gang involvement and walking down a different path.

Problems can arise if risk factors outweigh protective factors in a youth's life (O'Brien et al., 2013). The risk and protective factors must be studied together to be able to develop prevention strategies. Hill et al. (2001) discussed the Seattle Social Development Project (SSDP), which is a longitudinal project that studied more than 800 youth on factors in their lives at the ages of 10–12 years and the likelihood that they would join a gang and stay in a gang when they were between the ages of 13 and 18. Most participants (70%) belonged to a gang for 1 year or less. Youth may join gangs because of antisocial tendencies in family and peers or influences in the neighborhood, poor school performance, and early problem behavior (Hill et al., 2001). Youth who had the most social and behavioral problems such as violent and externalizing behavior such as aggression and hyperactivity in childhood were more likely to be involved in gang life for multiple years (Hill et al., 2001). The study found that the peak age for joining a gang was 15 years, but prevention should start earlier in later elementary grades with prevention efforts targeting all areas of the youth's life (Hill et al., 2001). Taking all of these factors together can be key in developing prevention strategies to help dissuade youth against gang involvement. Schools are the major institutions that youth are involved with on a daily basis, which can be primary places where these prevention strategies can take place.

Protective factors for gang involvement are broken down into several domains including family, school, and peer/community/social environment.

8.3 Tying Risk and Protective Factors Together

Youth who join gangs join for a myriad of reasons. If there are many risk factors in play, then there will be a higher risk of joining a gang. Risk factors are found across the domains of individual, family, school, peer, and community/social environment. The more risk factors, the more likely a youth is to join a gang. Protective factors across the domains of family, school, peer/community, and social environment can work together to prevent youth from joining gangs. Strengthening the protective factors in a youth's life is an important part of gang prevention.

References

Alleyne, E., & Wood, J. (2014). Gang involvement: Social and environmental factors. *Crime & Delinquency, 60*(4), 547–568.

De Vito, K. (2020). Seeking a secure base: Gangs as attachment figures. *Qualitative Social Work, 19*(4), 754–769.

Del Carmen, A., Rodriguez, J., Dobbs, R., Smith, R., Butler, R., & Sarver, R. (2009). In their own words: A study of gang members through their own perspective. *Journal of Gang Research, 16*(2), 57–76.

Dishion, T. J., Nelson, S. E., & Yasui, M. (2005). Predicting early adolescent gang involvement from middle school adaptation. *Journal of Clinical Child and Adolescent Psychology, 34*(1), 62–73.

Esbensen, F., Peterson, D., Taylor, T. J., & Freng, A. (2009). Similarities and differences in risk factors for violent offending and gang membership. *The Australian and New Zealand Journal of Criminology, 42*(3), 310–335.

Estrada, J. N., Huerta, A. H., Hernandez, E., Hernandez, R. A., & Kim, S. W. (2018). In H. Shapiro (Ed.), *The Wiley handbook on violence in education: Forms, factors, and preventions*. John Wiley & Sons.

Ezell, M. E. (2018). In H. Shapiro (Ed.), *The Wiley handbook on violence in education: Forms, factors, and preventions*. John Wiley & Sons.

Gorman-Smith, D., Kampfner, A., & Bromann, K. (2013). In T. R. Simon, N. M. Ritter, & R. R. Mahendra (Eds.), *Changing course: Preventing gang membership*. US Department of Justice, US Department of Health and Human Services & Centers for Disease Control and Prevention.

Gottfredson, G. D. (2013). In T. R. Simon, N. M. Ritter, & R. R. Mahendra (Eds.), *Changing course: Preventing gang membership*. US Department of Justice, US Department of Health and Human Services & Centers for Disease Control and Prevention.

Gover, A. (2002). The effects of child maltreatment on violent offending among institutionalized youth. *Violence and Victims, 17*(6), 655–670.

Guerra, N. G., Dierkhising, C. B., & Payne, P. R. (2013). In T. R. Simon, N. M. Ritter, & R. R. Mahendra (Eds.), *Changing course: Preventing gang membership*. US Department of Justice, US Department of Health and Human Services & Centers for Disease Control and Prevention.

Higgins, G., Wesley, J., & Mahoney, M. (2010). Developmental trajectories of maternal and paternal attachment and delinquency in adolescence. *Deviant Behavior, 31*(7), 655–677.

Hill, K. G., Howell, J. C., Hawkins, J. D., & Battin-Pearson, S. R. (1999). Childhood risk factors for adolescent gang membership: Results from the Seattle Social Development Project. *Journal of Research in Crime and Delinquency, 36*, 300–322.

Hill, K. G., Lui, C., & Hawkins, J. D. (2001). *Early precursors of gang membership: A study of Seattle youth* (pp. 1–6). U.S. Department of Justice. Office of Juvenile Justice and Delinquency Prevention Juvenile Justice Bulletin.

Howell, J. C., & Egley, A. (2005). Moving risk factors into developmental theories of gang membership. *Youth Violence and Juvenile Justice, 3*(4), 334–354.

Huesmann, L. R., & Guerra, N. G. (1997). Children's normative beliefs about aggression and aggressive behavior. *Journal of Personality and Social Psychology, 72*(2), 408–419.

Li, X., Stanton, B., Pack, R., Harris, C., Cottrell, L., & Burns, J. (2002). Risk and protective factors associated with gang involvement among urban African American adolescents. *Youth & Society, 34*(2), 172–194.

McNulty, T., & Bellair, P. (2003). Explaining racial and ethnic differences in serious adolescent violent behavior. *Criminology, 41*(3), 709–748.

National Gang Center. (n.d.-a). https://www.nationalgangcenter.gov/

O'Brien, K., Daffern, M., Chu, C., & Thomas, S. (2013). Youth gang affiliation, violence, and criminal activities: A review of motivational, risk, and protective factors. *Aggression and Violent Behavior, 18*(4), 417–425.

Robertson, A. A., Baird-Thomas, C., & Stein, J. A. (2008). Child victimization and parental monitoring as mediators of youth problem behaviors. *Criminal Justice and Behavior, 35*(1), 755–771.

Santiago, C., Wadsworth, M., & Stump, J. (2011). Socioeconomic status, neighborhood disadvantage, and poverty-related stress: Prospective effects on psychological syndromes among diverse low-income families. *Journal of Economic Psychology, 32*(2), 218–230.

Sharkey, J. D., Shekhtmeyster, Z., Chavez-Lopez, L., Norris, E., & Sass, L. (2010). The protective influence of gangs: Can schools compensate? *Aggression and Violent Behavior, 16*, 45–54.

Walters, G. (2016). Someone to look up to: Effect of role models on delinquent peer selection and influence. *Youth Violence and Juvenile Justice, 14*(3), 257–271.

Wolff, K. T., Baglivio, M. T., Klein, H. J., Piquero, A. R., DeLisi, M., & Howell, J. C. (2019). Adverse childhood experiences (ACEs) and gang involvement among juvenile offenders: Assessing the mediation effects of substance use and temperament deficits. *Youth Violence and Juvenile Justice, 18*, 1–30.

Zeldin, S. & Handler, J.F. (1993). Losing generations: *Adolescents in high-risk settings*. The National Academies Press: Washington, D.C.

Chapter 9
Warning Signs of Gang Involvement

9.1 Identifying Warning Signs

Youth often show early signs that they are either on the path to joining a gang or that they may be involved already. It is very important for staff in schools to get regular training on how to identify these signs. School staff need to be aware of the different warning signs that may indicate that a youth is either at risk of joining or affiliated already in a gang. Once these signs are recognized, prevention or intervention methods may be utilized. Some signs are more outwardly visible signs, and some are more behavioral in nature. The following list of warning signs is from the National Gang Center and New Jersey's Online Gang-Free Community. Pictures (Figs. 9.1, 9.2, 9.3, 9.4, 9.5, 9.6, 9.7, 9.8, 9.9, 9.10, 9.11,9.12, 9.13, 9.14, 9.15, 9.16, 9.17, 9.18, 9.19, 9.20, 9.21, and 9.22) were provided with permission of the East Coast Gang Investigators Association.

9.2 Visible/Physical Signs

Showing symbols of gang membership, such as clothing, tattoos, painting graffiti, and hand signs, are ways that gang members display they are a part of an organization (Decker & Van Winkle, 1996). These various symbols serve different purposes. The symbols show cohesiveness and bonding of the gang and also show outward allegiance that others can see, including rival gang members (Decker & Van Winkle, 1996). These other individuals can quickly see an article of clothing, a hand sign, or a tattoo and know which group the person is representing. This also sends a message to rival gang members to stay away and can help one be easily identified to drug customers or to recruit others (Decker & Van Winkle, 1996).

Fig. 9.1 Picture of a street sign here depicted in black and gold, the colors of the Latin Kings. (Photo: Edwin Torres. Used with permission from East Coast Gang Investigators Association)

Fig. 9.2 Picture of the flag representing MS-13, in the colors blue and white. (Photo: Edwin Torres. Used with permission from East Coast Gang Investigators Association)

9.2.1 Colors

Gangs use certain colors to represent their affiliation and unity. Gangs each have their own sets of colors which can represent their gangs. School staff may notice that a certain group of children are suddenly all wearing the same colors or have the same identifiers. Jay Franklin, a Gang Specialist and Captain of Security and Safety Manager for Riverside County, California, talked about colors and clothing: "Colors, and any gang identifying in a particular community, any gang-related clothing…But definitely with the colors." Special Agent Edwin Torres, President of the East Coast Gang Investigators Association, spoke about some of the colors of some of the major gangs:

9.2 Visible/Physical Signs

Fig. 9.3 Picture of the Latin King Manifesto as well as beads representing the Latin Kings in their colors of black and gold. (Photo: Edwin Torres. Used with permission from East Coast Gang Investigators Association)

Fig. 9.4 Picture of a patch in green and white, representing the Trinitarios gang. (Photo: Edwin Torres. Used with permission from East Coast Gang Investigators Association)

> You'll see shying away from certain colors or the use of certain colors…You have the traditional gangs or the major jurisdictional gangs, like we call them. Your Bloods will wear red. The Nortenos, which is a Latino-based gang out of the northern section of California, wear red as well. The Crips will wear blue. The Sureños out of southern California, a Mexican Latino-based gang, wear blue as well. MS-13 likes blue and dark black (Fig. 9.2). You have Latin Kings, which like black and gold (Fig. 9.1). Sometimes, they will wear red. So those are the big major colors. There is also Trinitarios, which is a Dominican gang, one of the fastest growing gangs in the area. They like red, white, and blue or red white and green, the colors of the Dominican flag. Pretty much every color has been taken by a gang somewhere. (Torres, 2019, Unpublished)

Fig. 9.5 Picture of Bloods hand sign and markings on hand. (Photo: Edwin Torres. Used with permission from East Coast Gang Investigators Association)

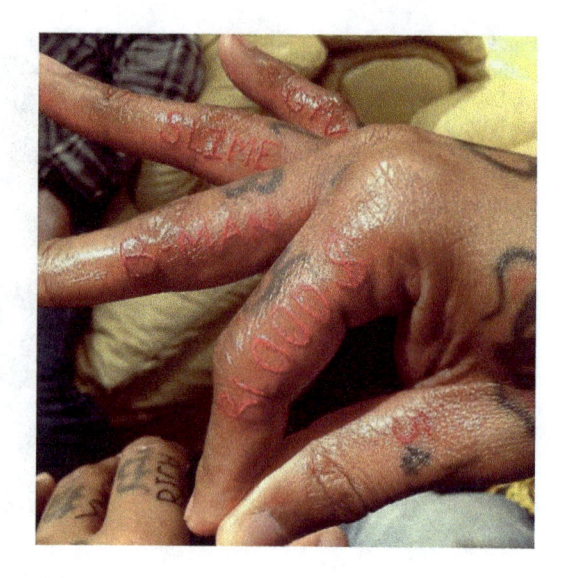

Fig. 9.6 Picture of Ñetas hand sign. (Photo: Edwin Torres. Used with permission from East Coast Gang Investigators Association)

Colors can take on special meaning for certain gangs. It is important for school staff to be able to recognize when colors take on the meaning of being identified with a gang so they can begin to intervene as needed.

When working in certain communities, it is important to have an awareness of what is happening in that area in terms of gang population. Gerald Mallon, LCSW, DSW, Associate Dean of Scholarship and Research at Silberman School of Social

9.2 Visible/Physical Signs

Fig. 9.7 Picture of Trinitarios hand sign. (Photo: Edwin Torres. Used with permission from East Coast Gang Investigators Association)

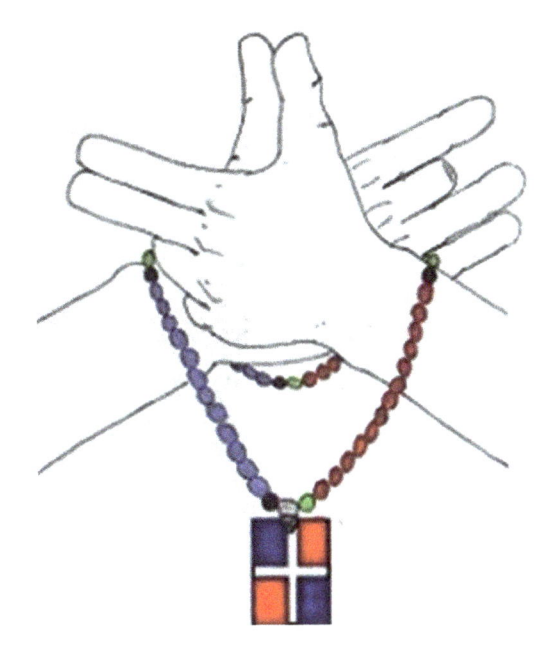

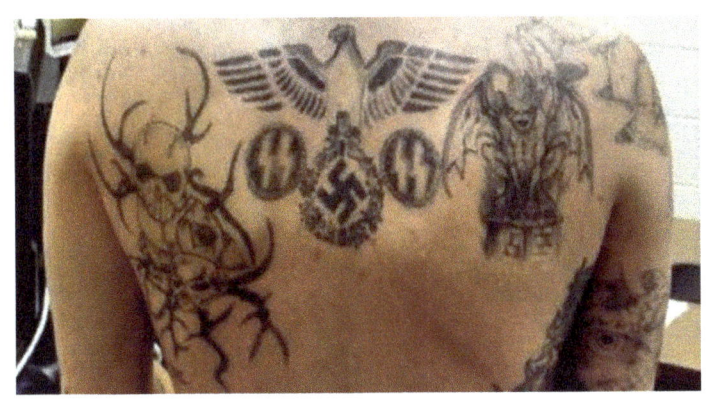

Fig. 9.8 Picture of an Aryan tattoo. (Photo: Edwin Torres. Used with permission from East Coast Gang Investigators Association)

Work at Hunter College and a Julia Lathrop Professor of Child Welfare, talked about running a project in East Harlem, where the staff ran into difficulties in the community related to wearing certain color T-shirts:

> We ran a project called a Navigator Project, a community project in East Harlem [in New York]. And we had navigators stationed in housing projects, and they would have these blue shirts that they would wear. All of a sudden, they started getting really hassled because one of the gangs had that color as their color and people when they would come in would associate them with that gang because they had that color. So they did have to deal with some of that, and we quickly had them wear white shirts or something completely different, because it put them at risk in that community. (Mallon, 2020, Unpublished)

Fig. 9.9 Picture of Blood branding on skin depicting blood burden, blood oath, and blood set. (Photo: Edwin Torres. Used with permission from East Coast Gang Investigators Association)

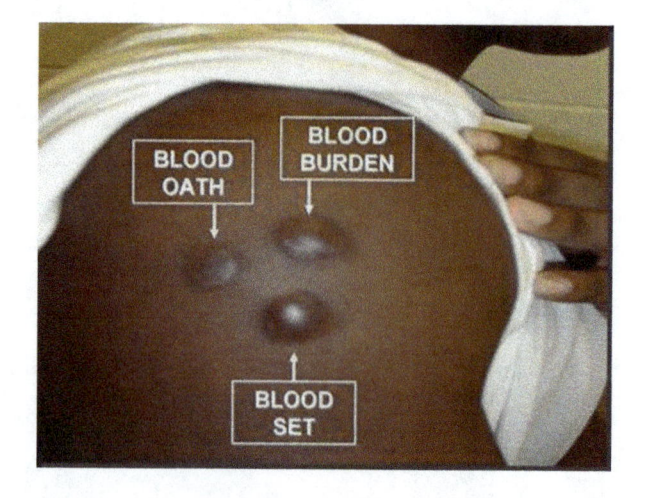

Fig. 9.10 Picture of Blood tattoo. (Photo: Edwin Torres. Used with permission from East Coast Gang Investigators Association)

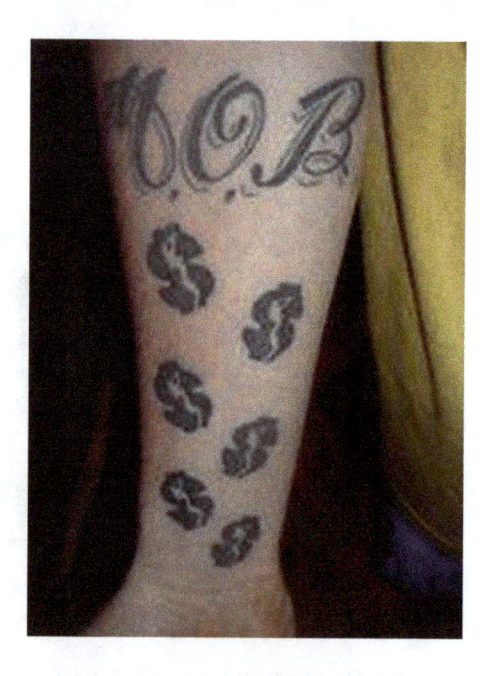

Colors can show unity with a certain gang. However, in wearing colors that are of one gang and then entering a territory of a rival gang who align with different colors, difficulty can arise. Wearing those opposing colors, even if not intentionally to represent the rival gang, can leave one vulnerable to violence.

9.2 Visible/Physical Signs

Fig. 9.11 Picture of MS-13 tattoo. (Photo: Edwin Torres. Used with permission from East Coast Gang Investigators Association)

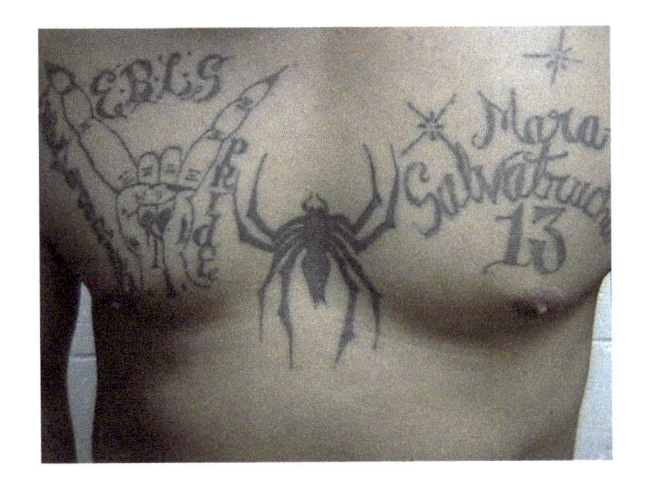

Fig. 9.12 Picture of West Side tattoo. (Photo: Edwin Torres. Used with permission from East Coast Gang Investigators Association)

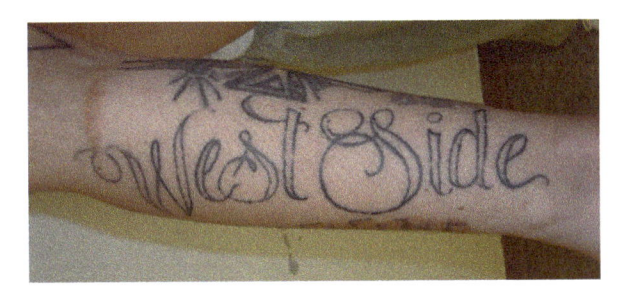

9.2.2 Clothing and Accessories

Youth in gangs often wear items in certain colors such as bandanas, T-shirts, hats, shoes, shoelaces, hair bands, and jewelry, such as beaded necklaces or belts (Figs. 9.3 and 9.4). Gangs will also use sports gear as a way to represent affiliation. Some will also alter the sports item slightly to show a partnership with a particular gang. Gang members like to wear bandanas and beads with the colors that are representative of their gang. Special Agent Torres said, "You'll see patterns, sports teams that they're going to wear that they used to not wear before" (Torres, 2019, Unpublished).

9.2.3 Hand Signs

Gangs use gestures, handshakes, and slang to communicate their affiliation (Figs. 9.5, 9.6, and 9.7). These various hand signs can be used to communicate with each other about gang-related activities in front of those who are not in the gang, such as the police. For example, the Crips make a "C" with their hands to represent their gang.

Fig. 9.13 Picture of Aryan symbol. (Photo: Edwin Torres. Used with permission from East Coast Gang Investigators Association)

Fig. 9.14 Picture of Ñetas symbol. (Photo: Edwin Torres. Used with permission from East Coast Gang Investigators Association)

9.2.4 Tattoos

Gang tattoos show affiliation, rank, crimes committed, and loyalty to a particular gang (Figs. 9.8, 9.9, 9.10, 9.11, and 9.12). These are additional visible signs that show allegiance. For example, Bloods may brand their bodies with dog paws, three dots, meaning blood burden, blood oath, and blood set (Fig. 9.9).

Additional Warning Signs 123

Fig. 9.15 Picture of Folk Nation symbol. (Photo: Edwin Torres. Used with permission from East Coast Gang Investigators Association)

Fig. 9.16 Picture of gang symbols. (Photo: Edwin Torres. Used with permission from East Coast Gang Investigators Association)

9.2.5 Symbols

Symbols are a way for gangs to show allegiance and mark territory (Figs. 9.13, 9.14, 9.15, 9.16, and 9.17). Students may have pages in their books or areas on their notebooks with symbols or gang language.

Fig. 9.17 Picture of gang symbol. (Photo: Edwin Torres. Used with permission from East Coast Gang Investigators Association)

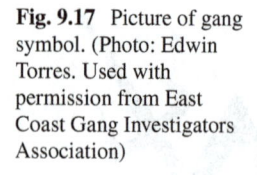

Fig. 9.18 Picture of Crips graffiti. (Photo: Edwin Torres. Used with permission from East Coast Gang Investigators Association)

9.2.6 Graffiti

Graffiti is a way for gangs to mark their territory and show off their unity (Figs. 9.18, 9.19, 9.20, 9.21, and 9.22). Graffiti identifies gang territory, which is important to gangs (Decker, 1996). Gang members may cross out already existing gang graffiti to add their own gang graffiti, as a way of disrespecting the other gang. This show of disrespect can spark violence between rival gangs. Using violence as a way to respond to the defacing shows cohesion and identity (Decker, 1996). Youth may have spray paint, markers, or sketch books.

Fig. 9.19 Picture of Ñetas graffiti. (Photo: Edwin Torres. Used with permission from East Coast Gang Investigators Association)

Fig. 9.20 Picture of Crips graffiti. (Photo: Edwin Torres. Used with permission from East Coast Gang Investigators Association)

9.3 Additional Warning Signs

9.3.1 Social Media

Social media can be a space for gang members to communicate, socialize, recruit members, represent their affiliation, post threats against rival gang members, and promote gang activities for gang members.

126								9 Warning Signs of Gang Involvement

Fig. 9.21 Picture of gang graffiti showing disrespect toward the Bloods and MS-13 gangs. (Photo: Edwin Torres. Used with permission from East Coast Gang Investigators Association)

Fig. 9.22 Picture of gang graffiti. (Photo: Edwin Torres. Used with permission from East Coast Gang Investigators Association)

9.3.2 Music and Movies

Young people may show a sudden interest in gangsta/gangster rap or movies, which highlight gang culture, which they may not have had before.

9.3.3 Money/Theft

Youth may suddenly have money or expensive items without explanation and may have incidences of theft. Special Agent Torres said, "There may be some incidences with theft. There may be some displays of wealth that they didn't have before like expensive items that they didn't have before, etc." (Torres, 2019, Unpublished).

9.3.4 Safety Worry

There may be a sudden preoccupation with safety and constantly surveying the area for danger. Youth may suddenly be afraid to go to school or leave the house because of a concern of a threat to their personal safety.

9.3.5 New Friends

Youth may suddenly withdraw from longtime friends and establish a new friend group. Jay Franklin, a Gang Specialist and Captain of Security and Safety Manager for Riverside County, California, said, "Warning signs are grouping, who they're hanging out with" (Franklin, 2019, Unpublished), having a whole new group of friends and leaving their old friends behind, especially if that new group is involved in criminal or delinquent behavior or getting into frequent trouble in school.

9.3.6 Use of Street Names

Youth may suddenly have a new nickname that they did not have before, which is a street name. Special Agent Torres said, "You'll also hear the use of nicknames that they didn't use before, street names. That's an outward display" (Torres, 2019, Unpublished).

128   9 Warning Signs of Gang Involvement

Fig. 9.23 Quick reference guide on breakdown of warning signs and ways schools can help

9.3.7 Behavioral Changes

There may be a sudden need for secrecy, displaying anger, aggression, deviance, and withdrawing from family and community. Special Agent Torres said:

> Some of the key warning signs are drastic changes in behavior, like opposition toward school authority. They will become withdrawn…absenteeism, truancy. They're not going to be coming to school as much if they're getting involved…Combative behavior, disrespectful language, you'll see a different change in their persona because gangs demand that different attitude and that change. (Torres, 2019, Unpublished)

Youth that suddenly have a totally different behavioral pattern is a warning sign. A student that might never get detention or never get in trouble in school may start having infractions. They may start to skip school because they are involved in gang activities, which become more important than academics. The gang has an influence on the language and their emerging disrespectful behavior, especially toward authority figures like school staff or police.

Mr. Franklin talked about witnessing isolation with youth:

> And then we tell parents look at their behaviors. If they start being more isolated from the family and more aggressive within the family. Used to go out for breakfast, now doesn't want to go. Some parents think they're just teenagers now and into other stuff. But when that's happening and when they're being more aggressive toward siblings and parents, take notice. (Franklin, 2019, Unpublished)

Many teenagers start wanting to spend less family time together and more time with their friends as they try to assert themselves toward independence. However, when there are other signs mixed in with isolation, such as being aggressive, then it can mean something else.

9.3.8 Drug Abuse

Showing signs of drug abuse or finding drug paraphernalia on them or at home can be a sign. Some youth will also get caught selling drugs or delivering drugs as part of gang activity.

9.3.9 Weapons

Possession of firearms or weapons could be a sign of criminal or gang involvement. These weapons could be found on them, or in their school locker, or at home.

9.3.10 Fighting

Young people can have nonaccidental injuries from being beaten or injuries to the hands and knuckles. They may come home with some new injuries that they didn't have before.

Special Agent Torres talked about warning signs in youth of gang involvement in schools and what school staff should look out for:

> What I try to tell teachers especially, what you want to look for is patterns. If you know your school, you'll know the rhythm and flow. So you want to look for patterns that change. So if you have a pattern that changes, you start asking questions. Why are kids wearing certain things that you're not used to? And it'll stand out if you're in touch with your kid. (Torres, 2019, Unpublished)

School staff can be in tune with their students and their patterns of behavior. If something starts to stick out and become unusual, then it's time to take notice and investigate. When something is unusual, it is best to look into it.

Mr. Franklin also spoke about the dangers of gang activity in school making detecting warning signs all the more important:

> These kids have no clue. Once they get in, they really have no clue. The one thing they do know is that they have to prepare. Schools is where they practice for the street because in the street it's real. They practice at school so they can do it right in the street. (Franklin, 2019, Unpublished)

Often, youth will conduct gang activity within school. They may deal drugs or try to recruit new members. They may try to start trouble with rival gang members. Staff members who know their schools and their kids will be able to spot things that are out of the ordinary.

Figure 9.23 is a quick reference guide offering a breakdown of warning signs and ways schools can help. There is a complete list of warning signs including colors, social media, clothing and accessories, sports items, graffiti, hand signs and slang, safety worry, music and movies, new friends, tattoos, evidence of fighting, change in behavior, firearms and weapons, money and jewelry, evidence of drug abuse, and symbols. A quick guide to components of gang prevention in schools includes how to involve students, get students connected, involve support staff, connect with parents, link with law enforcement, strengthen community, create a safe environment and awareness, and teach social skills.

References

Decker, S. (1996). Collective and normative features of gang violence. *Justice Quarterly, 13*, 243–264.

Decker, S., & Van Winkle, B. (1996). *Life in the gang: Family friends and violence.* Cambridge University Press.

National Gang Center. (n.d.-a). https://www.nationalgangcenter.gov/

References

National Gang Center. (n.d.-c) *Parents guide to gangs.* https://www.nationalgangcenter.gov/Content/Documents/Parents-Guide-to-Gangs.pdf

National Gang Center and Office of Juvenile Justice and Delinquency Prevention. (n.d.). *Gangs in schools.* https://www.nationalgangcenter.gov/Content/Documents/Gangs-in-Schools.pdf

New Jersey's Online Gang-Free Community. (n.d.). NJGangfree.org

Chapter 10
Prevention: Building a Safe Haven

> *When you turn 18, there's going to be no place like this [school] that wants to help you. You want to think about where you're going, where you want to be, and what you want to do next. You have to figure out what you want to do. You all have hopes and dreams. No one dreams about being dead. No one dreams about being in jail. Whatever your dreams are, find out who that person is that is going to help you get there. If that person next to you is not a person who is going to do that, then find someone who will. Plain facts. (Torres, 2019, Unpublished)*
>
> – Special Agent Edwin Torres, President of East Coast Gang Investigators Association, excerpted from a gang prevention presentation conducted at an urban high school

10.1 Building an Oasis

Schools can become an oasis for students that otherwise do not feel safe in their world. It can be a place of safety and consistency for students. van der Kolk (2014) said it is important for schools to create a predictable environment where students can feel seen, known, and safe with other people and form meaningful connections, which are all important to mental health. Children who are abused, neglected, and traumatized will find the greatest refuge in a school where they can learn self-regulation skills, form a sense of agency, and can feel seen and known by others (van der Kolk, 2014).

Schools are also a prime environment for enacting gang prevention. Providing a safe environment without fear is the most important thing that schools can do to prevent gang involvement (Gottfredson, 2013). Creating an environment with a strong anti-bullying and anti-harassment program is key. Having consistent rules and discipline is also important. Schools should build relationships with families and supports within the community and help with mentoring and coaching as well as offer other activities (De La Rue & Forber-Pratt, 2018). Father Greg Boyle, Founder of Homeboy Industries, talked about how to address gang involvement and preventing youth gang involvement in schools, which involves creating an environment where they feel valued:

> We think it's about behavior or morality, or we think it's about ignorance and how can we educate them around this. But it's not about convincing or winning the argument, it's not about grabbing them by the shirt and saying, "Don't you see that this will end in prison?" So it's not that kids don't know that joining a gang means that in all likelihood that you will die or go to prison. It's not like they don't know that. It's that they don't care that that is the case. So we're so reliant on content. If only we teach these kids. Show these kids. Instruct these kids. If only they listened so we could tell them. It's never about content. It's about context. And if only they knew that gang involvement could lead to death or prison, but it's not about any of that. It's only about wound, and it's only about healing. Can you create a place of love and cherishing where they feel valued and worthy and nurtured? And then they can find their way to having enough hope to resist gang life. But we have it so backwards, we think they're so ignorant, and they don't know. Obviously, they know better than any of us because they're closer to it. But you kind of want to have a greater reliance on context. Can you create a culture that cherishes, a culture of tenderness? (Boyle, 2020, Unpublished)

Educating kids about gangs when they are young is important. When they are young, they may not have the knowledge about the danger of gangs, so they need to be educated. However, as Father Boyle said, when they do get older, it's not that they don't know the dangers when they join. They know that joining a gang will likely lead to prison or death, but they are making the choice to join anyway. I had a student once tell me that he knew within five years he would be dead or in jail. He accepted his fate. He had no interest in changing anything about his life because he did not think he could. He also had a lot of trauma in his early childhood life. Had we intervened earlier, perhaps we could have made a difference in his life. Creating that place of safety and trust in school is so important.

10.2 Counselors as Secure Base

In De Vito (2020), all of the participants in the study had family of origin issues and some disruption in their relationships with their primary attachment figures causing a lack of consistency in their homes and lives. Having consistency in life growing up as a child is very important. Not having consistent love, support, comfort, and safety at home can cause youth to look outward for those things, and if gangs are readily available in their area, they may turn to them. Ainsworth (1989) talked about other adults stepping up and fulfilling the role of attachment figure if the primary caregivers cannot provide that secure attachment. Students come to school daily and have access to the same consistent staff members, sometimes for years. Staff members, especially school counselors or social workers, can become role models, tremendous resources, supportive allies, and advocates. In addition, they can be that protective factor, that secure base, and step into the role of replacement attachment figures in that youth's life.

School counselors and school social workers can be a great resource within the school system for at-risk youth. They can provide a great many resources and assistance to students and their families throughout the school day. School-based counseling can help students with emotional and behavioral problems (Rupani et al., 2012; Allen-Meares et al., 2013; Cooper et al., 2015). Counselors can help with emotion regulation and can team up with parents and caregivers to help them with emotion regulation as well (Kim & Page, 2013). In addition, school counseling can be a vital resource because some students may only have the opportunity to get mental health counseling within the school environment. It is convenient because students are at school daily, and it's a way to bypass stigma and cost of receiving private mental health counseling (De Vito, 2017). School is also a place where a lot of issues arise in a youth's life, so counselors are on the frontlines there ready to assist.

10.3 Need for Acknowledgment of Gang Problems

It is common for school administrators to not admit there are gang problems in their schools (Gottfredson, 2013; Ezell, 2018). Therefore, this may get in the way of prevention programs being put in place. The National Gang Center reported that there are reasons why school staff may not recognize the existence of gangs (National Gang Center, n.d.). They may not recognize gang activity when it occurs, which is why training is key for school staff. Also, school administrators may feel that by admitting that there are gang problems and gang members attending school, they cannot control the school climate. However, if a gang problem is not recognized and addressed, then the whole school suffers, including staff and students. Administration needs to overcome the stigma and acknowledge there is a gang problem and work together to find a solution. Jay Franklin, Gang Specialist and Captain of Security and Safety Manager for Riverside County, California, spoke about this issue:

> Acknowledgment. If your school sits in a community that has gang problems or gang issues, the school administration has to accept that there is a potential for a gang issue at the school. Once they identify that we're in a gang area and they're not trying to sweep things under the rug, and they realize they're not immune to it, that's huge. One thing that I had to do to really get schools on board, because they are scared of that stigma that comes with gangs, or to acknowledge it, I started doing trainings with administrators. I made it very clear. With a room full of administrators, I asked a question, "How many of you think that your school has gang issues?" I didn't even say a gang problem. Only one out of a room of 40 administrators raised their hand. One or two. I work deeply in this community...and I know there are gangs in the community, so you have gang issues. I'm not saying it's a problem or that you're not monitoring your school, or controlling your school, or being a good leader, but for you not to acknowledge that, that's crazy...Once the administrators knew that the superintendent brought this to their attention, not to point fingers, and say it's real and they need to address it, they were more apt to be honest and address it at the training. After that, we were able to get deeper into the conversation. A lot of good stuff came out of it. It's not to judge you. It's not pointing fingers. It's saying it's real and we need to address it. (Franklin, 2019, Unpublished)

Acknowledgment is imperative. There are administrators who do not want to admit there are gang issues in their school and district for various reasons. Perhaps they feel it reflects poorly on their leadership or their ability to provide a safe environment in their buildings. However, once they can admit there is a problem, the real work can begin. Even if they do not feel there is a problem, having prevention efforts put into place before a problem even begins is also a good idea.

10.4 Components of Gang Prevention in School

Gang prevention in schools is a team approach. The Office of Juvenile Justice Delinquency and Prevention (OJJDP) recommended a multidisciplinary approach (National Gang Center, n.d.). Law enforcement can report on criminal activity with students and their families while local organizations may have knowledge of community factors affecting the family. The school social worker or counselor may know about the student and family as well. Teachers and administration can speak on the student's school performance. This group can come together and discuss what they feel will work and not work with each individual student. Special Agent Torres said it is all about a team approach when it comes to gang prevention in schools. He said:

> Peer interaction, parent involvement, law enforcement engagement on a positive level. So I think there are some good components where you've got schools, the community, parents, and students, and law enforcement all working together. I know it's difficult. I've been at a lot of PTA [Parent-Teacher Association] or school functions where a lot of parents don't show up. But when you have that synergy, it's a great thing. (Torres, 2019, Unpublished)

Working together as team, all of these components can come together to help a student. Each component can attack a different problem and come at the problem at different angle. Parent involvement is going to be at the core of any intervention.

10.4.1 Target At-Risk Youth

Based on a combination of warning signs and identifying risk factors, students deemed at-risk for gang involvement could be targeted for focused prevention efforts. Mr. Franklin talked about targeting at-risk youth for prevention efforts and about having that one person they can go to consistently for help:

> When you're talking about gang prevention or intervention, a lot of times, it's that one person that they connect with or [get] that one message from, whatever it may be, that person that really got them to start thinking differently. Now I'm in high school, and Mr. Jay is at the middle school, and I know he gave me some tools, but this is a whole different beast out here. And then they start sliding back. When they made that point that at the elementary schools that we have a longer time to impact them, that became our focus. (Franklin, 2019, Unpublished)

If a youth has one person in their lives that can help make a change, it can make all the difference in the world. I see it in my work with students in working at a school.

A lot of times, they don't feel as if they have anyone at home they can go to for help with their problems or to confide in and get some help. That's why working in a school is such a great opportunity because staff are with the students every day for long periods of time. They have a chance to get involved and make a difference.

10.4.2 Involve Students

Kids will want to feel seen and connected to others and will do almost anything for it (van der Kolk, 2014). Making sure that students are engaged in school and with staff is vitally important. Create positive peer interactions for youth. Having a high investment in school is a protective factor against youth getting involved in gangs (McNulty & Bellair, 2003; O'Brien et al., 2013; Walters, 2016). Students can join activities during and after school, like sports and clubs, to increase attachment to school, to keep them involved with positive groups, and to learn positive skills. Getting students involved in after-school activities gives students a safe place to spend their time and access to positive groups and positive adult role models during critical times where they may otherwise be unsupervised at home (De La Rue & Forber-Pratt, 2018). Prevention should focus on reducing or disrupting antisocial involvement opportunities, as well as reaching younger siblings of delinquent youth, which may show a reduction in gang membership (Hill et al., 1999). Students need to feel as though they belong in their school and that there is a positive school climate where they feel as though teachers care about them (Zeldin & Handler, 1993). Student engagement will then likely increase. OJJDP reported that students who feel a sense of being valued and belonging at school are far less likely to become involved with gangs (National Gang Center, n.d.). Having that involvement gives them something to look forward to and gives them access to coaches and club advisors as well, positive role models they can bond with who can make a difference in their lives. The National Gang Center reported that police also offer some after-school activities in areas, such as the Police Athletic League (PAL) (National Gang Center, n.d.) Special Agent Torres said:

> Peer engagement is great. I think kids are thirsting to be a part of something. And I think that we, as adults, don't listen as much as we should to kids and ask them, "What do you guys need?" But we are quick to tell them what we think they should need. So I think sometimes they'll tell us. There was a project here in Union County [New Jersey] one time, where kids in a special services school made a power point and told them what they needed in terms of how to prevent gang violence, and they came in with a power point on what they'd like to see. It was very short, but very powerful, and they talked about what they needed in terms of recreation and things that they thought would help. They were spot on because they saw it from their level. (Torres, 2019, Unpublished)

Listening to what the kids want and need is very important. In working with students in schools, I have found that they will be very upfront and honest about things they want and don't want and things that work and don't work for them. Many times, they have requested supervised recreational activities, such as open gym nights at the local Y. They can be their own best advocates at times. In listening to them, we can gain valuable information.

Getting youth involved in activities is an important part of prevention. Gerald Mallon, LCSW, DSW, Associate Dean of Scholarship and Research at Silberman School of Social Work at Hunter College and a Julia Lathrop Professor of Child Welfare, talked about in terms of prevention, how important it is to get youth involved in activities and to keep them busy and to give them a sense of belonging:

> I do a lot of work in Louisiana. Mardi Gras in Louisiana is a huge thing. Everyone who isn't from there thinks it's just parades and they throw beads, and it is, but there are so many youth-oriented groups that young people get involved in to participate in Mardi Gras-oriented activities. If Mardi Gras happens in February, in October, they start coming together and practicing for these things. So they have cheerleader groups, flag twirler groups, and they have all kinds of dance groups, band, brass band, and they have stuff on horseback. I love going to these parades, because you see hundreds of young people, teenagers, high school kids, even younger than that participating. I always think, what a great thing for them to be a part of. Because in the absence of being part of a constructive thing, they're hanging out at home doing nothing, or getting involved in something that's negative. And I always think, there's this kid blowing his horn, or there's this girl shaking her bootie and having a great old time being a cheerleader. What I love about Louisiana, there's none of this, oh you have to be a skinny little girl to do this, everybody is welcome. You've got these thick kids, all kinds of kids, little tiny skinny kids. You know it's a really wonderful thing and they're so proud of themselves. You know they're marching in this parade. The funny thing is that sometimes I'd see four parades in one day and I'd see the same band because they recycle the same band, so they're in multiple parades. That kid that's been playing his horn has been practicing for months and months and that keeps them busy, which is a great thing and gives them a sense of belonging to something great. I know from raising my own kids. When they were busy, they were okay. When they weren't busy, they found some kind of drama to get involved with. (Mallon, 2020, Unpublished)

Getting kids involved in activities is crucial. Looking at the example Dr. Mallon gave, having students involved in something that is meaningful for them, such as the Mardi Gras parades, can keep them interested and invested in something. If the activity means something to the young people, they are more likely to stick with it. Keeping them involved in something positive, with positive role models and mentors, will also keep them off the streets.

Schools can be a great resource for helping kids. Dr. Mallon also talked about how getting kids involved is important but how in some poverty communities, schools may need to go the extra mile in terms of funding:

> Getting kids involved in situations, if it's in poor communities where it doesn't require money, because in all my years of working with families…I mean I love it when schools say, tell your mother to send $5 in tomorrow. Well, that mother didn't have $1. She couldn't even buy one cigarette or a quart of milk. So asking a kid to come in and bring in $5 to participate in activities, that's just not going to happen. I mean there is no money. They have to be activities that are no cost or very very low cost. Or where the school can really really subsidize them. But I think that getting them involved in activities of some sort that engage them and that they really enjoy doing, and it's just not sports, although for some kids, sports work really well, but for some kids, it's just not their thing. And I think that some kids are really into group activities, such as kids who are attracted to gangs, or there are those who like the group/peer thing. There's also probably older/younger stuff too where the younger ones are looking up to the older ones. (Mallon, 2020, Unpublished)

Fundraising for school clubs and sports can help to subsidize some of the money that parents would have to spend on activities. Having peers that younger kids can look up to involved in these activities is also really impactful. They can also become good role models.

10.4.3 Incorporate Mentors/Positive Role Models

Mentors can be positive role model in a child's life. Having positive role models for youth is a key protective factor in dissuading gang involvement (Higgins et al., 2010; McNulty & Bellair, 2003; Walters, 2016). Schools have an opportunity to set up positive role models for at-risk students, like positive peers, and staff members, such as coaches and teachers. Teachers and administration can get to know students on a personal level, which can help create meaningful relationships, which will connect students to school and decrease the chance of gang involvement (De La Rue & Forber-Pratt, 2018). Positive relationships with school staff where students feel they are cared for make it more likely students will stay in school and feel like they can be successful (De La Rue & Forber-Pratt, 2018). Staff can become mentors for students. They can get to know students on a more personal level and offer support.

Mentoring programs can be used to help with youth delinquency and isolation from living in poverty communities, such as by pairing up adults and older adolescents with younger people who have successful leadership positions in government and business (Zeldin & Handler, 1993). Big Brothers Big Sisters of America Program is a mentoring program that can also be helpful. They use a targeted prevention approach which identifies at-risk youth based on risk factors. They are then selected for prevention efforts through after-school programs. They can provide that mentoring and support to at-risk youth as well. Father Boyle talked about the importance of a positive experience with teachers and school staff to combat the possible negative home environment:

> It's tough in inner-city poor communities of color. The school is an oasis, but they have to go home. So that's the challenge. The Baptists say you may be the only Bible anybody reads. Well, you the teacher may be the only loving, caring adult this kid is encountering. So it's just another way of underscoring how absolutely essential and important a teacher is, far beyond instruction, is the loving, caring adult because you may be it in their life. People always lament are we supposed to be social workers also. No, but to the extent that you can love these kids that could well carry them past a horrific home life. (Boyle, 2020, Unpublished)

Being a teacher, or a school counselor, or staff member, may be the only caring, supportive adult that some students have in their lives. As school staff members, we may not be able to take away the pain and dysfunction of their home life. But we can offer them support and a positive relationship that can help mediate what they are experiencing at home and try to get them on the right path. We can connect them to resources outside of the home to help as well.

Dr. Mallon weighed in on how important it is to have a meaningful adult in children's lives:

> They spend millions and millions and millions of dollars on these studies looking at kids exiting foster care, what kids need, and they always come up with the same finding. If the kid had one meaningful adult in their life, one connected person who was good with them in their life, they did better. It's very interesting to me. The same things we knew 45 years ago about connection are still the important things. Why is that such a big miracle to have? We work with these kids and we can't find one adult that can be part of their life? We look at evidence-based practices and all these interventions and they're all fine. But in reality, they still need to have a meaningful relationship with one person who shows them that they really care about them. That's the other piece. The kids need to know that that person really cares about them. And that's what makes the difference. (Mallon, 2020, Unpublished)

There are many young people who do may not have any positive adult figures in their lives due to various life circumstances. Having a meaningful adult in one's life can make a huge difference in the world of a youth. Having that consistency with a person is what will really impact them. School staff members see these kids daily so they have the biggest chance to make a difference in that way.

Dr. Mallon went on to give a pertinent example of what happened to a youth that did not have a connection:

> It was the same thing when I ran a group home. We used to have these treatment team meetings, and I would always say, for example, "Who is connected to H?" And it would be like nobody. Nobody's connected to H. "No, he's never here, he's really weird, he doesn't talk to people, he runs in, and then he goes to his room." Well, what have you done to reach out to him? "Um…well he's really weird and he doesn't want people to reach out to him." And so, what does H do? H is mentally ill, not going to school, and one day he gets so angry that he picks up a broken bottle and he slashes the secretary across the face with it. And then it's like, how did that happen that none of us could really see that something really bad was gonna go down here? And it was because no one had a connection with him. And the ones who we did have a connection with, even when it could have gotten that bad, somebody could pull them aside and say, what are you doing? Let's go out and have a soda and walk around the park and talk a little bit because you're really messed up and I need to have a conversation with you. And sometimes just that act alone would sometimes stop whatever horrible negative thing was going to come. Now I'm not going to say it always did, but many times it did. And I think that was the strength of relationship and while I think it's great for kids to be involved in sports or activities or clubs but they still want to have or need to have that one meaningful relationship. And sometimes when kids are in the band or whatever, they're connected to the leader of the band, and they want to make that person feel good that they're a part of it, they want to be connected to them, and good adults who run those activities know that and know that it's just not about band, it's also about the connection to that kid that's blowing the horn. (Mallon, 2020, Unpublished)

Showing young people that you care and taking the time out to speak to them and help them can make a difference in their lives. When I speak to my students, I make sure they feel heard. I make sure they feel like I am really listening to them. I also make sure they realize I am an advocate for them and am there to support them. That meaningful relationship many times over the years has made a difference in many outcomes of situations in their lives. Having that attachment mediated many adverse situations.

Looking at it from an attachment perspective, Arthur Becker-Weidman, CSW-R, PhD, DABPS, founder of the Center for Family Development, talked about what schools can do in terms of gang prevention:

If schools can put in place an effective evidence-based gang prevention program that would be useful. On a one-on-one basis, if a teacher can develop a connection with a child, but it's the kind of thing where one semester or a year is insufficient. That's why I'm not a really big fan of mentor or big brother programs because the people in them tend to stick around for a year or so then they disappear. To be an attachment figure, you need to be consistently there over the long haul. That's why sometimes coaches can function in that way. Religious figures…if someone goes to the house of worship regularly, the person can. But that's what you really think you need. That's why for example, AA [Alcoholics Anonymous], the way it functions, it provides that sense of safety, security, and comfort and when you have a sponsor, they're really available to you 24/7. When people stick with it and continue with it. That's what enables them to achieve a reasonable level of sobriety. A replacement attachment figure is someone who is able to be there on demand for years. Could be a family member, religious figure, a mentor of some kind, someone who can be there as needed who is going to be in the person's life for years, not weeks or months. (Becker-Weidman, 2020, Unpublished)

School social workers and other school counselors often forge relationships with students that last for many years. Even after students have left the building I worked in, I would still hear from them years later to check in. Having that close attachment can help to influence how they interact with other people in their lives and in their future relationships. Coaches and mentors, if they are consistent, can also do the same thing. Even teachers can provide this as well if the relationship persists over time. The student does not have to have the teacher every year for class. I know students who have close relationships with a teacher they had for one class, but that close relationship lasted for years afterward.

10.4.4 Assess Needs and Create Awareness

Gang prevention should be tailored to each school. It is important to assess the school's needs first before deciding on individual needs (Gottfredson, 2013). A gang problem in California schools might look very different than a gang problem in New Jersey's schools. Each school district will have a unique set of needs. What is universally important is to provide education to staff, parents, and students. The National Gang Center recommended ongoing and regular yearly updated trainings by law enforcement who are informed of local trends for parents and educators (National Gang Center, n.d.). The trainings should be focused on the dangers of gangs and teaching how to recognize the various warning signs that are often seen in youth who are at risk of joining or are already involved in gangs. Education for students is focused more on the dangers of gangs, to give them awareness of the realities of being a gang member, and to provide resources for support for these students who need to talk to someone about their struggles, or if they are involved, help on getting out (National Gang Center, n.d.). Special Agent Torres said:

You really need to individualize [prevention] programs for that community. What may work in Union County [New Jersey (NJ)] won't work in Burlington County (NJ). I've seen people bring in prevention programs from Los Angeles [California] and try to make it work in NJ and the gang problem in NJ is entirely different from the gang program in Los Angeles.

> The gang problem in Newark (NJ) is 100 percent different from the gang problem in Camden (NJ). You have to individualize a program to suit the needs of the forces that drive whatever the issues are in that individual community. (Torres, 2019, Unpublished)

Each school district needs to make gang prevention programs fit their needs, as each school district will have a different gang problem in their area. Each community will also have different needs based on the gang issues in that particular community.

Creating awareness about gangs in the community is important. Mr. Franklin also weighed in on creating awareness:

> Being aware of what gangs are in your community and have an understanding of gangs. Anyone can come in and you can tell them you're going the wrong route and gangs are bad. But what does that really mean, you know? They really need to understand that there's real consequences even, with the laws. What additional [prison] time do gang members get? What's going to happen when you're identified as a gang member? To have these different people come in and bombard them with that…But when they hear it from a cop, when they hear it from a street worker or ex-gang member, when they're hearing it from school staff members, it's that same consistent message. When they're hearing it from a parent. Hopefully at some point from the prevention side, that kicks in. Doing good preventive work, we're giving good messages to these kids. When I was dealing with elementary school kids, I started bringing some of my teenagers in. They related to the adults, but they definitely related to teenagers that they look up to giving them that same message. Like wow, why is this kid saying that? He's a kid, he's younger. It just impacted our prevention program so much more. With the hardcore kids, we were really able to reach them with high school kids. (Franklin, 2019, Unpublished)

Hearing that same consistent message from different places is useful. If a parent, school staff members, street workers, ex-gang members, peers, and cops are all delivering the same message, it is more impactful. I have found that having peers who have been through a situation, speaking to another peer who is going through something similar, is very helpful to them. Teens tend to listen to other teens before they will listen to adults.

10.4.5 Engage with Parents and Caregivers

School staff should forge relationships with parents and caregivers, partner with them, and get them involved in their child's education. Youth spend most of their time at school during the day, and it is also a place where parents and service providers can work together (Zeldin & Handler, 1993). If school staff are concerned about a student's potential at-risk behavior or potential gang involvement, that parent or caregiver needs to be notified. Youth who have heightened parental supervision and have a consistent and involved family are less likely to join a gang (McNulty & Bellair, 2003; O'Brien et al., 2013; Walters, 2016). Support measures need to be put in place working with the parent. It is important to have a positive relationship with parents and caregivers and keep them informed. The more they are involved and aware of their child's life, the better. High parent involvement helps to change school culture and has benefit on students by enhancing academics (Zeldin &

Handler, 1993). Having parent-focused intervention that supports them to take on nonviolent solutions to problems and conflict is also important for prevention (Hill et al., 1999).

Increasing therapy services and giving training to parents on communication, monitoring, and parenting skills to parents who have a history of abuse and neglect allegations can all help reduce problematic behaviors in youth and also lower rates of future maltreatment (Robertson et al., 2008). Family interventions can also help youth who are already involved with the juvenile justice system (Robertson et al., 2008). Social and life skills training and parent skills training that help with supervision and nurturing behavior have been found to be useful (Robertson et al., 2008). Mr. Franklin also spoke about the importance of being involved with parents and caregivers:

> Notify parents…When things pop up at the school, anything with kids wearing colors or intimidating other kids, or grouping up, parents need to be notified immediately. Not after they have a big blow out and now the parents are finding out at a school meeting that their kid is actually involved in a gang. All those precursors [need to be notified], even if you're not 100 percent sure if the kid has the potential to be gang-involved. If they're wearing certain colors, [it is] something you may want to look into. Giving the parent that input to me is very huge. I've been in numerous meetings, where the parents are hearing it for the first time that their kids are deep in it and schools had the knowledge or the information and it was never brought to the parent's attention…There is definitely a collaborative effort with parent involvement. In any type of prevention program, that is huge. (Franklin, 2019, Unpublished)

Making sure that parents know what is going on with their kids is imperative. They need to be the ones to hear firsthand what is going on with their kids and not be the last to know. Knowing as much information as early as possible can enable them to start getting involved in intervention.

10.4.6 Connect with Support Staff

School support staff, including social workers, psychologists, guidance counselors, and school counselors, are invaluable resources for any school district. Get counselors involved. They can assess for risk, provide mental health counseling, and also refer to outside counseling resources. Father Boyle talked about how to instill hope in youth:

> No hopeful kid has ever joined a gang ever, ever, ever in the history of the world. So it's about who can cling to hope, who can imagine a future, and those are the things that compel a kid to keep his butt in his desk at school and work. So it's not a moral thing. It's traumatized damaged folks trying to find their way in life. (Boyle, 2020, Unpublished)

Helping kids to imagine a future that takes them further than the neighborhood they live in is powerful. Support staff can be figures to help students see there are other options for their future. Getting the student connected and to be able to see a brighter future and to have hope can motivate them to do better in the present.

Including intervention that is focused on problem behaviors, like aggression, and resisting negative peer pressure and influence can be helpful (Gottfredson, 2013). Research shows that programs with a cognitive behavioral component are most effective at reducing problem behaviors (Gottfredson, 2013). Cognitive behavior therapy is an intervention based on the fact that thoughts have an effect on feelings and then behavior. By engaging in this type of intervention, youth can learn to manage their thought, which will impact their feelings, which can then help to change and lessen problem behavior. Special Agent Torres said:

> I do know that prevention programs that consist of cognitive behavioral therapy seem to be the most effective programs. Those programs seem to have the most data behind them to show some kind of effectiveness. As far as kids in crisis, I believe that anything with a good cognitive behavioral base seems to have the most data behind it that it's effective for kids at high risk behaviorally. (Torres, 2019, Unpublished)

Cognitive behavioral therapy is an evidence-based therapy that has been proven to work well with different mental health issues, including anxiety and depression. I use components of this therapy when working with students on various issues including behavioral problems. I can see how it could be a useful tool to use when working on prevention programs since it targets thoughts which affect feelings and then behavior.

School-based counseling can be especially effective because those counselors are consistently there on a daily basis to be a resource and support. They are on the front lines when a lot of things occur during the school day. Schools can help kids to foster resiliency so they may be better equipped to deal with the trauma of their home lives (van der Kolk, 2014). If the parents are not around because they are working numerous jobs or they are not able to function as parents effectively for whatever reasons, schools can step up to the plate and take on that role where they can teach kids self-leadership and internal locus of control (van der Kolk, 2014). They can also be a link between home and school to assist in helping parents to get resources as well. Mr. Franklin talked about how some young people are entrenched in gangs because their families are also involved, making them more entrenched and making it more difficult to get out. But a counselor or school staff member can come in and help:

> Some families have attachment, but the attachment is gangs. Some families come from certain neighborhoods that are gang infested [and are] a big strong family. But they all adopted the gang culture and they all fall right in place with that. Some families support it. For those kids that are on the front end of it, [it's important] to have conversations. Because kids that are that entrenched when their families are that entrenched, they see both sides of it. But these other kids just see the glamour or the fascinating stuff. But to let them know, especially if they are speaking to someone knowledgeable enough, and have those in-depth conversations. I know how you feel when your dad went to jail and your brother got shot. Not that cool conversation, but that real conversation of that grief and the pain that comes with this lifestyle. Once they know that I relate to that, then they can relate to me in a bigger way. (Franklin, 2019, Unpublished)

It is very difficult for a student to say no to joining a gang if the family is already involved. The gang becomes the family and that becomes the attachment. Joining a gang may seem like the natural progression. Sometimes, having a peer that has been through it or an adult that has also been through the same thing to help, it can make a difference in terms of dissuading gang involvement.

School staff are in a position to provide positive relationships that can provide positive experiences for students. Youth who are gang-involved are more likely to have a history of trauma and negative life experiences, such as victimization and broken relationships (De La Rue & Forber-Pratt, 2018). Counseling can help address trauma and negative life experiences (De La Rue & Forber-Pratt, 2018). School counselors can be a supportive system for youth and help get them involved and invested in school and activities. They can help with behavioral changes and help them to avoid gang activity. When schools have more counselors and mentoring programs, violence and gang involvement decrease (De La Rue & Forber-Pratt, 2018). Schools should be employing more funding to employ more counselors (De La Rue & Forber-Pratt, 2018). In addition, peer counseling and group discussion have been found to be helpful with youth in the areas of violence prevention and substance abuse (Zeldin & Handler, 1993). Violence prevention programs have youth talk about violent behaviors with their peers to identify different ways to handle anger (Zeldin & Handler, 1993). Having that peer support and group discussion has been found to be promising and helpful.

10.4.7 Build a Safe Environment

Creating a safe school environment is a protective factor against gang involvement. Gang presence is higher in a school where students do not feel safe. Those involved in gangs experience more violent victimization while in school, and research shows that there is a lack of a feeling of safety within schools among staff and students if there are gangs in that school (Fisher et al., 2018). Schools where students feel safe have a lower chance of gang participation (De La Rue & Forber-Pratt, 2018). The National Gang Center reported that gangs often engage in intimidation and threats, bullying, both physical and cyberbullying, and criminal activities such as the use of weapons, sex trafficking, assault, illegal drug sales, and vandalism (National Gang Center, n.d.-a). The 2017 School Crime Supplement (SCS) of the National Crime Victimization Survey (NCVS) (2017), which is the result of a survey administered to students ages 12–18 years who are enrolled in school, noted that students who reported having gangs in their schools had a lower percentage (73%), reporting strict following of school rules. If a school rule is broken, most students said they knew what the punishment will be for that consequence (82%), in comparison with students who do not report gangs to be present at their schools (90%). Students who noted that there are gangs in school also had fewer positive views of school discipline.

Creating a healthy school climate is crucial. A good school climate where adults expect that students do not harm each other and everyone treats each other with respect and kindness is preferable (De La Rue & Forber-Pratt, 2018). In general, school climate is affected by gangs within the school because it creates an environment that allows more violence and victimization (Fisher et al., 2018). Increased measures of safety in schools can also contribute to an environment of fear, which can lead youth to see gangs as more appealing and cause more joining, which then continues the cycle of fear (Fisher et al., 2018). Fisher et al. (2018) found that students' perceptions of gang presence within the school and administrators' perceptions of gang activity within the school were linked with a lack of students feeling safe in school and a higher chance of physical altercations among students and drugs being offered to students as well. Research shows that gangs are also associated with a higher rate of drug usage (Fisher et al., 2018).

School staff who create a consistent safe environment that provides emotional and social support where students will feel safe and have a sense of support will create an environment that helps to regulate student behavior. Schools can improve safety, strengthen the bonds between student and school, and have increased support from staff and teachers to decrease gang involvement (Estrada et al., 2018). A way to improve safety is to have a safety plan including a strong antibullying and harassment program in school. Providing effective conflict mediation between students is also helpful. The National Gang Center also recommended creating a safe-passage-to-school program to provide safety for students who may need to walk through gang territories to get to and from school (National Gang Center, n.d.).

Making sure staff are all on the same page when it comes to rules and discipline is also imperative. Teachers need to provide a consistent positive learning environment within the classroom. Having that consistency and limit-setting helps to set up a positive and safe environment. Staff members need to be able to recognize risk factors and signs of gangs and address and eliminate problem behaviors by enforcing rules and consequences consistently (Gottfredson, 2013). Kirk "Jae" James, DSW, MSW, BA, AA, Clinical Assistant Professor at NYU Silver School of Social Work, talked about youth needing a safe place to go:

> Even in my own growing up, one of the things that was really good, we had spaces we could go. When you look at the gang culture, many of those young folks will say they didn't feel safe anywhere, like there wasn't a place they could go that felt safe. There wasn't an after-school program that felt safe, there wasn't community spaces that felt safe. And eventually this was it. (James, 2020, Unpublished)

Putting in place somewhere for youth to go to where they can feel safe can make a huge difference. Having something such as an after-school program, community center, religious center, or school events that can give them a safe place to engage in meaningful activities and where they have access to good role models can be helpful in dissuading a youth from gang involvement.

10.4.8 Implementing Dress Code

School dress codes and school uniforms are another way to implement gang prevention in schools. Consistent rules and consequences for behavior are important, such as having a dress code and not allowing gang paraphernalia to be worn. Fisher et al.

(2018) found that school dress code policies may have a positive effect on the perception of gangs within that school with teachers reporting lower rates of gang activity but students reporting no difference. Fisher et al. (2018) found that having a school uniform policy is a good way of lowering students' perception of gangs within the school, increased their feelings of safety, and lowered the likelihood that students reported engagement in a physical altercation or were offered drugs in the semester prior.

10.4.9 Link with Law Enforcement

The National Gang Center said that it is important that youth see law enforcement in a positive light and form positive relationships early on in their early elementary school years (National Gang Center, n.d.). Having a bond or a positive relationship can influence a youth's decisions long afterward in the future. Making sure that youth see law enforcement as helpful, instead of the enemy, can go a long way. Mr. Franklin said:

> Largest prevention impact that law enforcement has is when a kid is in trouble. This is what happens if you keep going that route. It's not cool. They need those hard conversations. They will receive an impact with that. When a kid is in trouble…law enforcement definitely…when it's going to linger with the courts. They can get in there and have those conversations when they're at that point of breaking and they share a lot of useful things…There's things in the street and gang culture that's totally against our everyday culture. How open am I really going to be unless I'm in trouble? They start telling on each other and everything just to get out of it. (Franklin, 2019, Unpublished)

Law enforcement can be helping in aiding in prevention efforts, especially when a youth is in trouble. Sometimes, it takes that one moment where they are really in trouble to make that turning point. Law enforcement can help them navigate the process and hopefully have a better outcome for themselves.

Schools are part of the larger community. Their collaboration with law enforcement is helpful. The National Gang Center said that law enforcement needs to be involved with school administration and community to be successful in gang prevention in schools (National Gang Center, n.d.). Law enforcement should link with school administration to create safety plans for schools concerning gangs (National Gang Center, n.d.). Law enforcement can take school staff concerns and can figure out whether there is gang risk or involvement. Their early identification of at-risk youth and gang trends can really help in the prevention aspect of things. Schools and law enforcement should also collaborate and share information, such as local gang trends and activity (National Gang Center, n.d.). This will give the police a view into what is happening in the school system, which will aid in helping to make the schools safer and the community also safer as well. Special Agent Torres said:

> Sometimes law enforcement gets involved at the tail end with schools. And they should be involved at the forefront. School resource officers should be a part of the school, not apart from the school. And they should be a resource, not just a school resource officer. And that

helps two ways. It creates a situation where kids see law enforcement in a positive light, and the law enforcement gets a chance to engage in the community at an early prevention level and get to know the kids. (Torres, 2019, Unpublished)

Having law enforcement as an ally in the beginning can be helpful in terms of prevention. Not seeing police officers as enemies and seeing them in a positive light can also be helpful. Having the police as a resource with schools and working in collaboration is immensely helpful.

10.4.10 Strengthen Community Ties

Preventing gang involvement also involves the community. Being attached to something in the community and having community involvement can aid in the prevention of gangs (McNulty & Bellair, 2003; Higgins et al., 2010; Walters, 2016). Research supports participation in the community and shows it has positive effects on youth, such as problem prevention and promoting achievement (Zeldin & Handler, 1993). Forming a collaboration with community agencies and faith-based programs, like churches, creates a strong sense of belonging in the community. Churches have youth programs, volunteer work, and also create an opportunity for people to come together as a community. There are also sports and recreational activities that are also tied to the community, which youth can become involved in, which can keep them occupied and off the streets. This is another place for them to meet mentors and positive role models.

10.4.11 Teach Students Social Skills

Another key component in gang prevention is teaching youth coping and social skills (McNulty & Bellair, 2003; O'Brien et al., 2013; Walters, 2016). Students can learn how to deal with their emotions more effectively and can learn how their bodies and minds work (van der Kolk, 2014). Social skills or life skills programs can help youth with things like learning skills to deal with stress management and interpersonal problems and daily living skills, such as impulse control, self-identity, ability to solve problems and comprehend the perspectives of other people, and school performance (Zeldin & Handler, 1993). These programs are shown to be successful and can easily be worked into school curriculums and helped along with counseling as well (Zeldin & Handler, 1993). Teaching anger management, conflict resolution, emotional awareness, social skills, and how to say no to peer pressure are all important prevention skills. This is where school counselors can be useful resources as well. School counselors can provide counseling services to teach students these skills. In addition, these kinds of skills can also be taught in the classroom through a life skills curriculum. Some at-risk young people are lacking the skills needed in these areas to be able to say no to peers or to make more positive decisions, even if it's not the most popular decision and goes against the crowd. Being able to channel anger in a more productive way, being able to handle conflict, and be able to resolve conflict in a nonviolent and healthy manner are key skills.

10.4.12 *Provide Other Options*

Underserved communities that struggle with poverty and low socioeconomic status need more opportunities. Students in school need to see that there are other options in life and that gangs are not the only option available to them. School counselors, guidance counselors, and coaches are great resources to provide those opportunities. They can link the students to programs and resources that can provide them with further opportunities. Outreach programs can be put into place in schools or in churches within the community to provide students with more opportunities for jobs and recreational activities. Many people believe that schools need to have a vocational program or school-to-work program that helps youth who are not college bound, to prepare students for transition from school-to-work programs (Zeldin & Handler, 1993). This can provide students with viable work options to consider rather than the street life. Father Boyle talked about alternative schooling as another option for gang members:

> The early days, I remember our local high school, the largest high school in the country, didn't throw out gang members. They'd have fights all the time, but they kind of worked with them. Until one day, they said we can't do this anymore. Then you have the birth of alternative school. And we were a lifeline. We had smaller classes and really individual wonderful tender care where gang members could thrive in that environment, so it kind of worked. (Boyle, 2020, Unpublished)

Smaller classes with more individualized attention can help students who need more support and resources. Students sometimes need additional help to be successful and motivated in school.

10.5 A Word on School Resource Officers

School resource officers (SROS) are law enforcement who patrol schools (De La Rue & Forber-Pratt, 2018). Thurau and Or (2019) in a report for Strategies for Youth: Connecting Cops and Kids reported that 71% of public schools have school resource officers (SROS). They also reported that although the federal and state governments spent about $2 billion to place these armed law enforcement officers into school buildings, there has not been evidence that says that these SROs are helpful in decreasing tragedies. There is little evidence that they contribute to the safety of schools (De La Rue & Forber-Pratt, 2018). Thurau and Or (2019) in a report for Strategies for Youth: Connecting Cops and Kids stated that if SROs are present, they do increase students getting arrested for small crimes and students of color, and those with disabilities are treated more harshly than others. Students might be criminalized for minor incidents if there is a police officer in the school building, when normally, school staff could have just handled the incident (De La Rue & Forber-Pratt, 2018). Officers in buildings has increased arrests by 300–500% annually, mostly for offenses that are not serious (De La Rue & Forber-Pratt, 2018). Thurau and Or (2019) in a report for Strategies for Youth: Connecting Cops and Kids suggested a need for regulation so that SROs are not pushing children into the juvenile justice system needlessly, so there has been a recent push to have SROs receive training in half the states.

The Youth Gang Involvement Risk Assessment Questionnaire (Fig. 10.1) includes family factors, school factors, individual factors, and social environment factors. This assessment questionnaire can be used to help identify students with risk factors for gang involvement.

10.6 Former Gang Members Speak About Prevention

In De Vito (2020), participants talked about things that could have prevented them from joining a gang. Participants also talked about their experiences with school and school staff members. Having a secure base within the family home with strong attachment to parents or caregivers could have prevented gang members from joining. Having a consistent homelife with parents who are at home and there to supervise are protective factors. Having different ways of making money or seeing there are opportunities outside of their neighborhood that do not involve gang life are also important. If there is a missing attachment figure in the home, another person could step into that role, such as a school staff member, counselor, or another family member. Getting counseling when there are risk factors can be a protective factor. Almost none of the study participants had counseling. As school staff, we can do better. We can offer that support for these at-risk youth.

10.6.1 *Lack of Attachment/Investment to School*

Johanna talked about how she did not like school because she felt like it was different for her. She wanted to be out on the street selling drugs. She had no interest in anything and no attachment:

> I didn't like school because you know for me it was a different dynamic. Everyone was always laughing and joking, but for me, I couldn't wait to get the fuck out of school so I could go sell some rocks to get me some new J's [sneakers]. It was just boring to me, not that I was stupid or dumb. I was highly intelligent. I could ditch school and come to school on Fridays and pass my test… It was just basically like it was too slow for me. I felt like you

Youth Gang Involvement Risk Assessment Questions

Created by: Katherine De Vito, DSW, MSSW, LCSW

Family Factors

Yes / No
- Does the student live with both parents?
- Is there a good relationship between parents or guardians?
- Are there any family members involved in criminal activity?
- Is the student left home unsupervised frequently?
- Are there gang members within the family?
- Is the family experiencing any financial troubles?
- Is there a history of abuse and neglect?

School Factors

Yes / No
- Are the student's grades good?
- Is the student involved in any school activities (sports, clubs, etc.)?
- Does the student attend in-school counseling?
- Are there good relationships with teachers and staff members?
- Does the student have discipline/behavioral problems in school?

Personal Factors

Yes / No
- Does the student have trouble managing anger?
- Does the student desire/need to make money?
- Are there emotional difficulties or any mental health diagnosis?
- Does the student have a known learning disability?
- Does the student feel like he/she has opportunities available to be successful in life?
- Does the student feel like he/she has access to consistent reliable people?

Fig. 10.1 Youth Gang Involvement Risk Assessment Questionnaire

know what? These kids are just basically kids and adolescents, and in my mind, it was almost as if I was an adult already. (Johanna, 2019, Unpublished)

Johanna was not interested in school at all because she was so focused on making money and being in a gang. If Johanna had a mentor or attachment to school,

Social Environment Factors

Yes No
☐ ☐ Is there any involvement in church?
☐ ☐ Is the student involved in any community activities?
☐ ☐ Is there involvement in sports or clubs outside of school?
☐ ☐ Has there been a history of involvement in criminal activity?
☐ ☐ Does the student have friends involved in criminal activity?
☐ ☐ Does the student have friends who are gang members?
☐ ☐ Is the student living in a low-income neighborhood?
☐ ☐ Is there a gang presence in the neighborhood?
☐ ☐ Does the student feel unsafe or feel the need for protection?

Student Name: _____

This assessment was created based on the research and practice of Katherine De Vito, LCSW. You may use for professional or personal purposes.

References:
Alleyne, E. & Wood, J. Gang involvement: Social and environmental factors. (2014). *Crime & Delinquency*, 60(4), 547-568.
Berger, R., Abu-Raiya, H., Heineberg, Y., & Zimbardo, P. (2016). The process of desistance among core ex-gang members. *American Journal of Orthopsychiatry*, 87(4), 487-502.
Del Carmen, A., Rodriguez, J., Dobbs, R., Smith, R., Butler, R., & Sarver, R. (2009). In their own words: A study of gang members through their own perspective. *Journal of Gang Research*, 16(2), 57-76.
De Vito, Katherine, unpublished work
Gover, A. (2002). The effects of child maltreatment on violent offending among institutionalized youth. *Violence and Victims*, 17(6), 655-670.
McNulty, T. & Bellair, P. (2003) Explaining racial and ethnic differences in serious adolescent violent behavior. *Criminology*, 41(3), 709-748.
O'Brien, K., Daffern, M., Chu, C., & Thomas, S. (2013). Youth gang affiliation, violence, and criminal activities: A review of motivational, risk, and protective factors. *Aggression and Violent Behavior*, 18(4), 417-425.
Pyrooz, D. & Decker, S. (2011). Motives and methods for leaving the gang: Understanding the process of gang desistance. *Journal of Criminal Justice*, 39, 417-425.
Ruble, N. & Turner, William. (2000). A systematic analysis of the dynamics and organization of urban street gangs. *The American Journal of Family Therapy*, 28, 117-132.

powered by
PIKTOCHART

Fig. 10.1 (continued)

perhaps things would have been different in her life. If there was something to attach her to school so she could form that attachment, maybe she would not have chosen that path.

10.6 Former Gang Members Speak About Prevention

Some students would come to school but then leave to go to the streets. Or they would use being in the school environment to engage in gang activity like selling drugs. Archie gave an example:

> I was there [in school] for just some brief moment. I'd go to school and hit a couple classes, and then I'd go outside or in the locker room and sell weed. And we'd go take a ride somewhere and try to rob somebody, then come back to school. (Archie, 2019, Unpublished)

Similar to Johanna, both of these participants were not interested or invested in school. They were more interested in the gang activity. Perhaps in Archie's case as well, if he had something to tie him to the school, perhaps he would have chosen differently.

Students may not want to come to school because either it is not a safe environment or the walk to and from school is not safe. Evelyn talked about liking school, but because of not being in a safe environment, she had difficulty getting to and from school. She said:

> I liked school when I was in it. It kind of kept me away [from] what was going on…because of the gang influence that I had around me. I ended up becoming part of that gang, and I was getting jumped while I was going to school. It became hard for me to go to school. (Evelyn, 2019, Unpublished)

Having that gang influence around her in the streets is something that was an obstacle to getting to and from school. If something had been done in her community in terms of intervention, perhaps she would have not have felt that unsafe feeling going to and from school.

Kids need something to attach them and keep them anchored to school. Jerry had an interest in basketball through school, but because he did not have that attachment or investment across the board, he did not stay connected year-round. He said:

> I felt like my other peers, they weren't really my peers. They just were my peers by age… I thought I was like the teachers. So when I was in school, it wasn't too much you could tell me. I learned what I needed to learn, but other than that, after basketball season, it's also a wrap with school. (Jerry, 2019, Unpublished)

Attachment needs to go beyond one thing, such as basketball. Only one activity will not work. Once the sports season is over, then the investment will be over. I see this with students and their grades in school as well. They keep up their grades during sports season, but then the grades will slip during the off season because there is a lack of motivation to do well. The student needs more things to keep them attached and involved and invested.

Some students are not interested in school because they are more interested in learning how the streets work. Instead of being invested in school, Jamie saw the gang and street life as teachers for him. He said:

> I was smart. I was street-smart. So I looked at it as school. That was like night school for me. I leave school and I still be in school…Why do I say that? It's just like learning. It's like the gang members I was with was like tutors to me. They still teachin' me…So I can teach others in the long run. (Jamie, 2019, Unpublished)

The gang members became teachers for some youth. Instead of learning in school, they were learning things in the streets. Again, investment in school may have made a difference in this situation.

10.6.2 Activities/Mentors

Having mentors and a person to step into that attachment figure role at school is key for at-risk youth. Luis talked about his kindergarten teachers who were there for him when he lost both of his parents at a young age. He still went back and visited them. He also had a gym teacher who became his mentor in middle school, whom he used to visit as well. He explained:

> In kindergarten, there were two teachers…they understood what I was going through and they was really there. As I grew up…I would always go back to their class and stuff like that, but as I got to middle school, it was my gym teacher…that looked out for me all the way through…After 8th grade, in 8th grade, I felt as though that's when I stopped caring. (Luis, 2019, Unpublished)

Having teachers that were supportive and caring helped Luis. He had that attachment to them and went back to them even though he wasn't in class with them anymore as a student. Having a teacher looking out for you can give one that sense of safety and security.

It is important for children, especially at-risk children, to be involved in activities in school to give them a sense of attachment and belonging to school. Plus, it gives them an activity to get involved with so they won't be on the streets getting into trouble. Josue spoke about this and also about his coach giving him a sense of connection to school:

> School was cool. Math was easy, but I didn't know how to read. I didn't pick up reading until I went to prison. It was like my…shameful secret. Nobody knew that… I could read like cat, hat, that, at, anything with two or three letters I'd be good, but anything more than that was kinda hard for me…what I liked about school was I loved sports. I think that was always my reason for being a part of school…but then when you get to high school, your grades have to be a certain average to play sports and mine never were. And that's when I just stopped going to school…what connected me was my baseball coach. He was a solid dude. He was like the one I remember… using his own money to try to create things and stuff like that. (Josue, 2019, Unpublished)

Individuals such as teachers, coaches, and counselors can be mentors for students. Even if youth are not into academics as much, these individuals can help step in and guide them. They can help them find something to be interested in while in school.

Some mentors actually stepped in and changed the lives of some of these former gang members. Luis spoke about his mentor who really went out of the way for him and was there for him consistently, which was something that aided in him leaving the gang lifestyle:

> I met [my mentor] when I was a freshman. It was funny because…I was the type of kid when I was a freshman, like I wasn't beat for nobody. [I would just] come to school, show

up, do my work, and go on about my business after school…He came to my class one time talking about I need to change my life and I just let him have it. Yo, forget that, f this, f that, I ain't got time for that, father locked up again. I don't care. Who are you to change me? Get out of here. I was one of those type of kids. So when I said all that stuff…he checked my grades. He started doing like mad sacrifices because like as a mentor and counselor, you gotta meet the kids on their terms, so all he could get from me was all he could get out of me. There'd be days where I'd be like, yo…come see me and he'd just come to my mom's crib or he'd pull up on the block I was hangin' around and I'd be like, yo what you doin' here like you whack and this ain't that type of area. He still came, so he sacrificed that, which I appreciated him for that. We just got mad close and he was just showin' me every day. (Luis, 2019, Unpublished)

Having a mentor who works in the school and looks out for students is invaluable. They can step in and be an attachment figure for what they are missing in their homelife. In Luis's case, this one particular mentor even conducted neighborhood and home visits. Having adults in your life that will go the extra mile for you can make a huge impact, showing that there is someone that will be there.

Hector talked about his mentor that he had when he was young and in elementary school. His coach was influential in his life. But then as he got older, he started to become less involved in school and more involved in the gang life. Had he maintained that connection, it could have been helpful. He said:

I was [connected to school]. Actually, I met [my mentor] when I was probably about, maybe about eight or nine years old. Back then, he was coaching teams. I actually lived like a couple houses down from one of his relatives. And I went to school and stuff like that…he was like in the streets a little bit…So he knew everybody…But he always coached and stuff like that. Always did kids' youth stuff, always at the park, and I lived across the street from the park so, that was like my get away from my home. (Hector, 2019, Unpublished)

Having a mentor can be such a valuable part of growing up. Having someone there for you and looking out for you is what every child needs. If they don't have that, they may look for it in a gang.

10.6.3 Counseling

None of the participants had consistent counseling. Many were afraid of speaking to a counselor about what was going on at home, for fear of being removed from their home. Josue explained:

You don't really mess with counseling because what are you gonna tell somebody? I sleep on the floor cuz of drive-bys. I'm afraid to throw out the trash at night because of such and such. My house just got shot up. What's gonna happen? They're gonna take you, you know?…So you don't say nothing. You just smile, and you shake your head like everything's okay and you go home. So it's not that easy. And nobody wants to be separated from their family and nobody wants their family to be judged. (Josue, 2019, Unpublished)

The fear of a counselor finding out about what's going on at home is there sometimes with kids. I find that if you can build a close trusting relationship with them, they will eventually open up to you if there are issues going on. Then you can step in and get them the help that they need.

Luis talked about how he had an issue with anger and people in authority. He said that counseling would never have worked for him. But it also was not tried. He explained:

> I really had a problem with authority and people trying to tell me what to do. So even if you did try counseling for anger like that, it's not like gonna work because I still have this thing for authority, where if I feel as though you're telling me what to do, I'd know that I'd feel that my way is better than what you're telling me what to do. It's gonna go in one ear and out the other ear and I'm gonna do what I want at the end of the day. (Luis, 2019, Unpublished)

School social workers can assist with anger management issues. I have worked with many students over the years with anger management issues within the school system. Even with resistant students, there are things that can be tried to assist.

Johanna did not receive counseling in school. She only received counseling once she became an adult. So the benefits of school counseling for her are unknown. She said, "I didn't start receiving counseling till I became an adult and could see what the benefits of counseling was gonna be…therapeutic and helpful" (Johanna, 2019, Unpublished). Hector also talked about not feeling comfortable with participating in counseling when he was younger. He said, "I grew up in a different type of environment…whatever goes on at home stays at home…certain things that are personal [keep] to yourself" (Hector, 2019, Unpublished). In addition, Leo talked about how receiving counseling was life changing for him as an adult. So there is no telling how helpful it would have been had he had it at an earlier age in school. He said:

> [Learning to now] like being able to be like compassionate, loving, to myself though, you know. And like, being able to take the mask off and saying, you know, all along I was scared of certain things, and all along I was. I was a fragile, broken individual. And being able to like speak to those things and actually like have counseling and talk about a lot of that stuff, and the way that prison made me feel. That changed everything for me. It liberated me because I was dealing with all that stuff on my own. (Leo, 2019, Unpublished)

If these participants had had counseling growing up, perhaps it could have helped them get out of the situation they were in at the time. It may have helped them to deal with some of the issues they were having and may have helped to prevent gang involvement.

10.6.4 Community Involvement

It is important for youth to have some kind of connection to something positive in their lives. In addition to home and school, community is another place to forge that connection. Being involved in church is a great outlet for at-risk youth. Antonio said that becoming actively involved in church really changed his life:

10.6 Former Gang Members Speak About Prevention

> I was a little bit active in church. I was active and soon it changed my life – I went to a retreat, like a Christian retreat – and then that's what changed my life…I kind of regret it because there were four or five years that I was living that life….[I] could have been doing church stuff or I could have been more prepared. (Antonio, 2019, Unpublished)

I hear often that youth who are involved in a church community find it to be something of real importance in their lives. It forms a connection with a community of people who can help and support youth. In addition, it keeps them involved and attached to something and off the streets.

10.6.5 Former Gang Members Giving Back to the Community: Offering Lessons to Youth

Some former gang members chose to give back to their community, looking to make a difference. Jerry talked about finding his faith and speaking to kids today and giving back so they don't make the same mistakes that he did in joining a gang:

> You know what, I was just thinking like, see I look at the spiritual aspect now. So I look at it like…my experience is what makes me who I am today. So…I wouldn't take it back. But that's why I just try to talk to the kids and tell the kids something different…Like if you don't want to experience what I experienced, to finally recognize what I recognized now, and that's recognizing God. You've got to recognize Jesus, definitely. (Jerry, 2019, Unpublished)

Giving back to the community by speaking to youth about his experience and how to avoid making the same mistakes is a way of giving back to the community. Jerry also talked about finding religion and focusing on the spiritual aspect of life really helped him as well.

Johanna looked back on her gang membership and feels like she could have given something back to her community instead: "I feel like all that fake positive [from being in a gang] could have been turned into something really positive…really gave back to my community instead of taking from it" (Johanna, 2019, Unpublished). Another participant, Lamar, also talked about giving back to his community instead of taking from the community:

> I want to be about building bridges and helping people as opposed to destroying the community that I come from…I still come around and I speak to certain people and I let them know that, "Hey, man, if you need help, you know" … I'm trying to inspire hope. (Lamar, 2019, Unpublished)

Inspiring hope in the community is powerful. Being able to step in and offer help to someone going through the same thing you did can be invaluable to them. Being that person that offers a helping hand or some hope, can be what that person needs to change his or her life around.

Most of the former gang members would not have made the same choices to be involved in a gang if they could go back. Jerry talked about how if he could have it all over again, he would not have made the choices he made to join a gang:

> If I could do it all over again… the experience is like the best teacher or whatever, but truthfully if I could do it all over again, it wouldn't be this way, honestly. It really wouldn't be this way, no, hell no. It definitely wouldn't be this way... Like I find the good in the bad because I have been through so much. So it's kind of like that all comes from the experience in the streets. I didn't get no other experience but prison and the streets. Where else have I been? Shit, but to jail and a little bit of time that I got in my neighborhood. (Jerry, 2019, Unpublished)

Looking back on things, many participants would not have joined a gang. They would have made different choices for themselves after seeing what their experience was like in the end. Instead of experiencing other things life had to offer, they were experiencing prison and street life.

Josue talked about wondering why he chose to join a gang and the positive that came from it, which is helping other people who are going down the path of gang involvement:

> You have to ask yourself…what was my self-worth like to be involved in gangs? Looking at it now. What was my self-worth like? I mean the positive of everything is always to have an understanding…the only positive I can see is connecting with other people [and helping those] that are going down that path. (Josue, 2019, Unpublished)

Josue questioned what his self-worth was like to become involved in gangs. As he got older, he was able to look back and have an understanding more about himself. Focusing on understanding and now trying to help others from making the same mistakes are his focuses.

Giving back to the community is a positive. Archie talked about speaking to the youth in the community about gang prevention:

> The grace of God saved me to the point where I could turn this around, and it's a negative and try to give back to these kids as a positive. For them not to make the same mistakes. Because I'm no better than the next man. I'm still a sinner, but I know the truth. And if I can give somebody an opportunity to make that change before they make that mistake, thank you Jesus…. We didn't disrespect our elders the way these kids do today. They have no discipline. They have no morals…And it's sad. It's like you all are all about yourself, self-preservation instead of unity. What happened to let's ride together? …So I just thank God. I still go to juvenile halls out here…and try to get some of these young kids' information if they would allow me to give it to them, and it's up to them to take it…But I thank God that he gave me the opportunity to wake up and get my life and get me together so I can choose to make the right decisions and give these youngsters a different opportunity. (Archie, 2019, Unpublished)

Archie has spent much of his time trying to give back to the youth of his community. He is trying to take the negative that he was putting forth and turn it into something positive. Sometimes, hearing from someone who has already been through this can be the most impactful for young people.

10.6.6 Looking Back and Making Different Choices

Looking back on gang life, many former gang members said they would make different choices if they could do it all over again. Lamar talked about the sad part of losing people in the gang life:

> It's no telling who I would be today if I didn't experience what I did as a member of a gang…it's no telling…I'd probably be disconnected from the struggle of my community, but I come from the community…a lot of times when you go through what you go through to get to who we are today and I think it's obviously part of my strength base. I kind of went back, learned a lot in the streets. I lost a lot of girls. I lost a lot of friends. I've seen a lot of people come and go. That's the unfortunate part. That's the drawback. I know a lot of people dead, unfortunately, died, dead at a young age for nothing…So that's the bad part. That's the, the negative. Because a lot of people dead... Looking back, a lot of people who, who's killed and we're growing up without them in the name of a gang. And it's sad. (Lamar, 2019, Unpublished)

Examining the consequences of what gang life brought to their lives is an eye-opening experience. Many recounted a lot of traumatic experiences of witnessing violence or deaths in their lives. They realize that much of it could have been avoided if they just did not join a gang.

10.6.7 Learning Lessons from the Gang Experience

Learning lessons from gang experiences are different. The following former gang members talked about their experiences in being in a gang and how they would have done things differently if given the chance. Leo talked about the negatives he experienced while being in a gang: "[The negatives are] prison…trauma from being incarcerated. Not being able to trust people fully. Not being able to like share my emotions with anybody. Fear, anxiety. And you disconnect" (Leo, 2019, Unpublished). Lamar talked about what he learned from being in a gang and what positives he can take from his experience:

> I learned something [from] a lot of friends I developed…I love them to death…I've come to have a lot of respect for them, but I can't deal with them today…and it's sad…because they're still stuck in that, in their addiction and their lifestyle…That's a tough part. But if I take a positive out of everything, is that my struggles, my downfalls, my experience, going to prison, [police], and experiencing the trauma I did in the gang life, the witnessing of things I witnessed, it created a strength base for me. It helped make me the man I am today, which is different. Which is obviously different than who I used to be. (Lamar, 2019, Unpublished)

Leo and Lamar spoke about the difficulties attached to gang involvement. Leo had long-standing issues of fear, anxiety, mistrust, and trauma from incarceration. Lamar realized that the friendships he made he needed to step away from due to their continued involvement in the gangs. They are still in the lifestyle, but he has moved away from it. He has tried to find the positive in every experience he had and turn it into something greater for himself.

For many participants, life would look much different if they decided not to join a gang. Jay also talked about how much different things could be if he did not join a gang:

> If I understood it and knew what it meant and how it could wreck you or ruin your life, hell no, I would've never joined a gang, heck no... I've had to jump through the hoops just to turn my life around for the mistakes I've made. It's no, heck no. (Jay, 2019, Unpublished)

Jay realized that had he truly known what a gang could do to his life, he would not have joined. He has spent a lot of effort trying to rebuild his life after the gang experience. If he could take back the decision to join a gang, much like many other participants, he would have taken it back.

Many participants experienced a sense of regret about their experience in a gang. Jerry talked about having regrets:

> I have a whole bunch of regrets. I regret a lot of things, honestly because I wish we would have known some of the things we know now...I have a lot of buddies that got killed over the years...When I was 17 years old, my best friend died... (Jerry, 2019, Unpublished)

Former gang members have a lot of regrets due to their choices. Many believed that if they had known what it was really going to be all about, they would not have joined a gang. Education and awareness early on can be invaluable in a child's life. Getting to the kids when they are young and having that lasting influence could make a positive impact and help dissuade them from joining a gang.

References

The 2017 School Crime Supplement (SCS) of the National Crime Victimization Survey (NCVS). (2017). National Center on Safe Supportive Learning Environments. https://safesupportivelearning.ed.gov/survey/school-crime-supplement-scs-national-crime-victimization-survey-ncvs

Ainsworth, M. (1989). Attachment beyond infancy. *American Psychologist, 44*, 709–716.

Allen-Meares, P., Montgomery, K., & Kim, J. (2013). School-based social work intervention: A cross-national systemic review. *Social Work, 58*(3), 253–262.

Cooper, M., Fugard, A., McArthur, K., & Pearce, P. (2015). Estimating effectiveness of school-based counseling: Using data from controlled trials to predict improvement over non-intervention change. *Counseling and Psychotherapy Research, 15*(4), 262–273.

De La Rue, L., & Forber-Pratt, A. J. (2018). In H. Shapiro (Ed.), *The Wiley handbook on violence in education: Forms, factors, and preventions*. John Wiley & Sons.

De Vito, K. (2017). Schools fall short: Lack of continuum of care in public schools. *Reflections Narratives of Professional Helping, 23*(4), 4–19.

De Vito, K. (2020). Seeking a secure base: Gangs as attachment figures. *Qualitative Social Work, 19*(4), 754–769.

Estrada, J. N., Huerta, A. H., Hernandez, E., Hernandez, R. A., & Kim, S. W. (2018). In H. Shapiro (Ed.), *The Wiley handbook on violence in education: Forms, factors, and preventions*. John Wiley & Sons.

Ezell, M. E. (2018). In H. Shapiro (Ed.), *The Wiley handbook on violence in education: Forms, factors, and preventions*. John Wiley & Sons.

References

Fisher, B. W., Curran, F. C., Pearman, A., & Gardella, J. H. (2018). In H. Shapiro (Ed.), *The Wiley handbook on violence in education: Forms, factors, and preventions*. John Wiley & Sons.

Gottfredson, G. D. (2013). In T. R. Simon, N. M. Ritter, & R. R. Mahendra (Eds.), *Changing course: Preventing gang membership*. US Department of Justice, US Department of Health and Human Services & Centers for Disease Control and Prevention.

Higgins, G., Wesley, J., & Mahoney, M. (2010). Developmental trajectories of maternal and paternal attachment and delinquency in adolescence. *Deviant Behavior, 31*(7), 655–677.

Hill, K. G., Howell, J. C., Hawkins, J. D., & Battin-Pearson, S. R. (1999). Childhood risk factors for adolescent gang membership: Results from the Seattle Social Development Project. *Journal of Research in Crime and Delinquency, 36*, 300–322.

Kim, H., & Page, T. (2013). Emotional bonds with parents, emotion regulation, and school-related behavior problems among elementary school truants. *Journal of Child and Family Studies, 22*(6), 869–878.

McNulty, T., & Bellair, P. (2003). Explaining racial and ethnic differences in serious adolescent violent behavior. *Criminology, 41*(3), 709–748.

National Gang Center and Office of Juvenile Justice and Delinquency Prevention. (n.d.). *Gangs in schools*. https://www.nationalgangcenter.gov/Content/Documents/Gangs-in-Schools.pdf National Gang Center. (n.d.-a). https://www.nationalgangcenter.gov/.

O'Brien, K., Daffern, M., Chu, C., & Thomas, S. (2013). Youth gang affiliation, violence, and criminal activities: A review of motivational, risk, and protective factors. *Aggression and Violent Behavior, 18*(4), 417–425.

Office of Juvenile Justice Delinquency and Prevention (OJJDP). (n.d.). https://ojjdp.ojp.gov/programs/gang-violence-prevention

Robertson, A. A., Baird-Thomas, C., & Stein, J. A. (2008). Child victimization and parental monitoring as mediators of youth problem behaviors. *Criminal Justice and Behavior, 35*(1), 755–771.

Rupani, P., Haughey, N., & Cooper, M. (2012). The impact of school-based counseling on young people's capacity to study and learn. *British Journal of Guidance & Counselling, 40*(5), 499–514.

Thurau, L. H., & Or, L. W. (2019). *Strategies for Youth: Connecting Cops & Kids: Two billion dollars later: States begin to regulate school resource officers in the nation's schools a survey of state laws*. https://strategiesforyouth.org/sitefiles/wp-content/uploads/2019/10/SFY-Two-Billion-Dollars-Later-Report-Oct2019.pdf

van der Kolk, B. (2014). *The body keeps the score: Brain, mind, and body in the healing of trauma*. Penguin.

Walters, G. (2016). Someone to look up to: Effect of role models on delinquent peer selection and influence. *Youth Violence and Juvenile Justice, 14*(3), 257–271.

Zeldin, S., & Handler, J. F. (1993). *Losing generations: Adolescents in high-risk settings*. The National Academies Press.

Chapter 11
A Piece About Trauma-Informed Practice

> *If it's true that a traumatized person will cause damage, our philosophy at Homeboy Industries is that the cherished person will find their way to the joy of cherishing. So it's about healing because it's about wound. These are folks that are mentally injured. And we need to do a lot of things to help them. (Boyle, 2020, Unpublished)*
>
> – Father Greg Boyle, Founder of Homeboy Industries

11.1 Adverse Childhood Experiences (ACEs)

The Centers for Disease Control and Prevention (CDC) reported that Adverse Childhood Experiences (ACEs) are potentially traumatic events that are experienced during the childhood years, which are the first 18 years of life (Centers for Disease Control and Prevention, 2021.). There was a study conducted from 1995 to 1997 at Kaiser Permanente. The CDC-Kaiser Permanente Adverse Childhood Experiences (ACE) Study used surveys to investigate abuse and neglect in childhood, household challenges, health later on in life, and well-being (Centers for Disease Control and Prevention, n.d.-b). There are ten types of childhood traumas measured in the CDC-Kaiser Permanente ACE Study. Three are related to abuse: physical abuse (being beaten, hit, or physically hurt by a parent or adult in the home), verbal abuse (being put down, being sworn at, or being insulted by a parent or other adult in the home), sexual abuse (being touched in a sexual way or being forced to touch their body in a sexual way, or attempting to have sex with you, by an adult, or someone at least five years older). Two are related to neglect: physical neglect (an adult in your household never or did not try hard to make sure your basic needs were met) and emotional neglect (adults in your house did not make you feel protected or safe). Five are related to household challenges: intimate partner violence (parents or adults living in the home being physically violent toward each other, such as kicking, slapping, hitting, punching, or beating each other up), substance abuse in the household (someone living in the home was an alcoholic or

© The Author(s), under exclusive license to Springer Nature Switzerland AG 2021
K. De Vito, *Gang Prevention in Schools*,
https://doi.org/10.1007/978-3-030-82914-8_11

abused drugs), mental illness in the household (someone living in the home was mentally ill or depressed, or there was a suicide attempt), parental separation or divorce, and incarcerated household member (someone living in the home went to jail). Each type of trauma counts as one. According to the 2011–2014 Behavioral Risk Factor Surveillance System, emotional abuse was the most prevalent ACE, followed by parental separation/divorce, household substance abuse, and physical abuse (Merrick et al., 2018). Please see Fig. 11.1 for the ACES Questionnaire that identifies Adverse Childhood Experiences.

11.1.1 Impacts of ACEs in Childhood

The CDC reports that toxic stress from ACEs can impact and change brain development, impacting areas such as learning, stress response, attention, and decision-making abilities (Centers for Disease Control and Prevention, n.d.-b). When students enter school, the effects of trauma become more obvious (van der Kolk, 2014). van der Kolk (2014) reported that more than half of students who reported ACE scores of four or higher had behavioral or learning problems compared with 3% of students who had zero as a score. Children are sometimes diagnosed in school with learning and behavioral difficulties, like Attention Deficit-Hyperactivity Disorder, when their behavior is a direct result of ACEs exposures (Burke Harris, 2018). If children grow up with toxic stress, they may have trouble forming relationships that are healthy and stable and have instability in the areas of work and finance. They may also struggle with depression. All of this can impact and be passed onto their own children. Poverty is also found with ACEs exposures (Steele et al., 2016). Poverty increases the chance of experiencing different childhood adversity, including violence and cognitive deprivation (Lambert et al., 2017). Children with a lower socioeconomic status have higher amounts of stress, which can be chronic, and makes it difficult to regulate emotions, which causes them to develop maladaptive coping skills (Evans & Kim, 2013).

11.1.2 Future Impacts of ACEs in Adulthood

van der Kolk (2014) reported that growing older and maturing did not make the effects of these adverse experiences go away. In fact, it continued to affect their lives as adults. The body starts to show the effects of chronic stress. Depression in adulthood rises. Having an ACE score of six or more were linked to a 15% or greater chance of having one of the leading causes of death in the United States. The CDC reported that ACEs are linked to problems in adulthood with health, opportunity, and well-being, such as substance misuse, mental illness, and chronic health problems, and can also have a negative impact on education and job opportunities (Centers for Disease Control and Prevention (n.d.-b). Some examples of

11.1 Adverse Childhood Experiences (ACEs) 165

BRFSS Adverse Childhood Experience (ACE) Module

Prologue: I'd like to ask you some questions about events that happened during your childhood. This information will allow us to better understand problems that may occur early in life, and may help others in the future. This is a sensitive topic and some people may feel uncomfortable with these questions. At the end of this section, I will give you a phone number for an organization that can provide information and referral for these issues. Please keep in mind that you can ask me to skip any question you do not want to answer. All questions refer to the time period before you were 18 years of age. Now, looking back before you were 18 years of age---.

1) Did you live with anyone who was depressed, mentally ill, or suicidal?

2) Did you live with anyone who was a problem drinker or alcoholic?

3) Did you live with anyone who used illegal street drugs or who abused prescription medications?

4) Did you live with anyone who served time or was sentenced to serve time in a prison, jail, or other correctional facility?

5) Were your parents separated or divorced?

6) How often did your parents or adults in your home ever slap, hit, kick, punch or beat each other up?

7) Before age 18, how often did a parent or adult in your home ever hit, beat, kick, or physically hurt you in any way? Do not include spanking. Would you say—

8) How often did a parent or adult in your home ever swear at you, insult you, or put you down?

9) How often did anyone at least 5 years older than you or an adult, ever touch you sexually?

10) How often did anyone at least 5 years older than you or an adult, try to make you touch sexually?

11) How often did anyone at least 5 years older than you or an adult, force you to have sex?

Response Options

Questions 1-4	Question 5	Questions 6-11
1=Yes	1=Yes	1=Never
2=No	2=No	2=Once
7=DK/NS	8=Parents not married	3=More than once
9=Refused	7=DK/NS	7=DK/NS
	9=Refused	9=Refused

Fig. 11.1 ACEs Questionnaire. (Source: Centers for Disease Control and Prevention, n.d.-a. Behavioral Risk Factor Surveillance System ACE Data. https://www.cdc.gov/violenceprevention/aces/ace-brfss.html)

traumatic events include experiencing abuse, neglect, or violence, witnessing violence either within the home or in the community, and having suicide within the family. In addition, there could be things within the child's household environment that could impact his feeling of safety, stability, and bonding, such as having substance misuse, mental health problems, and parental separation or household members going to prison. Children who are exposed to ACEs such as abuse, neglect, and experience of a dysfunctional household can lead to risk behaviors in adulthood such as suicide, depression, mental health problems, long-term physical problems, alcohol abuse, HIV and risky sexual behavior, and increased poor health problems including cancer, diabetes, heart disease, and skeletal fractures (Murphy et al., 2014). The total count of ACEs categories can show the amount of childhood stress experienced (Murphy et al., 2014).

ACEs impact children in a negative way and are more likely if certain conditions are occurring. ACEs are more likely when a child grows up in a disadvantaged environment, and there is unfavorable parenting within the home where there is likely household dysfunction and an increased risk of abuse and neglect (Wolff et al., 2019). Socialization can then be more difficult when there is violence in the home, parents are in jail, or there is parental substance abuse (Wolff et al., 2019). Households with marital discord, drug and alcohol abuse, physical abuse, and sexual abuse also have a higher rate (Estrada et al., 2018). Arthur Becker-Weidman, CSW-R, PhD, DABPS, founder of the Center for Family Development, talked about ACEs:

> Children who are raised by maltreating caregivers, who have complex trauma, which refers to chronic early maltreatment within the caregiving relationship, typically have several adverse childhood experiences (ACEs) in their background. Maybe an abusive parent, maybe they were physically, emotionally, or psychologically abused. Maybe there was domestic violence. You might have a parent who is in prison. You've got at least four ACES right there, plus probably others, and research shows the more ACEs in your background, in addition to being more likely to develop a whole variety of physical medical disorders, you're also more likely to develop a whole range of psychiatric disorders. (Becker-Weidman, 2020, Unpublished)

Having numerous ACEs can affect a child profoundly when growing up and cause physical and psychiatric issues. More damage is created with each adverse experience (van der Kolk, 2014). Wolff et al. (2019) found that there is a positive association between ACEs scores and gang involvement. Children who have ACEs are more likely to join a gang than someone who has no ACEs. If that is the case, then it is more likely that a youth who joins a gang is more likely to have experienced trauma in his or her life in some way. Father Boyle talked about the impact of ACEs on the individuals seeking help from his organization and how we as a society should react with compassion instead of judgment and help:

> ACE is a one through ten checklist…like parents who are mentally ill, or one of the other parents is in prison, or sexual abuse. It's a checklist of ten. Just to give you some reference point, I'm zero on that list for adverse childhood experiences. Medical professionals will say if you have a kid who is a four or five on that list, then wow…cause for alarm. You are going to have health issues and socialization issues. Every single man and woman who walks through our doors at Homeboy is a nine or a ten on that scale. I say nine or a ten because it's hard sometimes, especially for the males, to acknowledge sexual abuse. So we'll go with nine or ten. So that's just off the charts difficult to navigate. Is that why they join a gang? Of course,…completely…Parents in prison, people using drugs, lots of domestic violence, neglect, lots of mental illness, if you look at that list of ten and you know gang

11.1 Adverse Childhood Experiences (ACEs)

> members are by and large experiencing nine or ten of that list…you can see the reasons why they join gangs. And it's hard. So navigating a nine or ten on the ACEs is really extraordinary and something as a society we should stand in awe and say, "Whoa, I personally have never had to carry anything like that." So once you stand in awe, you can respond compassionately and not with judgment. (Boyle, 2020, Unpublished)

Father Boyle spoke of youth experiencing trauma as the reason youth join gangs. If that is the driving force, then it would make sense that if there was some type of early prevention or intervention, that could swing the pendulum the other way and prevent the youth from joining. Many people judge gang members by what they see on the news or in the media. However, when you think about what must have occurred in that child's life for him or her to choose that path, it might be a little easier to think with compassion and think in terms of how can we intervene and prevent gang involvement in youth early on in life.

Gerald Mallon, DSW, LCSW, Associate Dean of Scholarship and Research at Silberman School of Social Work at Hunter College and a Julia Lathrop Professor of Child Welfare, talked about the impact of growing up with a difficult childhood on youth and how they may repeat the same patterns of behavior if there's no intervention:

> I live in East Harlem [in New York] and it's hard. I see a lot of single moms doing the best they can, and I also see kids not really well cared for or parents who are really abusive to them right in the street, and you think, gosh if they're abusive to them in the street, what are they doing to them when they're at home? And then the reverse with great loving parents who are doing wonderful things for their children. You start to see things. Whatever that kid is experiencing, then that is what they start doing when they're parents and when they're in relationships. It's just an ugly cycle and they don't know any better. The one thing I remember, this one mom was trying to get her kids back, and the worker said, "It's John's birthday next week, are you planning on doing anything for him?" And she said, "What do you mean am I planning anything? What should I do? So what?" And they were like, "What do you mean so what? Well, are you going to get him a cake? Are you going to get him a card?" She said, "No! Nobody ever did that for me." So yes, that's exactly now why you now pass this on to your child. They grow up without any kind of celebration for their birth, and people are not aware of that I think to some extent, so it's not like you can blame them or they're being mean, or they're being ugly, they just don't even know any better. How do you get people to get to a point where you can really say you need to do things differently? There are certain people who don't realize it ever, and it just becomes their life. I'm a believer that people can change and families can change, but they need some outside intervention to help them. And they have to want to change. Then they have to have some outside intervention to help them be sustainable and to change. And some people just don't get that. (Mallon, 2020, Unpublished)

Maltreatment and violence can be cyclical, and this type of behavior can be passed down from generation to generation. Wanting to change and accepting help and intervention are the ways to breaking that cycle. Individuals in this cycle need help to recognize and understand why they may engage in this type of behavior and need to be shown ways to break the cycle of behavior.

In the justice system, there are many people who have been impacted by ACEs. Kirk "Jae" James, DSW, MSW, BA, AA, Clinical Assistant Professor at NYU Silver School of Social Work, talked about those involved in the justice system and the prevalence of ACEs:

Everyone who has been in the justice system has ACEs. You won't find anyone in the justice system who doesn't have multiple ACEs. When you start to look at those ACEs, you start to look at issues of attachment. It makes perfect sense…gang involvement makes perfect sense. The behaviors we see are very much aligned with ACEs. (James, 2020, Unpublished)

Issues of attachment often coincide with ACEs. When there is trauma, there is often attachment issues involved as well. Youth involved in the justice system are likely to have many ACEs. If that is the case, then getting intervention, especially in terms of attachment, can be helpful. A good therapist can assist in helping to work through issues of attachment.

The ACEs Pyramid illustrates the mechanism by which Adverse Childhood Experiences can influence one's health and well-being through the life span of an individual. Please see Fig. 11.2 for the ACEs Pyramid.

Early Adverse Childhood Experiences can have a lasting impact on different areas of life such as injury, mental health, maternal health, infectious disease, chronic disease, risky behaviors, and opportunities. Please see Fig. 11.3 to learn about how early adversity has lasting impacts.

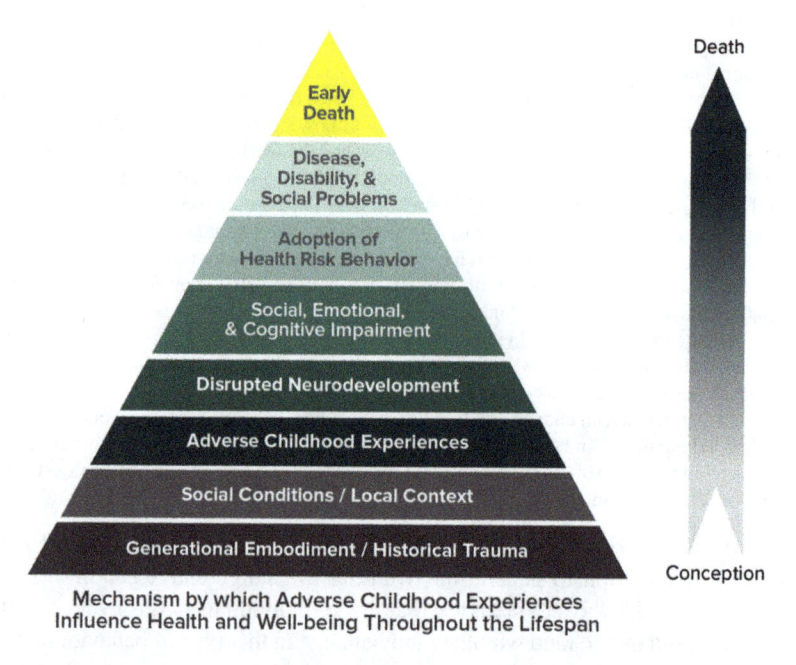

Fig. 11.2 ACEs Pyramid. (Source: Centers for Disease Control and Prevention, n.d.-b. About the CDC-Kaiser ACE study. https://www.cdc.gov/violenceprevention/aces/about.html)

Fig. 11.3 Early adversity has lasting impacts. (Source: Centers for Disease Control and Prevention, n.d.-b. About the CDC-Kaiser ACE study. https://www.cdc.gov/violenceprevention/aces/about.html)

11.1.3 ACEs Are Preventable

ACEs are preventable. The ACE study data revealed that the most serious and expensive public health problem in the United States is child abuse (van der Kolk, 2014). The overall cost of child abuse was more than heart disease or cancer (van der Kolk, 2014). If child abuse was eliminated, it lowers rates of depression by more than half, alcoholism by two-thirds, and IV drug use and domestic violence by three-quarters (van der Kolk, 2014). The CDC reported that children and families who experience safe, stable, and nurturing relationships and environments can prevent ACEs (Centers for Disease Control and Prevention, 2021). It is all about finding and creating those positive, supportive, and nurturing relationships for children. Having at least one person who is dependable, reliable, supportive, and loving and someone that that child can trust can make all the difference in the world. It just takes one person.

According to the CDC, some other things that can be done in areas of prevention include strengthening family economic supports such as having family-friendly work policies and strengthening financial security within the family; changing social norms and promoting anti-violence norms and positive parenting, such as having public campaigns that focus on enhancement and engagement and reducing corporeal punishment through legislation; providing children with a strong start in life with good-quality childcare, preschool enrichment, and family involvement; teaching skills like social-emotional learning and parenting skills which promote positive child development, such as early childhood visitation in the home and having a parenting skills and family relationship approach; connecting kids with adults in mentoring programs or through school; and intervening and including treatment to prevent harmful effects of ACEs, such as having enhanced primary care, behavioral parent training programs, treatment for exposure to abuse and neglect, and treatment which will prevent behavior problems and involvement in violence later on in life (Centers for Disease Control and Prevention, 2021).

ACEs are entirely preventable by doing things such as strengthening economic support to families, changing social norms to support parents and positive parenting, providing quality care and education early in life, enhancing parenting skills to promote healthy child development, and intervening to lessen harms and prevent future risk. Please see Fig. 11.4 to learn about how ACEs are preventable.

Strengthen economic supports to families
- Strengthening household financial security
- Family-friendly work policies

Change social norms to support parents and positive parenting
- Public engagement and enhancement campaigns
- Legislative approaches to reduce corporal punishment

Provide quality care and education early in life
- Preschool enrichment with family engagement
- Improved quality of child care through licensing and accreditation

Enhance parenting skills to promote healthy child development
- Early childhood home visitation
- Parenting skill and family relationship approaches

Intervene to lessen harms and prevent future risk
- Enhanced primary care
- Behavioral parent training programs
- Treatment to lessen harms of abuse and neglect exposure
- Treatment to prevent problem behavior and later involvement in violence

Fig. 11.4 ACEs are preventable. (Source: Centers for Disease Control and Prevention, 2021. Preventing childhood abuse and neglect. https://www.cdc.gov/violenceprevention/childabuseand-neglect/fastfact.html)

11.2 Effects of Violence on Youth

Schools that have a higher gang presence also have a higher level of victimization and violence (Clark et al., 2018). Youth who are violent offenders are more likely to be violently victimized as well (Clark et al., 2018). Taylor (2008) discussed the relationship between gang membership and victimization. Youth involved in gangs were more likely to be violently victimized than youth who were not members of a gang. Gangs produce violence, and violence can be a normative behavior for gang members, with violent victimization increasing once a gang member rather than protection from gangs (Taylor, 2008). Gang members may experience violence the most from their own gang, such as being initiated in a violent way upon entering a gang, and experiencing violent discipline from their fellow members for breaking gang rules (Taylor, 2008).

Youth who are involved in gangs may have a higher incidence of Post-Traumatic Stress Disorder (PTSD) symptoms due to the high levels of violence exposure (Li et al., 2002). Children who experience trauma may develop PTSD symptoms like distraction or hyperactivity, intrusive thoughts, and avoidance of things that are related to the trauma (Li et al., 2002). Li et al. (2002) said that higher PTSD symptoms could be due to the higher violence exposure due to gang activity or because the gang environment itself is stressful. They also found that the gang is associated with lower levels of resilience such as social problem-solving and family ties along with higher levels of symptoms of distress such as lack of belonging. In terms of prevention, programs should focus on providing a realistic picture for youth about the increased chance of violent victimization which comes along with being involved in a gang (Taylor, 2008).

11.3 Trauma-Informed Practice

van der Kolk (2014) reported that if we ignore the roots of trauma while attempting to treat trauma, we are likely to fail. The environment a person grows up in strongly impacts whether one winds up living a life that is safe and healthy. Income, housing, the structure of family, and opportunities for education and employment will impact whether someone will experience traumatic stress in his lifetime and whether there will be resources available to address the trauma if experienced (van der Kolk, 2014). Living in poverty, having schools that are lower quality, being socially isolated, unemployment, gun availability, and lack of quality housing are all factors that influence the development of trauma (van der Kolk, 2014).

Harden et al. (2014) described how trauma-informed practice tries to understand the impact of violence exposure on survivors of trauma. There are programs that train therapists and teach them strategies and interventions with violence survivors and help them understand how they are impacted by traumatic events (Harden et al., 2014). The National Childhood Traumatic Stress Network has a wealth of research and practice for childhood trauma (Harden et al., 2014). Therapy that is trauma-informed may be useful in treating youth impacted by violence, including gang violence. Dr. James talked about the importance of trauma-informed care:

> I think trauma-informed care is important. Looking at the genesis of most folks who end up in gangs, or experiences of those involved in gangs, and I think things that come up most for me are issues of attachment, looking at relational theory, and attachment and relational theory have to be closely connected. Because obviously your attachment then determines your quality and level of relationships with others and also motivational theory. Looking at where people are at in the change place and being able to support that and understanding that it's going to look different at different times. Sometimes, it's going to be stronger than others based on what's happening. There has to be almost an amalgamation of those theories and adequate service provision. (James, 2020, Unpublished)

Attachment has profound effects on your life. Future relationships are affected by attachment. Therapists who can work effectively with those with attachment issues can really help them change their way of viewing the world and their relationships. Treatment of those with attachment issues and complex trauma is important. Dr. Becker-Weidman discussed treatment of attachment and complex trauma:

> Complex trauma is different than PTSD. Simple trauma refers to some kind of traumatic event. Typically, it occurs later in life, typically it is an event, and typically it occurs outside of the primary care relationship. So the distressing event can somewhat be mitigated by the attachment security in the primary relationship. Complex trauma, on the other hand, refers to chronic (meaning repeated events, not one event, many events), early (meaning within the first five years of life), maltreatment, within the caregiving relationship, and that's where you get the driving your foot in the car with the foot on the break and gas experience, which causes attachment breakdown and then complex trauma, which can lead to impairment in one of seven domains of functioning, which is why assessment is so important. The domains being attachment, behavioral regulation, emotional regulation, biology, defensive functions, self-concept, and cognition…For disorders of attachment and complex trauma, the evidence-based treatment would be some form of attachment-focused therapy, specifically dyadic developmental psychotherapy. I always suggest that people go to the California Evidence-Based Clearinghouse for Child Welfare (n.d.). That organization independently evaluates different therapeutic approaches, gives them a rating based on the evidence from 1 to 5, and then gives them a rating of low, medium, or high for the relevance for child welfare. And so dyadic developmental psychotherapy has a rating of 3 for evidence-based, meaning there's been at least two studies with controls showing efficacy. And they rated it as highly relevant to the child welfare population. So that would be the approach to use. And that's the reason in my practice that I get families who have had one, two, three years of treatment with no improvement. And it's not because the therapist wasn't competent, or the treatment delivered was an off the wall kind of thing. It was not the right treatment for the underlying condition, which leads me to my second important point. A kid or a dad or mom calls you up, or a teacher calls you up, and says I've got this kid in my class, eight or nine, and he can't sit still. He's always calling out in class. He gets up from his seat. If there's a noise outside, he has to run to the window to see what it is. He is very disorganized. He's always losing things. So you'll be thinking, well, must have ADHD. If you look in the DSM 5, those are six of the required symptoms to meet that diagnosis. The sort of go to treatment, evidence-based treatment is a stimulant of one kind or another. However, you can get the same symptom constellation if the child had sensory integration dysfunction, if they had suffered a traumatic brain injury, if they were experiencing generalized anxiety disorder. Or if they were prenatally exposed to toxins like lead, or alcohol or drugs, and each of those you would treat differently. For attachment-related difficulties and complex trauma, dyadic

developmental psychotherapy is one of the more common evidence-based treatments for that. (Becker-Weidman, 2020, Unpublished)

According to the California Evidenced-Based Clearinghouse for Child Welfare (n.d.), dyadic developmental psychotherapy is a form of treatment for children and parenting of children with problems which are the result of abuse, neglect, or living in multiple placements. Children who experience these issues have not experienced dyadic interaction that occurs between parent and child, which is necessary for development to occur in a normal way. This form of therapy incorporates a foundation of empathy, acceptance, curiosity, and playfulness, as opposed to threats, use of power to force submission, intimidation, or coercion. The goals of the therapy are for the child to develop a more secure attachment pattern, symptoms of trauma to resolve, and to have a more secure and permanent connection with the caregiver. The goals for the parent are to increase attunement with the child, increase sensitivity, to use parenting approaches that are attachment sensitive, and to have reflective function.

11.4 How Can Schools Become Trauma-Informed?

School staff can learn to become trauma-informed. Some schools punish children for things like aggressive outbursts, tantrums, or spacing out in class, which can all be signs of traumatic stress, which can just create another traumatic trigger, instead of relieving the underlying problem (van der Kolk, 2014). van der Kolk (2014) said that the first step is to acknowledge the child is upset, then find out why, and discuss solutions. Having predictability and making sure expectations are clear are important. The National Child Traumatic Stress Network (n.d.) identified components of "Essential Elements of a Trauma-Informed School System" including identifying, assessing, addressing, and treating traumatic stress, teaching trauma education and awareness, establishing partnerships with students and families, having a trauma-informed learning environment which encompasses social/emotional skills and wellness, being culturally responsive, encompassing emergency management and crisis response, addressing staff self-care and secondary traumatic stress, examining and revising school discipline policies and practices, and forming collaboration across systems and forming partnerships within the community.

The next section discusses what administrators, teachers, and support staff can do to become more trauma-informed in schools (Dragun, 2019).

11.4.1 Administrators

Assess School Culture and Climate
Developing a positive school culture and climate is an important step. A school that has a positive climate and culture can create an environment that encourages learning and development. One way is to include Social Emotional Learning (SEL) into

the school curriculum. SEL curriculums help students to understand and manage emotions, make responsible decisions, understand empathy for others, form positive goals, and develop and maintain relationships.

Adjusting the Discipline Model

Adjusting the discipline model is also important. Students who have experienced trauma or neglect may experience difficult feelings associated with their trauma or ACEs if they are given punitive punishment at school. Therefore, discipline should not involve yelling or embarrassing the student and should instead be respectful and nonviolent and connect the consequence with the behavior and not the student. Keeping children in school and giving consequences there and avoiding out of school suspensions would also be useful.

Promote a Trauma-Informed Approach

Providing professional development for staff, educating them about trauma and the impact on students is helpful, as is modeling a trauma-informed practice by speaking to staff in a respectful empathic way as well is useful.

11.4.2 Teachers

Co-regulation

Modeling emotional self-regulation for students can help them to learn appropriate behaviors and self-regulation. Co-regulating is a skill that students learn, where they can focus on de-escalation and focus on feelings instead of the behavior. Remain calm, acknowledge the student's feelings, and give them time to calm down in a safe environment.

Culturally Responsive Trauma-Informed Approach

Be mindful of culture and have a culturally responsive trauma-informed approach by understanding each student's culture and lived experience. When students feel that a teacher understands them, they can grow and be successful.

Respond to Behavior with Curiosity

When a student is dysregulated, try to understand what is going on with the student at that particular time. Instead of engaging in a power struggle, nurture the connection you have with the student. Try to foster a connection with your student every day.

11.4.3 Support Staff

Recognize ACEs Prevalence and Signs

It is important for school social workers and other support staff to recognize the signs and effects of trauma and stressful life events. If these signs are recognized, then interventions can be put into place to help meet the needs of the student emotionally and protect them from harm in the future.

Bolster Resilience

Research has shown that resilience can counter the effects of trauma and ACEs (Moore & Ramirez, 2016). Resilience is built through positive relationships with important adults in the student's life, such as teachers and support staff, and it gives students a chance to learn how to manage their feelings and impulses (Blodgett & Dorado, 2016).

Trauma and ACEs Screening

It is important for school staff to include an ACEs Questionnaire when working with individually referred students. The results can reveal information that can lead to getting the student support that he or she needs.

11.5 The Importance of Trauma-Informed Care

Trauma can impact a child for a lifetime. Being exposed to violence and having Adverse Childhood Experiences (ACEs) can have negative effects on children that can be seen for years to come. Prevention, intervening, and providing help to these children is key. Having school staff working from a trauma-informed lens can be instrumental. School staff can be a piece of the greater picture of creating a trauma-informed environment that can help children feel more comfortable in school and be successful in the classroom.

References

Blodgett, C., & Dorado, J. (2016). *A selected review of trauma-informed school practice and alignment with educational practice*. CLEAR Trauma Center, University of California.

Burke Harris, N. (2018). *The deepest well: Healing the long-term effects of childhood adversity*. Houghton Mifflin Harcourt.

California Evidence-Based Clearinghouse for Child Welfare. (n.d.). *Dyadic developmental psychotherapy*. https://www.cebc4cw.org/program/dyadic-developmental-psychotherapy/

Centers for Disease Control and Prevention. (n.d.-a). *Behavioral risk factor surveillance system ACE data*. https://www.cdc.gov/violenceprevention/aces/ace-brfss.html

Centers for Disease Control and Prevention. (n.d.-b). *About the CDC-Kaiser ACE study*. https://www.cdc.gov/violenceprevention/aces/about.html

Centers for Disease Control and Prevention. (2021). *Preventing childhood abuse and neglect*. https://www.cdc.gov/violenceprevention/childabuseandneglect/fastfact.html

Clark, K., Pyrooz, D., & Randa, R. (2018). *The Wiley handbook on violence in education: Forms, factors, and preventions* (H. Shapiro, Ed.). John Wiley & Sons.

Dragun, A. (2019, May 19). *Recognizing student trauma: A trauma-informed guide for school staff*. https://alexiskaliades7.wixsite.com/mysite-trauma

Estrada, J. N., Huerta, A. H., Hernandez, E., Hernandez, R. A., & Kim, S. W. (2018). In H. Shapiro (Ed.), *The Wiley handbook on violence in education: Forms, factors, and preventions*. John Wiley & Sons.

Evans, G., & Kim, P. (2013). Childhood poverty, chronic stress, self-regulation, and coping. *Child Development Perspectives, 7*(1), 43–48.

Harden, T., Kenemore, T., Mann, K., Edwards, M., List, C., & Martinson, K. J. (2014). The truth n' trauma project: Addressing community violence through a youth-led, trauma-informed and restorative framework. *Child and Adolescent Social Work Journal, 32*, 65–79.

Lambert, H. K., King, K. M., Monahan, K. C., & McLaughlin, K. A. (2017). Differential associations of threat and deprivation with emotion regulation and cognitive control in adolescence. *Development and Psychopathology, 29*(3), 929–940.

Li, X., Stanton, B., Pack, R., Harris, C., Cottrell, L., & Burns, J. (2002). Risk and protective factors associated with gang involvement among urban African American adolescents. *Youth & Society, 34*(2), 172–194.

Merrick, M., Ford, D., Ports, K., Guinn, A., & Merrick, M. (2018). Prevalence of adverse childhood experiences from the 2011-2014 behavioral risk factor surveillance system in 23 states. *JAMA Pediatrics, 172*(11), 1038–1044.

Moore, K., & Ramirez, A. (2016). Adverse childhood experience and adolescent well-being: Do protective factors matter? *Child Indicators Research, 9*(2), 299–316.

Murphy, A., Steele, M., Dubic, S. R., Bate, J., Bonuck, K., Meissner, P., Goldman, P., & Steele, H. (2014). Adverse childhood experiences (ACEs) questionnaire and adult attachment interview (AAI): Implications for parent child relationships. *Child Abuse & Neglect, 38*, 224–233.

The National Child Traumatic Stress Network. (n.d.). https://www.nctsn.org/

Steele, H., Bate, J., Steele, M., Dube, S. R., Danskin, K., Knafo, H., Nikitiades, A., Bonuck, K., Meissner, P., & Murphy, A. (2016). Adverse childhood experiences, poverty, and parenting stress. *Canadian Journal of Behavioural Science, 48*(1), 32–38.

Taylor, T. (2008). The boulevard ain't safe for your kids youth gang membership and victimization. *Journal of Contemporary Justice, 24*, 125–136.

van der Kolk, B. (2014). *The body keeps the score: Brain, mind, and body in the healing of trauma*. Penguin.

Wolff, K. T., Baglivio, M. T., Klein, H. J., Piquero, A. R., DeLisi, M., & Howell, J. C. (2019). Adverse childhood experiences (ACEs) and gang involvement among juvenile offenders: Assessing the mediation effects of substance use and temperament deficits. *Youth Violence and Juvenile Justice, 18*, 1–30.

Chapter 12
School Prevention Programs

> *I can't imagine being locked up for 24 hours a day. We gotta do something. Talking to kids in jail isn't good enough. We gotta do something first to prevent them from getting in jail. I started to notice something that kids are all gangstered up. Everyone is a gangster. MOB…kids running around with grapes on their neck. Are ya'll making wine or something? Kids running around with crowns on their necks. Are you a king or something? Are you from England? I just kept noticing all these kids were coming in, going home, and dying. Just straight murder. [That's why] we started going around talking to kids and doing [prevention] stuff. (Torres, 2019, Unpublished)*
>
> *– Special Agent Edwin Torres, President of the East Coast Gang Investigators Association, excerpted from a Gang Prevention presentation at an urban high school*

12.1 Let's Talk About Prevention Programs

A great place for prevention to start is in the school system. Schools have access to children for the entire length of the school day. This is a great opportunity to reach students in the area of gang prevention. There are many gang prevention programs being utilized in schools today. Fisher et al. (2018) reported that schools have used nearly 800,000 prevention programs and various ways for combating gangs. Prevention programs take on two different approaches. One is an individual approach which targets the individual with attempts to provide the resources and skills necessary to lower interest in gangs by promoting distancing from gang activity, promoting prosocial engagement by engaging the student during the school day in place of class time, during in-school suspension, and during lunch, after school, or on a weekend (Fisher et al., 2018). The second approach tackles the whole school, by enforcing behavioral standards, which creates an environment that makes gang activity less possible (Fisher et al., 2018). This can also include counseling and parent classes for guardians (Fisher et al., 2018). It is important to target the entire school population when it comes to gang prevention, with giving individuals special attention who are identified as most at risk (De La Rue & Forber Pratt, 2018). Prevention programs in schools should address things such as impulse control, lack of attachment to school, and rules (Gottfredson, 2013). Helping youth to resist peer pressure and rewarding involvement in school are also important (Gottfredson, 2013).

12.2 Addressing Risk Factors

Combining the knowledge of risk and protective factors together with reducing risk factors and enhancing protective factors are crucial to gang prevention (Estrada et al., 2018). Due to a higher risk of gang involvement due to cumulative risk factors, programs should try to address as many areas as possible in the youth's life, including individual, family, peer group, school, and community/social environment. It is important to use multiple component prevention strategies addressing risk factors across all of the domains (Hill et al., 1999). In the individual domain, programs that strive to reduce impulsive and risk-taking behavior or that can focus them in more positive ways, such as sports or activities, or increase morality, a sense of responsibility and conscience, or wanting to do positive things, are helpful (Esbensen et al., 2009). In the peer domain, programs that supervise peers in activities that provide structure and help increase making positive prosocial friend choices and discourage association with negatively influenced peers, who engage in deviant behavior, are positive (Esbensen et al., 2009). In the school domain, helping to make students feel safe in school is important (Esbensen et al., 2009). In the family domain, linking families with parenting classes and supportive services, including counseling, may be beneficial. In the community domain, linking youth with supportive services and positive recreational services, such as faith-based services in the community would also be helpful.

12.3 Focused Deterrence

A way to focus intervention efforts is to use focused deterrence strategies. This type of strategy tries to understand the dynamics behind criminal activity and the conditions that sustain it and uses law enforcement, social services, and community involvement as a way to lower offending criminal behavior (Braga et al., 2019). The first step involves law enforcement agencies coming up with consequences for those offenders who engage in gang violence and then clearly communicating the consequences to that population (Engel et al., 2013). Second, those who want to get out of the gang are offered social and job services (Engel et al., 2013). Also, community leaders come up with community engagement activities and try to communicate a nonviolence message and rejection of violence within the community (Engel et al., 2013). Focused deterrence was found to reduce criminal activity, including gang activity (Braga et al., 2019). Using components of this method in prevention efforts may be useful to prevent gang involvement.

12.4 Addressing the Need for Prevention

Prevention is needed across the board. Gerald Mallon, DSW, LCSW, Associate Dean of Scholarship and Research at Silberman School of Social Work at Hunter College and a Julia Lathrop Professor of Child Welfare, talked about how important prevention is when it comes to at-risk youth and how more funding needs to be put into prevention:

> The criminalization of these young people when they get arrested and go to juvenile detention…let's keep them away from other youth because they have proven they form gangs; it becomes a juvenile justice criminalization type of discussion rather than looking at why they get involved in the first place. They make signs and the colors and the tattoos. People get really into that. Well, why does that start in the first place? What was going on there in the first place? That's where you can protect them…A parable comes to mind…it's a parable that this one village would find all these children floating down the river and some of them were dead or just in really bad shape and people were like, we have to stop this and we have to rescue these kids before this happens to them. And someone said, why don't we go to the source where this happens and see who is throwing them in the river, because that's where you would really need to go. So they go several villages away, and they find out that some children are being thrown in the river because they couldn't be cared for, or they had disabilities, or they thought that they were possessed, things like that, where they had to educate that village to deal with these things so they weren't dealing with the end part of the problem, they were dealing with the beginning. That is really what prevention is all about. They never put the same amount of money into prevention that they put into, for instance, in the areas of foster care or juvenile justice. It costs about $400 a day per kid to keep them in foster care, maybe more, and prevention would maybe cost $25 a day, but they don't put those resources there. Politicians and people are panicked about children being harmed and children involved in criminal activity, so they want immediate results. So they put the money into institutionalization of the kids and not into prevention. (Mallon, 2020, Unpublished)

Prevention comes in at the beginning. The earlier prevention can start, the better. As the example of the parable stated, it is much easier and more effective to come in at the beginning and prevent a problem than it is to come in at the tail end. It is harder to intervene once youth start to go down that path than it is to do things to prevent their involvement from the start.

Addressing prevention from another standpoint is by coming at it from two standpoints, immediate and long-term intervention. Each of these interventions are addressing social problems. Kirk "Jae" James, DSW, MSW, BA, AA, Clinical Assistant Professor at NYU Silver School of Social Work, talked about gang prevention and intervention and needing to look beneath just the surface of gangs. There are societal inequalities that need to be addressed first:

> We have to create safe communities. We go to the tip of the iceberg and then look deep beneath. If communities don't feel safe, if they're being targeted, whether it's by police or the lack of access creates inner targeting, we're going to see this. Whenever there is disproportionate disparity between the haves and the have-nots, in communities who don't have, there's going to be some type of response, and the response is often going to look like what we call gangs. They're just really creating equity. It's a by-product of the lack of equity we have in our society. If families are healthy and intact, then development looks a little bit different. I feel we often move toward an intervention that's not inclusive of the broader socioeconomics and broader experiences of families, and I think any intervention has to really be broad-scale intervention. We need to make sure people feel supported. A single mother raising five children at home and she's spending most of her time at work or spending most of her time self-medicating because she can't deal with the trauma she's experiencing, then we're going to still see these issues being very prevalent. I do feel that it requires not necessarily a Band-Aid approach, but even in a conversation around social justice, these things are intricately connected. We can't really solve the problems of gangs until we solve a lot of the ills that are a by-product of white supremacy and capitalism. What can we do? There are two levels of interventions. There's the harm reduction intervention, which is something that's more immediate that can we do in this moment, creating spaces for people to feel safe, to feel seen, to be able to feel that they have hope and opportunities. The long-term interventions need to be rooted in an understanding that gangs and "crime" are really based in an economy and a society that is often been oppressive toward broad segments of people and then looking at the trauma of that, looking at the attachment of that, and relational aspect of that, and understanding that those things are playing out in what we would say is crime or gang activity. (James, 2020, Unpublished)

Prevention programs that can start by targeting youth in disadvantaged areas are even more important. Creating safe communities, a place of safety, and being able to provide resources to youth is so beneficial. Dr. James refers to starting small in the short term by creating safety and hope for these youth. However, there is the broader issue in society of inequality and lack of access that needs to be address as well on a larger scale.

In gang prevention programs, it also is important to have good people implementing the programs, and there also needs to be consistency. Special Agent Torres said:

> I think in terms of gang prevention, it really boils down to the individual. There are really good programs out there, but it needs really good people to implement them…if there's a really good person implementing it and is really dynamic and takes an interest in the kids, it works. I think they need more faith-based programs out there. The problem with gang prevention is there is no consistency. There needs to be much more consistency when it comes to gang prevention programs. I think that's what kids are missing, that consistency in their lives. Gangs provide that consistency. Anything that is consistent in a kid's life that can counterbalance what gangs offer will be successful. (Torres, 2019, Unpublished)

Kids are missing consistency in their lives. The lack of consistency at home drives them to look outside for consistency, which they find in a gang. If prevention programs can offer a sense of consistency, they will be more successful. Having people in place who really care about the youth and take an interest, can be more impactful.

Having individuals that someone can trust and have a positive relationship with can really make a difference in a youth's life. Rios (2010) found that youth participating in the study had given up on themselves because they felt the system had given up on them and felt that school staff and police treated them negatively, which led to feeling detached from school. They have structural obstacles in their lives, such as a neighborhood without resources, uncertain labor market, or a school that is neglected and focused on expulsion (Rios, 2010). It is important for youth to create meaningful relationships within the community, such as with local institutions like school or college (Rios, 2010). Building positive relationships helped change youths' own self-perceptions because they could believe they could make it because they had positive relationships with people and knew that they cared for them and had a connection with them (Rios, 2010). In Rios (2010), youth only needed a small amount of resources to give them the power they needed to overcome obstacles, such as forming positive relationships with school staff and community members. It is best that organizations, such as school, programs, and labor market, work with at-risk youth to form positive relationships with them, and youth are also taught to take advantage of these opportunities as well (Rios, 2010). Once organizations become interested in helping at-risk youth, are genuine, and engage in respectful unconditional positive treatment, these youth often respond by feeling self-empowered, change obstacles into strengths, and return to school and away from crime (Rios, 2010).

12.5 When Should Prevention Start?

When is the right age to begin prevention programs? Prevention should start early in elementary school and should not wait until adolescence to begin (Hill et al., 1999). Starting prevention in the elementary grades could impact adolescent gang membership in a significant way (Hill et al., 1999). Elementary schools who can increase academic success for their students may reduce gang involvement (Hill et al., 1999). Most gang members will initiate between the ages of 12 and 15 years (Sharkey et al., 2010). Youth join gangs as early as 7 or 8 years old, but involvement ramps up at age 12 or 13 (Estrada et al., 2018). Special Agent Torres said:

> The most difficult and targeted age is the 5th- and 6th-grade age, 12- and 13-year-olds. I've seen them as young as eight. With the newer paradigm with the neighborhood-based gangs that we have seen, we're hearing kids as young as eight, nine, ten years old. Because they're so neighborhood-based, they don't have as much red tape as the larger major gangs. So we're seeing them younger and younger. So definitely, the beginning is around that middle school age. It seems to be the most problematic age. (Torres, 2019, Unpublished)

Most of the participants in my research study joined gangs when they were at the middle school age. However, the gang influence started much younger. In light of that information, prevention programs should ideally strive to be implemented as early as possible, in the elementary schools. Special Agent Torres said:

> In the more urban and larger suburban areas, you want to start gang prevention earlier because kids are more exposed to that gang mentality at an earlier age. The earlier you can get started, the better off you are. (Torres, 2019, Unpublished)

The earlier gang prevention programs are started, the better. The gang influence starts at a young age, often in elementary school or even younger depending on the area. Starting prevention early and having that early influence on youth is going to be the best way to go.

Jay Franklin, Gang Specialist and Captain of Security and Safety Manager for Riverside County, California, also talked about the importance of starting gang prevention programs as early as possible, in elementary school:

> Gang prevention should start in elementary school. But most school districts don't want to touch that. We had a school district in our county, and they were experiencing real gang issues, [like] elementary school kids getting jumped in; kids coming back to school because they're a part of this clique now; getting piercings in 2nd and 3rd grade. An elementary school kid's older brother had a shoebox. The shoebox had drugs in it, so he took it to school, not just to show kids what he had but to show them this is what I have and to try to get them to try it and buy some. When I had a meeting with the counselors, totally about gangs, what they said was, we have the biggest chance to make a difference in elementary school because we have them the longest. Because even in junior high, when people want to start prevention stuff in junior high… it's two quick years. It may not be enough if you don't follow them to high school or if you don't have a transition program. (Franklin, 2019, Unpublished)

Mr. Franklin recommended starting prevention programs in elementary school as well. Starting in elementary school is the primary place to begin. If we start prevention programs early, we can begin to show opportunities and options and warn of the dangers of gangs. Mentoring can also begin for students, especially those deemed at-risk, which can help dissuade gang involvement.

12.6 Gang Prevention Programs

The following are several gang prevention programs. Some are more school-based programs specifically, while others take on a wider range and go outside of the school environment as well.

12.6.1 Promoting Alternative Thinking Strategies (PATHS) (Source: https://pathsprogram.com/)

Promoting Alternative Thinking Strategies (PATHS) is a universal prevention program which teaches social skills in the classroom to students and addresses teacher classroom management practices (Gottfredson, 2013). The program promotes social and emotional competencies and works to lower behavioral issues and aggression in children at the elementary school level. The program uses Affective-Behavioral-Cognitive-Dynamic (ABCD) model, which links emotional competency to awareness of behavior. The program's goal is to help students to build skills so they can understand their emotions and also manage them.

A study that evaluated the program found fewer behavioral issues in elementary school with less conduct disorder and fewer arrests through high school (Gottfredson, 2019). According to www.pathsprogram.com, the program has been found to reduce teachers' reports of students' aggressive behavior by 32%; increases teachers' reports of students showing self-control by 36%; improves performance on state achievement tests in the areas of reading, math, and writing; increases students' emotional vocabulary by 68%; and increases students' scores on cognitive skills tests by 20%. It has also been found to have lower mental health and health services usage (Gottfredson, 2019). This program is promising because problem behaviors and delinquency are risk factors for gang involvement (Gottfredson, 2019). If these risk factors can be addressed adequately, then there will be a lower risk of gang involvement.

12.6.2 G.R.E.A.T. Program (Source: https://www.great-online.org/)

The Gang Resistance Education and Training (G.R.E.A.T.) Program is a cognitive-based, evidence-based gang and violence prevention program that is set in schools and run by law enforcement officers. Law enforcement officers come into schools and provide instruction for students in a classroom. At the middle school level, they do 13 weekly sessions, and at the elementary level, they do six weekly sessions. They also have summer activities and family strengthening components as well. The middle school curriculum also has a project called Making My School a G.R.E.A.T. Place, which gives students an opportunity to put their learned skills into practice. The goals of the program are:

1. Help youth avoid gang membership
2. Create a reduction in violence and criminal behavior
3. Create positive relationships between police and students (Clark et al., 2018; Connell et al., 2018).

The lessons in the program focus on learning problem-solving strategies, developing skills, and cooperative learning, as well as discussing gangs and violence, body language, calming others, goal setting, decision-making, peer pressure/refusal skills, anger and conflict management, communication skills, and responsibility and roles in society (Clark et al., 2018; Connell, et al., 2018). In addition, the courses address risk factors such as school performance and commitment, peer influence and association with positive or negative peers, self-control, guilt, involvement in activities, empathy, moral disengagement, and neutralization techniques (Clark et al., 2018). The elementary program for fourth and fifth grade students talks about decision-making and communication skills, anger management, violence prevention, and having respect for others (Connell et al., 2018).

Evaluation of a revised version of the G.R.E.A.T. program showed a 39% reduction in odds of a youth joining a gang after following participants for one year and less support for violent behavior (Connell et al., 2018). Participants had positive attitudes toward law enforcement, had more negative attitudes toward gangs, had better anger control, used more refusal, disliked risk, and had more concern for the well-being of others (Clark et al., 2018). It has been found to be the most successful gang and violence prevention program in schools (Clark et al., 2018). Special Agent Torres said, "I know that G.R.E.A.T. is a program that has been touted nationally. So there's been some data that it has some effect. It's a good program on an introductory level" (Torres, 2019, Unpublished).

12.6.3 Gang-Free Schools and Communities Initiative (Part of the OJJDP Comprehensive Gang Model) (Source: National Gang Center: www.nationalgangcenter.gov)

The Comprehensive Gang Prevention, Intervention, and Suppression Model is funded by the federal Office of Juvenile Justice and Delinquency Prevention (OJJDP). It has been shown to be effective in different cities in reducing gang violence. Researchers evaluated the model in six different cities. They did a comparison of youth and neighborhoods that received the programming with ones that did not receive it and found that in three of the six cities, there were reductions in gang violence. In two of the sites, there were less drug-related offenses compared to the other group. The Gang-Free Schools Program developed a school component to the Comprehensive Gang Model and developed programs within a school setting which links the school component to other community gang prevention activities. The program incorporates prevention, intervention, suppression, and reentry activities while using community resources already in place to sustain the program. The five major components of the Comprehensive Gang Model include:

Community Mobilization: Local citizens coordinate programs and staff functions throughout agencies.
Opportunities Provision: This component involves training, employment programs, and education development that are specifically for youth who are gang involved.
Social Intervention: Social intervention consists of having schools, faith-based organizations, law enforcement, youth service agencies, and juvenile justice organizations reach out to youth who are gang involved and their families and connects them to services.
Suppression: Suppression involves putting social control measures in place and having juvenile justice system and community agencies monitor and closely supervise youth who are involved in gangs.
Organizational Change and Development: This component consists of putting together and utilizing policies and procedures that produce the most useful and effective way of utilizing resources across agencies to deal with the gang problem.

12.6.4 Gang Reduction and Youth Development (GRYD) (Source: https://www.lagryd.org)

Gang Reduction and Youth Development (GRYD) is a program that was established by the City of Los Angeles Mayor's Office in 2007 to provide gang prevention and intervention services. The mission of the program is to strengthen youth, families, and communities with resiliency to gangs. The goals are to:

1. Increase the knowledge in the community and their capacity to address gang violence and involvement
2. Increase protective factors of youth against gang involvement for youth at risk of joining a gang and reduce gang joining among youth ages 10–15 years
3. Increase positive prosocial connections and protective factors for youth that may already be gang involved between the ages of 14 and 25 years and to facilitate communication and responses that are coordinated to address gang violence

The program promotes positive youth development, tackling the causes that lead youth to join gangs, reducing youth gang involvement, strengthening the relationships between law enforcement and the community, responding to gang violence immediately in an attempt to stop retaliation, and increase information sharing and collaboration and coordination of services between communities and the GRYD office. The program has seven components as described by The Year 2 Final Report: Evaluation of the Los Angeles Gang Reduction and Youth Development Program (Dunworth et al., 2011):

Primary Prevention: This includes community activities that are supposed to build gang activity resistance, such as the Gun Buy Back program, Community Action Teams, and Community Education Campaign.

Secondary Prevention: Services are geared toward youth and family, which are intending to inhibit gang joining in youth who are at risk in the 10–15 years of age range, who are not gang members currently.

Intervention Case Management: Intervention specialists target activities for youth 14–25 years of age who are already in gangs, trying to get them to disengage from gang life.

Community Intervention: Community Intervention Workers respond on an immediate 24/7 basis to violent gang-related incidents in the GRYD communities to try to reduce the retaliatory response and promote peacemaking.

Law Enforcement Engagement: Cooperation and coordination between LAPD patrol/gang unit officers with GRYD staff is done to try to enhance trust and cooperation with the community.

Suppression: Suppression is not something focused on in the GRYD program, but the program tries to coordinate prevention and intervention activities with the police.

Summer Night Lights (SNL): SNL offers free activities for the community in parks and recreational centers, operating four nights a week from July 4 through Labor

Day. It integrates prevention, intervention, and law enforcement into park activities during the summer months.

The Year 2 Final Report: Evaluation of the Los Angeles Gang Reduction and Youth Development Program (2011) reported positive outcomes for the GRYD component objectives. In terms of prevention, GRYD stakeholders cited improvements in perception of community safety, positive view of the Summer Night Lights program on safety and quality of life in the parks, gang prevention service availability, an increase in youth resistance to pressures to join gangs, and communication of other options other than gang life. Stakeholders also felt that the GRYD programs increased prevention and intervention services in the targeted communities. Over 60% of youth who had been enrolled in the program retested on the YSET assessment six months after, scored at a risk level that would make them ineligible for the program. Youth enrolled in the program showed significant improvement on all of the risk scales, a reduction in some criminal, delinquent, and gang-related behavior.

12.6.5 The City of Chicago's Youth Violence Intervention Plan (Source: https://youth.gov/youth-topics/preventing-youth-violence/forum-communities/chicago/brief)

The City of Chicago's Youth Violence Intervention Plan addresses the many factors that lead youth to violence, by combining prevention, intervention, and response (enforcement and reentry). The earlier violence can be prevented, the more effective the programs will be, which includes building up families and communities. The program initiatives include:

Prevention

Gang Intervention: Gang intervention is run by the Chicago Police Department, law enforcement officers, community figures, and service providers. The goal is to let gang members know that they need to stop the violence or face a response from the Chicago Police Department and federal partners. This is modeled on the Boston "Operation Ceasefire" Model.

Youth Shooting Review: Experts from nonprofit and governmental agencies come in to study the different factors that lead up to youth shootings. They will then come up with intervention strategies to prevent youth shootings in the future. This is based on a model from Milwaukee.

Intervention

One Summer Chicago: Run by the Department of Family and Support Services (DFSS), programs in Chicago will help keep youth busy and out of trouble by coming up with productive summer jobs for at-risk youth.

Cognitive Behavioral Therapy/Social Emotional Learning Initiatives: Youth can learn the vital skills on how to regulate their emotions and learn interpersonal skills. Cognitive behavioral therapy teaches youth how their thoughts impact their actions.

Safe Passage: The Chicago Public Schools established "Community Watchers," which are stationed along a safe route to keep students safe while they walk to and from school. This initiative will help students who may be afraid to attend school because of violence in the area.

Response

Gang School Safety Team: Run by the Chicago Police Department, this initiative's goal is to prevent retaliatory youth violence. If there is a victim of violence, officers go to the victim's home and try to discourage his/her associates from retaliating and escalating more violence.

SAFE Communities: Run by the Chicago Police Department, this program creates a collaborative network of stakeholders in the community to maintain order in the neighborhoods that have a lot of gang activity.

Chicago Safe Start: Run by the Chicago Department of Public Health (CDPH)'s office of Violence Prevention, this program seeks to reduce the impact of violence on younger children by raising awareness, expanding services, and educating agencies.

Jail Alternatives and Diversion: Cook County is trying to keep youth offenders from committing future crimes by using jail alternatives.

Aftercare Services: The Illinois Department of Juvenile Justice created this program to help youth who are leaving Illinois Youth Centers to reenter communities and prevent future crimes. An aftercare service plan is created for each individual youth. It also helps with mental health and substance abuse related issues.

12.7 Prevention: A Path Forward

Prevention is a path forward for our youth. Schools are a great place to do prevention programs because the students are there the majority of the day. Prevention needs to start as early as possible. Combining the risk factors and protective factors together is a way to come up with prevention programs. The various programs that are out there now, including G.R.E.A.T., Promoting Alternative Thinking Strategies (PATHS), Gang-Free Schools and Communities Initiative, Gang Reduction and Youth Development (GRYD), and the City of Chicago's Youth Violence Intervention Plan, are just a few of the noteworthy prevention programs. More research needs to be done to develop further ideas for prevention programs.

References

Braga, A., Weisburd, D., & Turchan, B. (2019). Focused deterrence strategies effects on crime: A systematic review. *Campbell Systematic Reviews, 15*, 1–65.

Clark, K. J., Pyrooz, D. C., & Randa, R. (2018). School of hard knocks: Gangs, schools, and education in the United States. In H. Shapiro (Ed.), *The Wiley handbook on violence in education: Forms, factors, and preventions* (pp. 203–226). John Wiley & Sons.

Connell, N. M., Riner, R., Hernandez, R., Riddell, J., & Medrano, J. (2018). Short school-based interventions to reduce violence: A review. In H. Shapiro (Ed.), *The Wiley handbook on violence in education: Forms, factors, and preventions* (pp. 303–320). John Wiley & Sons.

De La Rue, L., & Forber Pratt, A. J. (2018). When gangs are in schools: Expectations for administration and challenges for youth. In H. Shapiro (Ed.), *The Wiley handbook on violence in education: Forms, factors, and preventions* (pp. 287–302). John Wiley & Sons.

Dunworth, T., Hayeslip, D., & Denver, M. (2011). *Y2 final report: Evaluation of the Los Angeles Gang Reduction and Youth Development Program*. US Department of Justice Office of Justice Programs. https://www.ojp.gov/ncjrs/virtual-library/abstracts/y2-final-report-evaluation-los-angeles-gang-reduction-and-youth

Engel, R. S., Skubak Tillyer, M., & Corsaro, N. (2013). Reducing gang violence using focused deterrence: Evaluating the Cincinnati initiative to reduce violence (CIRV). *Justice Quarterly, 30*(3), 403–439.

Esbensen, F., Peterson, D., Taylor, T. J., & Freng, A. (2009). Similarities and differences in risk factors for violent offending and gang membership. *The Australian and New Zealand Journal of Criminology, 42*(3), 310–335.

Estrada, J. N., Huerta, A. H., Hernandez, E., Hernandez, R. A., & Kim, S. W. (2018). Socio-ecological risk and protective factors for youth gang involvement. In H. Shapiro (Ed.), *The Wiley handbook on violence in education: Forms, factors, and preventions* (pp. 185–202). John Wiley & Sons.

Fisher, B. W., Curran, F. C., Pearman, F. A., & Gardella, J. H. (2018). Do school policies and programs improve outcomes by reducing gang presence in schools? In H. Shapiro (Ed.), *The Wiley handbook on violence in education: Forms, factors, and preventions* (pp. 227–248). John Wiley & Sons.

G.R.E.A.T. Program. (n.d.). https://great-online.org/Home/GREAT-Home

Gang Reduction and Youth Development (GRYD). (n.d.). https://www.lagryd.org/to

Gottfredson, G. D. (2013). In T. R. Simon, N. M. Ritter, & R. R. Mahendra (Eds.), *Changing course: Preventing gang membership*. US Department of Justice, US Department of Health and Human Services & Centers for Disease Control and Prevention.

Hill, K. G., Howell, J. C., Hawkins, J. D., & Battin-Pearson, S. R. (1999). Childhood risk factors for adolescent gang membership: Results from the Seattle social development project. *Journal of Research in Crime and Delinquency, 36*, 300–322.

National Gang Center. (n.d.). *OJJDP Comprehensive Gang Model Overview*. https://www.nationalgangcenter.gov/Comprehensive-Gang-Model/Online-Overview

Promoting Alternative Thinking Strategies (PATHS). (n.d.). https://pathsprogram.com/

Rios, V. (2010). Navigating the thin line between education and incarceration: An action research case study on gang-associated Latino youth. *Journal of Education for Students Placed at Risk, 15*(1–2), 200–212.

Sharkey, J. D., Shekhtmeyster, Z., Chavez-Lopez, L., Norris, E., & Sass, L. (2010). The protective influence of gangs: Can schools compensate? *Aggression and Violent Behavior, 16*, 45–54.

The City of Chicago's Youth Violence Intervention Plan. (n.d.). https://youth.gov/youth-topics/preventing-youth-violence/forum-communities/chicago/brief

Chapter 13
Being the Change: Making a Difference

> *My lockdown unit in Jamesburg [in New Jersey] was the worst unit on the ground…you get to know kids a lot…no one cares about you when you're in jail. I was doing a count. I see a pair of legs hanging in the window in one of the units I'm walking through. So I start screaming…the kid, we'll call him Jay, had taken each strand of the blanket and little by little braided it into a rope, so he could put it into the vent, so he could choke himself with it. He braided a piece of yarn to braid it into a rope so he could hang it up. Which means it took a while to do it. We ripped the rope off his neck. We start to perform CPR. He used to call me Uncle T…I'm not letting go of this kid. I knew this kid over four years…He would pick up the telephone, and he would talk to the operator just to have someone to talk to. His mother would never accept his phone calls. She never wrote him. In the four years he was in Jamesburg, he never had a single visit from anyone in his family. Nobody ever came to visit. The only time I ever saw him have a visit was from DYFS [Division of Youth and Family Services]. His legal guardian was his grandmother. She never came to visit because she was elderly, and she was too sick to visit. So we doing CPR and someone told us, sir he's dead. And I said I don't got time for that. Get the paddles on this kid. He's a young kid. He's only 16. You gotta give him a chance. Put the paddles on him. Inject him with something. He's only 16… So they took him. On his neck, you could see the marks where he changed his mind, and he tried to pull off the rope. And I thought to myself…I don't know where he was at in his life… Jay was a kid who lost hope. Had no real family… His clique and crew that he hung around with used him to do dumb stuff. He followed along because he just wanted to belong. You all know anyone like that? Just wants to belong. Just wants to be with somebody. He'd do anything you want him to do, and they'd just laugh at them because he's dumb enough to do what you want. Believe it or not, we all play that role at some point in your life…He never surrounded himself with people who were going to get himself to that next level. (Torres, 2019, Unpublished)*
>
> *– Special Agent Edwin Torres, President of the East Coast Gang Investigators Association, excerpted from a Gang Prevention presentation at an urban high school*

13.1 Surrounded by People Who Can Get You to That Next Level

The story from Special Agent Edwin Torres, President of the East Coast Gang Investigators Association, captures the pain felt when losing a life of someone that you cared about. Witnessing the aftermath of a suicide of someone so young who had his entire life ahead of him brings a tremendous amount of sadness and a feeling of helplessness. What could have gone differently for this young man in his life? Along the way, was there something someone could have done to intervene and change this outcome? Special Agent Torres knew this young man for years. This young man had no support system at home, no real family, and wound up involved in a gang. He was likely seeking something out in a gang that he was lacking at home. The consequences of the gang activities left him locked up with no hope. He had no invested family. He had no real friends. He had lost hope in life. What if he had had someone in his life to help mentor and guide him? What if he had been surrounded by people who could have gotten him to that next level in life? There is no telling what this lost life could have turned into had he had the opportunity to see something different for his life.

13.2 Lack of Consistency

When there is a lack of consistency within the home, such as a lack of attachment to a primary caregiver, youth may look outward to replace that missing consistency with something else. This young man did not have that consistent family within his home. Youth may seek a replacement family if there is not a solid foundation within the home. Peer groups are very important during adolescence. If a youth is looking to flee something within the home, such as abuse or neglect, they may look toward something else as a replacement, such as a gang, if gangs are available in the area. The young man mentioned in the story above did join a gang, and it did not serve him well. Having that consistency in the home, community, or school environments could be what keeps youth on a different path than a gang. If this young man had had someone in his life to guide him on the right path, perhaps his outcome would have been different.

13.3 No Other Option: Gangs Enter the Picture

When youth feel that there are no other options, there are multiple risk factors in play, and there is a lack of protective factors, they may turn to a gang. Those who have grown up with the gang influence in the area may feel it is the natural progression in life to join. Coming from a poverty or a low socioeconomic status community and seeing gangs as a faster, easier way to make money for their families may be a driving force for gang membership as well. Youth who are hopeful, have positive goals in life, or feel they have many options available to them would likely not join a gang. Special Agent Torres mentioned that this young man had lost hope in life. He did not surround himself with positive people who could get him to that next level in life. If he had had the right people around him or saw that there were other more positive options for him, perhaps he would have not joined a gang.

13.4 Creating a Safe Haven

As this book has shown, schools can be a safe haven in a world that does not otherwise feel safe for youth. Being trauma-informed adds to the level of safety and trust that a school provides. Operating with an awareness and sensitivity to possible traumas that students have experienced in their lives is paramount. Many young people are living in worlds that are chaotic and devoid of a real sense of family. There are issues at home, and they need support, guidance, and to be shown that there are other options out there. There are other options other than death, jail, or serious injury. Schools can provide that safe haven and that support that they may not be getting at home. Staff members can be there to guide and show that there are other options available to them other than gangs. Many staff members within school systems can provide multiple levels of support, care, and guidance. Perhaps in providing those things, it can be enough to carry youth forward, despite the circumstances at home or in the environment.

13.5 Looking Ahead

There are many things that can be done in the way of prevention in schools that were already mentioned in this book, including being informed on gang trends, getting students involved, having mentors, working with law enforcement and families, implementing a dress code, strengthening community ties, teaching students social skills, providing students with other options, creating awareness, getting mentors and school support staff involved, and providing a safe consistent environment. Future research is needed on gang prevention programs for schools and communities. Each would need a gang prevention program tailored to the specific needs of that district or community. Many of the social problems that contribute to gang problems, such as lack of opportunities in lower socioeconomic status communities and poverty, need to be addressed in general, as was discussed as well. If those larger issues were addressed, they would filter down and affect youth everywhere.

13.6 Making a Difference

Youth do better if they have at least one person in their lives with whom they have a meaningful connection. This is especially true if the person has attachment issues. If there is a lack of attachment in the home, that child could be in search of a secure base. That person could be a family member, a friend of the family, coach, teacher, mentor, counselor, or religious figure, just to mention a few examples. If the person is working in a school, it is even more likely because that is where we have access to students for the majority of their days. If you are reading this book and you are in a position where you are working with at-risk youth, please do not downplay your role. Your role could be a powerful change agent in that child's life. Being there for that child and providing support and a meaningful connection could be the one thing that causes a shift in that young person's path. Together, we can deliver messages of hope to the youth that we work with on a daily basis. You can join me in trying to be that one person who can make a difference in a child's life.

Index

A
Abuse, victims of, 33, 34
Adverse Childhood Experiences (ACEs), 163
   adulthood, impact of, 164, 166, 167, 169
   childhood, impact of, 164
   prevention, 169
   violence, effects of, 171
Age, 3
Aggressive behavior, 98, 101
Anger, 93, 94
Attachment, 79, 82, 83, 86, 88, 90, 92–94, 172
Attachment theory, 92, 93
   abuse, victims of, 33, 34
   classical attachment theory, 19, 20
   clinicians, 25–27
   gangs and, 23–25
   gangs, influenced by family members in, 35–37
   insecure attachment, 23
   lack of family consistency, 27–29
   lack of supervision at home, 34, 35
   modern attachment theory, 22, 23
   parents absent, 31–33
   single mother home, being raised in, 29, 30
   types of attachments, 20–22
Awareness, 191

B
Band-Aid approach, 180
Behavioral disabilities program, 79–81, 83, 84
Behavioral management problems, 93
Behavioral Risk Factor Surveillance System, 164
Brotherhood, 41–43
Brotherhood, Sisterhood, Unity Gang as Replacement Family, 41
   brotherhood, sisterhood, unity, 41–43
   conditional love, 48
   gang as replacement family, 43–46
   growing up with gang members, 46, 47

C
California Evidence-Based Clearinghouse for Child Welfare, 172, 173
CDC-Kaiser Permanente Adverse Childhood Experiences (ACE) Study, 163
Center for Family Development, 64
Centers for Disease Control and Prevention (CDC), 163
Child Study Team evaluation, 81
Classical attachment theory, 19, 20, 82
Cognitive behavior therapy, 144
Community Mobilization, 184
Community/social environment risk factors, 107, 108
Complex trauma, 172
Conditional love, 48
Consequences, of leaving gang, 65, 66
Consistency, 20
Counseling, 80, 81, 85–89, 91–93
Counselor, 79–82, 85, 86, 88, 91, 92, 94
Court-ordered anger management counseling, 81

D
Death, 66, 67, 69, 70
Destiny, 59

Disengage
    consequences for leaving, 65, 66
    factors for disengagement
        better life outcome for themselves and families, 66, 69
        gang disillusionment, 72–75
        getting out of the gang, 75–77
        incarceration, 71, 72
        moving on, 77, 78
        witnessing/experiencing violence, 69, 70
Disrupted attachments, 90
Division of Child Protection and Permanency, 82
Drug addiction, 32

E
East Coast Gang Investigators Association, 66
Education
    gangs and, 5, 6
Emily case Illustration, 86–89, 91, 92
Emotion regulation, 135
Ethnicity, 4, 5

F
Faith-based programs, 148
Family, 79, 81, 84–88, 90, 91, 93, 94
Family consistency
    lack of, 27–29
Family protective factors, 111
Family risk factors, 102–105
Family systems
    gangs and, 39–41

G
Gang
    as replacement family, 43–46
Gang disillusionment, 63, 72, 74, 75
Gang internal processes, 39
Gang involvement
    clothing and accessories, 121
    colors, 116
    hand signs, 121
    symbols, 123
    tattoos, 122
    visible/physical sign, 115
    warning signs
        behavioral changes, 129
        drug abuse, 129
        fighting, 130
        money/theft, 127
        music and movies, 127
        safety worry, 127
        social media, 125
        use of street names, 127
        weapons, 129
Gang involvement theories
    developmental model of, 10
    gang membership, 13
    gangs as attachment figures, 14, 15
    interactional theory, 9, 10
    limitations, 17
    methodology
        participants, 15–17
    multiple marginalization theory, 11
    self-control theory, 13
    social control theory, 12, 13
    social disorganization theory, 11
    social learning theory, 12
    strain theory, 11, 12
    systems theory, 12
Gang lifestyle, 47, 63, 68, 69, 76
Gang members, 7, 58, 63–78, 97, 98, 103
    and lifestyle, 57, 58
Gang prevalence, 2
Gang prevention
    activities/mentors, 154, 155
    awareness, 141, 142
    community involvement, 156–158
    community ties, 148
    counseling, 155, 156
    dress code implementation, 146
    law enforcement, 147
    learning lessons, from gang experience, 159, 160
    mentors/positive role models, 139, 140
    parents and caregivers, 142, 143
    safe school environment, 145, 146
    school support staff, 143–145
    schools, 133, 134, 136
    students social skills, 148
    targeting at-risk youth for, 136, 137
Gang problems, 107
Gang Reduction and Youth Development (GRYD), 185
Gang Resistance Education and Training (G.R.E.A.T.) Program, 183
Gangs, 3, 6
    and attachment theory, 23–25
    and education, 5, 6
    and family systems, 39–41
Gang violence, 61, 97, 102, 109, 111
Grief counseling, 89

Index

H
Homeboy Industries, 64, 98
Hope, 64, 65, 67, 77, 78
Hyperactivity, 98

I
Incarceration, 67, 69, 71, 72
In-Class Resource classes, 84
Individual risk factors, 98, 101, 102
Interactional theory, 9, 10

J
Jail, 66, 67, 71, 72, 75, 77
Juvenile justice criminalization, 179
Juvenile justice system, 150

K
Kyle case Illustration, 79, 80, 82–84, 86

L
Law enforcement, 147, 191
Leaving a gang, 63, 64, 66, 70, 77, 78
Lifestyle
    idolizing gang members and, 57, 58
Low socioeconomic status, 51, 57

M
Mallon, Gerald, 40, 51
Mentoring programs, 139
Modern attachment theory, 22, 23
Multiple marginalization theory, 11

N
National Child Traumatic Stress Network, 173
National Gang Center, 2–5, 101–103, 105, 107, 135
Negative life events, 101
Negative peer influences, 101
Neighborhood, 51
Normative beliefs, 98

O
Office of Juvenile Justice Delinquency and Prevention (OJJDP), 136
Opportunities Provision, 184
Oppositional Defiant Disorder, 81

Organizational Change and Development, 184
Outreach programs, 149

P
Peer and community/social environment protective factors, 111–113
Peer engagement, 137
Peer group risk factors, 105–107
Peer groups, 39, 58
Physical injury, 69
Police Athletic League (PAL), 137
Positive consistent family role model, 40
Post-Traumatic Stress Disorder (PTSD) symptoms, 171
Poverty, 57
Primary caregiver, 88, 92–94
Probation, 81
Promoting Alternative Thinking Strategies (PATHS), 182, 183
Protective factors, 109
Pull factors, 63, 67, 68
Push factors, 63

R
Race, 4, 5
Reflections Narratives of Professional Helping, 79
Replacement family, 24, 79
Risk factors
    community/social environment risk factors, 107, 108
    family factors, 102, 104
    family protective factors, 111
    gang membership, 98, 103
    individual risk factors, 98, 102
    peer and community/social environment protective factors, 111, 112
    peer group risk factors, 105, 106
    pull factors, 98, 105
    push factors, 98, 102, 104
    school protective factors, 111
    school risk factors, 105
    tying risk and protective factors together, 113
    tying risk factors together, 108, 109

S
Scheduled counseling, 89
School-based counseling, 80, 81, 86, 135
School counseling, 1

School counselors, 145
School prevention programs
   City of Chicago's Youth Violence Intervention Plan, 186
   elementary school, 181, 182
   focused deterrence strategies, 178
   G.R.E.A.T. Program, 183
   GRYD, 185
   Promoting Alternative Thinking Strategies (PATHS), 182, 183
   prosocial engagement, 177
   risk factor, 178
School protective factors, 111
School resource officers (SROS), 149
School social work, 1, 2, 79, 80, 86
Seattle Social Development Project (SSDP), 112
Secure attachment, 82, 92–94
Seeking safety, 52
Self-control theory, 13
Self-regulation skills, 133
Sensitivity, 191
Sisterhood, 41–43
Social control theory, 12, 13
Social disorganization theory, 11
Social emotional learning (SEL), 173
Social environment
   gang violence, 61
   grew up in, 53–56
   idolizing gang members and lifestyle, 57, 58
   playing cards, 59, 60
   way of life, 58, 59
Social Intervention, 184
Social learning theory, 12

Social skills, 101
Social support system, 83
Societal inequalities, 179
Solution-Focused Therapy, 83
Special Agent Torres, 102, 104, 106, 108, 112
Special Education and Related Services, 81, 89
Strain theory, 11, 12
Superintendent Suspension Hearing, 81
Suppression, 184
Systems theory, 12

T
Therapist, 82, 93
Trauma-informed practice
   co-regulating, 174
   discipline model, 174
   impact of violence exposure, 171
   school culture and climate, 173
   staff support, 174
   trauma-informed care, 175
Trust, 80, 82, 88, 91, 93
Turnaround, 71

U
Unity, 41–43

V
Violence, 51, 55, 69
   and gangs, 3
Violent victimization, 145